Your OLD TESTAMENT TOOLBOX

Your OLD TESTAMENT TOOLBOX

Study Helps for the Hebrew Scriptures

Tom V. Taylor

GOSPEL FOLIO PRESS
304 Killaly Street West, Port Colborne, ON L3K 6A6
Available in the UK from JOHN RITCHIE LTD.
40 Beansburn, Kilmarnock, Scotland

YOUR OLD TESTAMENT TOOL BOX: STUDY HELPS FOR THE HEBREW SCRIPTURES
by Tom V. Taylor
Copyright © 2005 Tom V. Taylor
All rights reserved.

Published by
GOSPEL FOLIO PRESS
304 Killaly St. W.
Port Colborne, ON, L3K 6A6 Canada
1-800-952-2382
orders@gospelfolio.com
www.gospelfolio.com

ISBN 1-897117-16-7

All Scripture quotations from the New King James Version
unless otherwise noted.
New King James Version © 1979, 1980, 1982, Thomas Nelson, Inc., Publishers

Cover design by J. B. Nicholson, Jr.

Printed in the United States of America

FOREWORD

The Old Testament was the Bible of the Lord Jesus. He came to earth in order to fulfill its promises. On many occasions we read testimonies similar to these words from Matthew 26: *"All this was done, that the scriptures of the prophets might be fulfilled"* (v. 56).

With three verses from the book of Deuteronomy, He turned back the devil's temptations. Similarly He pressed His critics: *"Do ye not therefore err, because ye know not the scriptures, neither the power of God?"* (Mk. 12:24)—a warning we might well take to heart.

The early disciples also found in the Old Testament a rich resource of fulfilled prophecies, illustrations of biblical principles, and inspired poetry. Believers *"searched the scriptures daily"* (Acts 17:11) and from it Paul *"reasoned...out of the scriptures"* with those who did not yet believe (v. 2). It was with only the Old Testament in hand that Apollos *"mightily convinced the Jews... showing by the scriptures that Jesus was Christ"* (18:28).

In two verses, the apostle Paul succinctly and clearly explains the role of the Old Testament scriptures in the lives of New Testament Christians. They are for our *warning* and for our *learning*: *"Now all these things happened to them as examples, and they were written for our admonition, upon whom the ends of the ages have come"* (1 Cor. 10:11, NKJV). *"For whatsoever things were written aforetime were written for our learning, that we through patience and comfort of the scriptures might have hope"* (Rom. 15:4).

Since this is true, we need to give ourselves seriously to the study of these thirty-nine often neglected books. But those who have tried to do some study in the Old Testament acknowledge that the process is challenging, to say the least. Proverbs and metaphors; history and biography; poetry and prophecy—the Old Testament presents to the reader a bewildering array of word pictures and a rich variety of literary styles. In the same way that we shouldn't read a mortgage as we would a love letter, so we need to learn what to look for in the varied kinds of Scripture in order to hear them as they were originally intended. Where can we find trustworthy help?

This book is just what we need.

Until the publication of *Your Old Testament Tool Box,* these helpful aids to the Hebrew Scriptures were available only to the author's students. That wasn't fair. While it was true that the refreshing and practical ministry of Tom Taylor had reached thousands through Bible conferences and over regular radio programs, his real area of expertise—helping believers unlock the riches of the Old Testament books—was largely out of reach. Now you hold it in your hands.

While there are many helpful resources available to the English reader, this book is unique. With three levels of study for the beginner, intermediate and advanced student, this volume will give a wide range of help and can be used to expand our biblical horizons. It will equip us as we explore both familiar and uncharted territory for truths that will enrich both our lives and ministries.

The editor's prayer is that, as you give yourself to the careful study of the Old Testament, you will sense the companionship of the Lord Himself, that He will walk beside you as He did on the Emmaus road, expounding to you *"in all the scriptures the things concerning Himself"* (Lk. 24:27).

J. B. NICHOLSON, JR.
Grand Rapids, Michigan

TABLE OF CONTENTS

Dedicated to our Lord
and to my wife, Ruth,
who has been my constant companion, critic, and confidante
in this effort of writing about the Old Testament

PREFACE

WHY THIS BOOK WAS WRITTEN

Why another book on Old Testament studies? At a publisher's seminar some years ago, I heard Dr. A. W. Tozer say something like this: "If we read the books that were written yesterday, we would not need to write any more books today—but we don't, so we must."

In any subject there are both basic and more advanced materials. This book will suggest basic materials and offer some direction on further study materials as well. It is intended to provide instructional aids for the study of the Old Testament. It is not its intent to set out a detailed methodology but to sketch in for the student items of particular importance that render study more meaningful.

It is highly unlikely that anyone working with the subject can anticipate all the questions that may come to the mind of the student in pursuing such a study. This work can hardly be an exhaustive treatment, but it is hoped that it will give some practical steps to the understanding of the Hebrew Scriptures and will thereby encourage a greater appreciation and use of the Old Testament. *"Every word of God is pure,"* says the writer of Proverbs (30:5), and *"all scripture is given by inspiration of God"* (2 Tim. 3:16) that we might be complete in our understanding and competent in our witness, *"thoroughly equipped for every good work."*

SOME BASIC IDEAS

The Old and New Testaments constitute the sacred Scriptures. The adjectives "old" and "new" are terms of accommodation and should not be allowed to infer superiority or inferiority. The Old Testament is foundational to the New and, as is often said, "The New is in the Old concealed; the Old is in the New revealed."

We believe the Old Testament as given by the Lord: infallible, inspired, and inerrant. We will not argue these things at this point, but they are first principles and are fundamental to our approach.

By *inspired* we mean that God breathed it through the instruments of service—holy men of His choosing; by *infallible* we mean that it will not mislead us in teaching or understanding; by *inerrant* we mean that it is accurate in all matters it teaches to the extent to which they are taught.

The Bible displays a progressive revelation as, age by age, God reveals His will. Truth is cumulative throughout, but the experiences of mankind are built on the particular truths known at a given time. This simply means that Noah, for example, offered sacrifices without the benefit of the Levitical laws of the Mosaic economy. Later worshippers could not ignore the additional revelations concerning appropriate worship, excusing themselves by saying that they were just doing what the earlier communities did. The growing light of greater revelations brought both greater privilege and greater responsibilities.

The reading and studying of the Scripture is vital to our growth. But we cannot do it all at once, so we need to study progressively—book by book, theme by theme—and allow the Word of God to direct us and enrich our lives in worship and devotion.

VALUABLE HELPS

There are those who think they will simply study the Bible by itself. Our point is not to argue or disagree with those who wish to proceed that way, but for most of us there are some invaluable helps[1] in furthering our study:

1. *Software programs:* Some Bible programs have valuable study helps included. Not available to all, these helps should not be over-

looked when it is possible to take advantage of them.

2. *A Bible concordance:* Either *Young's Analytical* or *Strong's Exhaustive* will be acceptable.

3. *A Bible dictionary:* Useful for defining terms and explaining institutions. Vine's *Complete Expository Dictionary* is valuable and the single volume by InterVarsity Press, *The New Bible Dictionary*, is likewise useful. There are many others, and since the dictionary often moves into theological themes, you should attempt to have one that takes a view honoring the Bible as the Word of God.

4. *A Bible commentary:* There is a wide variety of commentaries, and the usefulness of them is not uniform. A work by one author gives uniformity in approach. Individual book commentaries are also valuable so long as one remembers that these are to be a help to the Bible study, not a substitute for it. William MacDonald's *Believers Bible Commentary* has been found helpful by many.

5. *A study Bible* is also useful. The Scofield or Ryrie, for examples, are meaningful helps. I have received much help from Newberry's *Annotated Bible* and the *Companion Bible* but, as with the commentaries, there is a tendency to allow the notes of the authors to become more important than the text, a danger that must be avoided.

6. There are, today, a great number of more sophisticated helps in language study and in analytical Bibles, etc. One needs to survey these carefully before becoming involved. The old axiom, "If it looks too easy, it's not," is still true.

THE STUDENT'S ATTITUDE

Needless to say, the attitude of the student is of paramount importance. It is an unhappy fact that many of us do not attempt to learn from the Bible as much as we do to work into the Bible some idea or random thought. One of my friends used to say, "Wonderful things in the Bible I see, hidden there by preachers like me." Unhappily that is often the case.

The student should come with an attitude of *thankfulness* to the Lord for His provision of this truth for us. *Humility* is a needed characteristic in which we see ourselves as learners, not as lecturers. *Industry* is part of the proper student attitude, indicating a willingness to work, and *teachability* goes with humility. If we are determined to learn from the Scriptures and to profit by the truth, the Holy Spirit certainly will be our great Teacher as we are yielded to His guidance.

LIFE APPLICATION

In applying our studies in the Old Testament to life, we must learn to distinguish *didactic* (teaching) material, *demonstrative* (illustrative) material, and simple *narrative* (story) material. If not, we may incorrectly apply to ourselves some advice given by the Lord to a particular party—but by no means given to all people. Some grasp such advice and make a doctrine of it.

To take an obvious example, the Lord told Ezekiel (3:22) to come out and meet Him in a field where He would meet with him and talk with him. That is a particular word to Ezekiel and does not suggest that prayer meetings should always be held out of doors in a field.

More will be said about this later. For the moment we note that the Scripture is to be applied to life, but distinguishing the character of the material will greatly aid one in knowing how and where it should be applied.

ARRANGEMENT OF THE MATERIALS

Some years ago I aspired to teach Latin and asked a venerable Latinist how much Latin I would need to know to teach it. Her reply was, "Everything!" I was rather crestfallen since I knew then, and really know today, that no one ever knows everything about anything. Our knowledge is always partial. But there are some things that are basic and foundational, and other aspects are built on these.

One can see a good illustration of it in mathematics. We do not start with calculus (it almost ended me!); we begin with the simple numbers. So for each of the areas in the Old Testament that will be considered, the study material is divided into three groups or levels. These three levels (and the sections for all students to read) can be easily located by the distinguishing marks in the columns: 1 or 1 for Level One, 2 or 2 for Level Two, 3 or 3 for Level Three, and A or A for all three levels of students to read.

The first discusses the basics that should be known as one approaches the subject. The second is a group of somewhat more detailed matters that add to one's total knowledge, and the third group addresses the most complicated issues. One may (or must) study the Bible at every level. But rather than say, "One must know it all," we may learn basic materials first and develop one's learning from there. This is not a matter of academic excellence or spiritual superiority; it is simply a matter of growing in the truth.

A LESSON FROM EXPERIENCE

It was 1943. World War II was in progress. I was fifteen—soon to be sixteen—and living on a farm in Western Pennsylvania. I had made teaching a life goal and knew that I would have to go to college. But we were poor. I needed a job that would pay more than the customary seventy-five cents a day plus lunch if I ever hoped to get college money.

Then my mother heard that a local tree surgery company was hiring boys my age since the men it needed were mostly in the army. I applied and got the job (I think they would have hired anyone). I told Mr. Black, the proprietor, that I did not know much about tree surgery and he told me I would be taught what I needed to know.

I have never known a boy who could not climb trees, but I was looking at trees 60-80 feet tall with no lower limbs and my heart failed within me—several times. But I soon discovered that I did not have to learn the whole job at once.

One day I learned how to climb with ropes, how to tie the right knots, how to use a double footlock on the safety line for protection. Another day I learned where to make the right cuts on tree limbs and the proper methods for cutting them out without hurting myself. In time I learned how to use the power tools and make borings for dynamiting tree stumps. But I went a step further and learned all of the common trees in our area by their botanical names as well as the common names. There was no white oak tree; it was *quercus alba*.

In fact I almost learned too much! When a client said, "What are you spraying?"

I politely replied, "Dichloro-diphenyl-trichloroethane."

My answer left the client looking perplexed and annoyed—until I explained we were using DDT. He looked relieved.

It is a long way from the tree business to Bible study, but there is this much in common: we do not need to know it all in one day. We need to learn things progressively and become more proficient as we move along. We will always be kept humble, incidentally, by the simple fact that we will never know it all—at least in this life.

THE DIVISIONS AND BOOKS OF THE OLD TESTAMENT

In Hebrew culture the Old Testament is called *Tanakh* (or *Tanaach*), a composite word built out of the initial Hebrew letters of the three divisions of the Old Testament Scriptures: the Law (*Torah*), the Prophets (*Nevi'im*) and the sacred writings (*Ketuvim* or *Kethubim*). This division is historic and was certainly known and understood long before the coming of the Lord.

The Law (*Torah*) consisted of the five books of Moses and today is called the *Pentateuch* (Gk. for "five containers," where containers presumably refers to scroll cases in which these books were kept).

The Prophets (*Nevi'im*) consisted of the former prophets (Joshua, Judges, Samuel, Kings) and the latter prophets (the three major prophets: Isaiah, Jeremiah, Ezekiel with the twelve minor prophets: Hosea, Joel, Amos, Obadiah, Jonah, Micah, Nahum, Habakkuk, Zephaniah, Haggai, Zechariah, and Malachi).

The Sacred Writings (*Hagiographa* was the Greek title; *Ketuvim* is the Hebrew term) included the poetic books: Job, Proverbs, Psalms; the Rolls (*Megilloth*): Ruth, Esther, Song of Solomon, Ecclesiastes, Lamentations; and the Histories: Chronicles, Ezra, Nehemiah, and Daniel.

Chronicles is the last book in this arrangement of the Old Testament. The antiquity of it is seen in the statements of the Lord in Matthew 23:35. There He charges the Pharisaical community for being guilty of shedding innocent blood from the blood of Abel (Gen. 4) to the slaying of Zecharias in 2 Chronicles 24:20-21 or, as we would understand it, from one end of the Bible to the other.

These divisions probably originated with the readings in the temple/synagogue worship services of Israel. They are not to be regarded as inspired but as a practical means of assembling the literature for reading and instructional purposes.

THE OLD TESTAMENT CANON

The term *canon* indicates a standard or rule, as well as the results of applying that canon or rule. When we speak of the Old Testament *canon*,[2] we are first defining the principle by which books were accepted for the Bible. Secondly, we are indicating the results of that work. The principle by which books were accepted for the religious life of Israel was simple: Did God give it? If a work came from God it was accepted as authoritative and normative.

Later rabbinical schools would speak of these works as "defiling one's hands." The rabbis considered these books to be so clean or holy that they made anything close to them look unclean, making their carefully washed hands look filthy by comparison.

While the five books of the Torah were foundational and had the divine imprimatur of the Lord speaking to Moses, the later books were tested along points of truth taken from Deuteronomy 13 and 18. There were many other books, of course, and some of real value but none deemed as having the signature of God.

The books of the modern *Apocrypha* (from the Gk. for "hidden") were not accepted into the biblical canon because they did not "defile the hands." While they make interesting reading, a quick perusal of the historical mistakes in Judith and the theological mistakes in Tobit will show why these books could not come up to the standards of divine authorship.

The same may be said for such works as the "Book of Jasher" and the many *pseudo-epigrapha* (false authorship claims) that were current at the time of the Lord and some much earlier.

Man is a literary creature, and the more we know of ancient civilizations, the more we marvel at the preservation of the Word of God through the centuries of time. For Old Testament study in general, we do not need to know all of the technicalities behind these things, but it is good to know what the sacred books are, and what part they play in the Bible as a whole.

APPROACHING THE SUBJECT

The historical books of the Old Testament will be the first item of consideration. Following this we will look at Old Testament Poetry and Prophecy. There are overlaps of material in a study like this. Not all the poetry is in the poetic books, for example, and some of our basic materials will be repetitive—one does not need a totally new category for each consideration. Following these major portions, many other subjects will be analyzed on the same basis.

What do we need to know to make the study more fruitful? It is important that the student does not look at the Old Testament as a book of carefully guarded mysteries but as a repository of truth about God and His people, and therefore providing a sound foundation for our spiritual learning and experience.

But it needs to be stressed that, before beginning any study of a passage of the Word of God, there should be an exercise of prayer and a thorough reading of the passage. Neither should be overlooked. Read the passage as often as practical in your time allowance. It is a good idea to develop an outline of the passage or to consult one of the reference Bibles to get an overall grasp of the content. In other words, having a familiarity with the text will allow you to effectively use the study tools we will introduce.

I
OLD TESTAMENT HISTORY

The material to be studied in this chapter will relate to the historical books, regardless of which portion in the canon they are found. We will include historical segments from other books that are not primarily historical records—from the poetry sections and from wisdom literature, for example. The material will be treated together as a type of literature. The goal is to understand the ways of God with His people and to see how His programs are accomplished in the face of the opposition of the world and its contrary forces.

Level One: THE HISTORICAL SECTIONS

Level One is suggested for the beginner in Old Testament studies, but in one sense we are all beginners, so it is not wrong to check every basic step.

Four items are enumerated for this level. Some may seem very simple, others more complex, but they are all important foundation points for this study.

1. *A survey knowledge of Bible history:* One should be acquainted with the accounts of creation, the fall, and the flood, as well as the call of Abraham and the beginning of the Hebrew economy (Gk., *oikos* house + *nemein* to manage; the arrangements God made with the Hebrews for operations in Israel).

This survey knowledge would also include Israel's Egyptian experience, the conquest of Canaan, and the establishment of the monar-

chy as well as familiarity with the time of the division of the kingdom and the subsequent fall of Israel (the Northern Kingdom), the
separate history of Judah with the Babylonian Captivity and the
return of the exiles. The age of the final prophets of the Old
Testament and a brief knowledge of the inter-testament period would
be rewarding. A broad overview of these events enables one to
understand the historical context in which something occurs. That is
often very useful in interpreting a passage. There are many Bible
surveys that will meet that need (see BIBLIOGRAPHy for suggestions).

2. *An understanding of the Ages and Dispensations:* Throughout
history God has progressively revealed His truth and given more
exact data about His ways and dealings with His creation. The periods of time in which He has done this are called by many scholars
"dispensations," although today it is very common to hear them
called "ages."

It might be helpful to distinguish these words as follows: ages are
distinct periods of time marked out by God, revealing to man a new
dispensation or stewardship. Although each age is charged with
some particular accountability factor revealing God's will for His
people, some aspects of these stewardships often carry over into
other ages. For example, human government's responsibility to deal
with premeditated murder, given in Noah's time, is still in effect.

The truth that God gives is cumulative, of course, but one cannot
expect Noah to understand the rules for camp life given to Moses
hundreds of years later. The truths given to Noah are valid matters
of belief, but the data given Moses are much more detailed and enter
into many more areas of life. Thus we speak of the age of Innocence
(in the garden of Eden), Conscience, Human Government (through
the flood), then Promise (especially in the days of Abraham and the
patriarchs), the Law (with Moses and Sinai), the Church (grace), and
to many the seventh age will be the Millennium.

This way of identifying distinctive changes in God's dealings with
His creatures is not a test of orthodoxy, but the progression must be
observed. If another system of names is used, we still must understand that God through time has increased our blessing and knowledge, and we need to see the reality of it in our Bible study.

It is important to note that salvation is accomplished in every age by the same vital media: the grace of God. The perspective may be different in that, for example, the Old Testament worshippers looked forward to the coming of the promised Redeemer while the New Testament worshippers look backward. From God's point of view, the matter is settled in Revelation 13:8—the Lamb was slain *"from the foundation of the world."*

Noah, we are told, found grace in the eyes of the Lord (Gen. 6:8), the saving factor in every age. The law could never save and the blood of bulls and goats could never take away sin (Heb. 10:4), but God used such means to cause mankind to look to Him, and their belief—faith in God—was accepted by Him. (Heb. 11:6). It has always been grace that saved and such will be the case forever!

The moral *character of God* does not change with the ages, but the *government of God* is expressed in different ways. In Noah's day there was the flood while in Moses' day there was the plaguing of Egypt. Yet God's character is marked by justice and love in every case and it can readily be seen how the Lord is always dependable. An easy example of this varied expression of government may be seen in the priesthood:

- In Genesis 3, God was the first priest, providing the sacrifices
  - then the patriarchal heads of families served as priests
    - until God established a priesthood through the family of Levi
      - eventually, in the Church Age, every believer is a priest.

This priesthood of all believers is anticipated in the Old Testament (Ex. 19:6) but not seen until the pronouncement of the New Testament (1 Pet. 2:9). Today it is one of our joys to serve as priests to the Lord of the Universe.

3. *An understanding of the program of redemption:* Redemption is the great theme of the Bible so far as our experience is concerned. Although there is a great deal of theology related to this theme, the student of the Old Testament should at least understand the reality of sin and the total lostness of mankind, the love of God, and His outreach in grace. The key thing is to know personally the reality of salvation and grace, and have a thankful response to the Lord who gave Himself for us.

In coming to grips with this concept, the prophetic promise of

Genesis 3:15 is fundamental. The reality of sacrifice and God's acceptance of a substitute for our sin needs to be understood. Messianic promises of a wider sort (Gen. 49:10, Deut. 18:15*ff*, Isa. 53) also need to be considered. We see God's care for Israel and the protection given to the promised line of the Messiah. We also can trace out the character of the Messiah. The fulfillment of these promises from the Old Testament by the Lord Jesus makes it clear that the Redeemer has come, and God has announced that *"whoso-ever believes in Him shall be saved."* That the cross is the central point of our personal history, as well as religious and world history is a fact that should not be denied.

As we study, then, in the historical books, we will often be arrested by some incident and may wonder why it is recorded until we see how it augments the program of redemption.

4. *One should have access to sound bibliographic material:* The bibliography for this work contains numerous references catalogued to go with the presentations in the text. It is important that if the student comes on a word he cannot define, discovers a place name and has no knowledge of where it is, or reads of an object he cannot identify or the name of a person whom he does not recognize, that he look it up in an appropriate work. The more knowledge one may have about the text, the more likely one is to enjoy its study.

Incidentally, if pronouncing the names is a problem to a student, virtually every Bible known to me has a pronunciation gazetteer within its pages. The sad comment is that many of us are just not used to looking things up or seeing the importance of having them in good form. But the details of Scripture are not trivia: *"Every word of God is pure"* (Prov. 30:5).

Level Two: THE HISTORICAL SECTIONS

Level Two deals with the next area of materials helpful to the study of the historical books and passages. These are important but not so basic—I am not suggesting they are unimportant, but that they come in a second line of study.

Please remember that these levels are not platforms of academic excellence or spiritual superiority, just the practical tools to advance your study. Students often become impatient with basic things, but it is the understanding of them that makes further study possible. Without that understanding, one is handicapped in the enjoyment of the study and in the benefits that come from it.

There are five items in this study, and while the order in which they are given may not suggest relative importance, it is an order that will keep us on the subject.

1. *Understanding the Covenants and Promises of God:* Generally speaking, a covenant is a commitment between parties requiring certain performance. Some covenants are referred to as *monotheke,* meaning the covenant is one-sided, often imposed by the stronger party on the lesser party. Others are called *diatheke,* meaning they are arranged by the parties working together. In our day the terms "unilateral" and "multilateral" are used in similar ways. A promise may be part of a covenant relationship, but more generally a promise is simply a commitment to fulfill some obligation.

Covenantal promises must be kept in context; we must note carefully to whom they are given. While we may learn a good bit from every promise made, we should not simply transfer them to other parties. The chorus we used to sing in Sunday School, "Every Promise in the Book is Mine" was a nice singable tune but not theologically accurate. There are promises made to Abraham (Gen. 12) that were uniquely his. They may be thought of as mine in the sense that they are teaching me something about the Lord, but regarding the actual terms of the promise, they are not mine. I should not go to Palestine and lift up my eyes on the land and claim God has given it to me! This is a hard point for some, but necessary for our correct understanding of God's Word.

In my older King James Bible, in the prophetic books especially, the editors have labeled all the blessings given to Israel as promises to the Church, while the passages of judgment they identified as "wrath upon Israel." It is a classic example of not observing to whom the promise is made, or with whom the covenant is arranged.

No attempt here is made to list all the covenants, but one will observe the covenant made with Adam, with Noah and the generations following Noah, and the covenant with Abraham (Gen. 12 and elsewhere), with regard to a land, a seed, and the fulfillment of the redemptive promise.

The covenant is "renewed," we might say, with Isaac, Jacob and Joseph and with all of Israel as a nation coming out of Egypt. This detailed formulation of the covenant at Sinai is usually called the Mosaic Covenant. The book of Deuteronomy gives the exacting details of this covenant, with the blessings and cursings and all the data that are incumbent on such covenant making.

There is the Davidic Covenant and the promise of the continuance of his kingship with the necessary warnings that, if his people do not follow in the ways of God, they cannot expect all the blessings of God. In fact this covenant is continued to a remnant group, and the ultimate fulfillment of it will be seen in the great reign of the Lord Jesus on this earth, events still to come.

There is also a Gospel Covenant: all who call on Him will be saved.

This is obviously not the end of the study of the covenants, but it is a brief introduction that one needs for any work in the historical books and other historical accounts.

It should be noted that many of the promises of God are outside the covenantal umbrella, such as the promise of the Lord regarding the Church in Matthew 16. But wherever God makes a promise, we know His word is the final authority, and in all of life the only certainty that we really know is that of the Word of God.

The study of the covenants should not be confused with "covenant theology," a theological alternative to looking at biblical history as the unfolding of progressive ages. It represents the whole of Scripture as covered by one or a few covenants made within the Godhead. This is an oversimplification but it is not the purpose of this book to resolve theological difficulties. The student must first study the Word of God as a basic unfolding of truth, and then develop a comprehensive view based on one's understanding of His complete revelation.

2. *An Understanding of Priesthood:* So much of the historical material centers around priests and kings and religious controversy that an understanding of the priesthood becomes vital for a complete picture of many historical occurrences. A priest was one who served as a functionary between God and man, although the first priest was

God Himself, His priestly service being the providing of animal sacrifice for the benefit of Adam and Eve. But after this simple act of grace, a great deal of priestly order and ritual developed.

Although we are not told how it was learned or passed on, the concept of priesthood eventually settled in the patriarchal head of a family. We see Cain and Abel responsible for their own acts of sacrifice and worship. It is plain that the Lord had informed them enough about the propriety of what they were doing that Cain was guilty when he did not do what was right. The Lord informed him that if he had done the right thing he would have been accepted. So it may be that the patriarchal responsibilities were established or became known after the family situation was developed.

The question is asked at times: Why did there need to be any set order at all? Why not allow every person to be his or her own representative before God as the situations allowed? Let me suggest that such a proliferation would have resulted in an enormous number of wrong practices; the truth of the concepts (which were ultimately to lead to the perfect Priesthood of Christ) would have been utterly lost.

At any rate, we see the patriarchal priest in prominence from the days of Noah until the giving of the revelations at Sinai.

An interesting study in this regard is seen in the life of Job. In chapter 1, he offers sacrifices on behalf of his children who *may* have done that which was wrong before God. (The Hebrew is remarkable in this passage, but that is not the point here.) The children are not little boys and girls, but seemingly grown adults; they are off on a party experience while Job offers sacrifices for them— just in case.

Of course we are familiar with the Abraham accounts and the patriarchal privilege that was his. We need not go further in individual cases, but must observe that the worship and serving of the Lord was then, and is now, serious business. Those who were to be involved in it needed to observe all that the Lord had given them. The propriety or impropriety in these matters is an item which influences many historical passages in the life of Israel.

This becomes more plain when we come to the Levitical laws detailed in the books of Exodus, Leviticus and Deuteronomy. God instituted a new program for the blessing of His people. The patriarchal priesthood was set aside in favor of a priesthood invested in the family of Levi and eventually more specifically in the family of Aaron (Lev. 8; Mal. 2:4). This was a selection made by God, ironically fulfilling a prediction given years earlier in Genesis 49.

This priestly order had its duties well defined, and with the judgmental deaths of Aaron's sons (Lev. 10) it became apparent that the service of God was serious business. In this capacity the priests both represented man to God and God to man—it was a two-way communication. In a very practical way the Levitical priest showed the face of God to the people about him.

Every aspect of the priest's life was important. He was to be physically whole, morally upright, and spiritually alert. His family status was also important (Lev. 21–22) but his yieldedness to God was basic to everything else.

There were many failures in the priesthood, however. In the study of the historical books we often find the cause of tragic situations traced to a priesthood that did not function after the divine order. Valuable material on this line may be seen in Malachi, especially in chapter 2 where Levi is praised for his service at the founding of the Levitical order, and the priesthood of Malachi's day is taken to task for its inadequate representation of the work and will of God.

In having an understanding of the priesthood, it is good to know many of the terms that are used, what they mean, and how they are translated. Many of the measurements, technical details, and major worship terms are given brief definition in APPENDIX 2. But these are sometimes too brief for the serious Bible student, so when encountering such details, it is important to have the right bibliographic material nearby.

When looking up the meaning of *ephah,* for example, you are not likely to forget it. As a measurement, it would be approximately 28 quarts (very close to a bushel) and when it is pronounced properly, one will never confuse the *ephah* with the *ephod.* Pronunciation is important!

3. *Language and Word Usage:* One might wonder about this item in a course preparatory to Bible study, but the fact is that we often are not wise with regard to our own language. Someone may completely misunderstand a passage just because a speech device was not understood. I saw a friend shocked one day when I asked anoth-

er companion if he had the "loot." The shocked party took "loot" to mean something illegitimate but my other friend understood perfectly and handed me a twenty dollar bill for the admission money we needed for our venture. We understood it among ourselves, but to someone else it might seem to be a case for the police!

The study of language and language usage is long and complicated, and in this work I will reduce it to three segments:

- language variety
  - speech figures
    - literary devices

More will be said about language when we look at the poetry of the Old Testament, but it is necessary to lay a groundwork for that study and this is the most convenient time.

Essential variety in language. Basically language is used in three ways. We identify them as literal, allegorical, and typical. The ideas are intermingled, of course, and overlapping is common, but the major ideas are well served.

i. LITERAL LANGUAGE indicates that the term used is a concrete description of the item discussed. It is to be taken in its plain and obvious sense. It is not necessarily *letteristic,* in which the exact word is used for an exact thing (i.e., bread = bread), but the terms that are used depict accurately what is in focus (bread could also be described as a loaf, a morsel, a piece, or a mouthful; similarly wine could be called *"the fruit of the vine"*).

When we are told that a particular number of fish was caught when the apostles followed the instruction of the Lord, that is a literal statement. Had one been there and counted them, that is the number there would have been in the net. Literal language has the advantage that it is plain, easily understood, and means what it says.

There can be some overlap when literal ideas are drawn from a speech figure. When Jesus spoke of Herod and referred to him as a *"fox"* (Lk. 13:32), He was using a metaphorical speech figure but was still speaking literally in that the proverbial character of foxes for being wily, sneaky, deceptive, and duplicitous creatures was exactly what Herod was.

ii. ALLEGORICAL describes language usage in which the terms do not portray the subject exactly but describe it in figurative terms. However, these figures at the same time *mask* the real subject, yet give enough clues that anyone knowing the general matter will understand what is discussed. Ezekiel makes great use of allegory when he speaks of the kings of Judah and Babylon in the eagle account of Ezekiel 17. The Lord Jesus uses allegorical language in John 15 and the "True Vine" discussion.

An allegory needs to be identified in the text or made plain by the contrasting absurdity that would exist if it was interpreted literally. This should be obvious when Christ speaks of the bread He gave His disciples to eat at the first Lord's Supper. *"This is My body,"* He said of the bread, while still *in* His body. No one should doubt that He was speaking of the bread as a symbol of His body.

This particular language usage is often called "figurative" and sometimes "spiritualistic" but the preference in this work is to call it allegorical since figures are used in all forms of language, and "spiritualistic" does not accurately enough describe a language art that uses one form to depict another.

SEE PG 40

iii. TYPICAL language is that used to take one entity and predict or describe another (type + antitype, not the opposite of the type but something put over against the type to make an obvious comparison). It is also figurative, but *pre*figures something or someone yet to come. Daniel's stone cut without hands (Dan. 2:34, 45) is typical language both in its character and in its action. We will look at the study of types in another section of our work and, while there is not a lot of typical language in the Old Testament, there is enough to make it an important part in our study.

So at this level when reading an historical account we should ask:

• "Is this written so that I may know exactly what happened?" If the answer is yes, the language is literal.

• "Is this written to make me think of something similar in another circumstance?" If the answer is yes, the language is allegorical.

• "Is this written to predict and direct me to something that is to come?" If the answer is yes, the language is typical.

Occasionally, an historical account may involve all three! But the

student who knows that possibility is ready to explore and seek
fuller definition and, being forewarned, is being forearmed.

Figurative Language and Speech Figures. This is a giant subject! A figure in this sense is something that is used to identify or
define something else. We use figurative language constantly. In
fact, it is hard to communicate without it. It must be remembered
that the use of a figure in language does not mean the literal character is lost. That is important. If I say, "he runs like a rabbit" everyone understands that I am speaking of speed, not of going on all
fours with his arms being shorter than his legs!

APPENDIX 1 gives a list of the most common speech figures along
with a brief definition and an example from the Bible. The great
work on this subject is that of E. W. Bullinger in a massive book,
Figures of Speech Used in the Bible. (Bullinger is also the author of
the *Companion Bible* and a work on Numbers in the Bible as well as
several other books. His work dates from the 19th century.)

To fail to understand the speech figures[3] is to lose a great deal of
meaning in all parts of Scripture. But we must be especially careful
in this area: there is a tendency in a technical study like this to
become very complicated and make the Bible more a book of veiled
mystery than a revelation of truth.

Literary Devices. In this category we include fables, riddles,
dirges, love songs, and so on. More will be said of these in our poetic section, but you need to be aware that they exist in Scripture.
Jotham's fable, which describes the trees in the forest selecting a
king (Jud. 9:7*ff*), is a good example of such a literary device.

I once had a student come to me in a perplexed manner, asking
when this council of the trees and bushes happened! He could hardly believe such a thing would be mentioned in the Bible. But the
telling of it in such a graphic way illustrates the historical event in a
memorable way, an event that would greatly affect Israel's history.

While there are not many of these devices in the Old Testament
(the New Testament adds many more), it is important to see them.
The Bible student does not have to be a master in every field of language study, but we should be sufficiently informed so that we can
identify the device used and can be blessed by it.

4. *An understanding of the Legal Strictures of the Lord:* The study of the Law of God is a more formal study than can be made here. But an understanding of the legal restraints in the Old Testament is necessary to save ourselves from personal legalism or from general confusion. The fact is that many of the legal statements in the Old Testament are conditioned by time and place. While they have much to teach us, they are not the governing principles of our lives.

However, since much of the historical material in the Old Testament centers in Israel's obeying or defying the laws of the Lord, it is important that we be able to make these distinctions in a general way at least. This discussion, then, is very broad, but gives some facts about the law that should be known when one studies the historical sections.

There has always been order in the universe based on God's law. We can see it in the creation of the world, when God spoke and it was so. We see it in the Garden of Eden. And we can see it in the early day of human history leading up to the Flood. It is not hard to see how God graciously governed His people by the truth of His own person and the limited edicts that showed His justice and mercy.

It should be noted that laws—related to the use of offerings, the keeping of the Sabbath, the taking of man's life, *et al*—are as old, almost, as creation itself. But the structure of Law comes into plain view with the Mosaic economy and the revelation at Sinai (Ex. 20*ff*), where God gave the formal statements of the covenants in the book of Deuteronomy. With these matters come the priestly laws, many domestic laws, and societal ordinances.

Some believers think we should live under these laws today, but the New Testament makes clear that the context of time and place must determine these divine strictures. The principle of Law could only condemn; sinful flesh was unable to meet such divine standards. The *"righteousness of the law"* could only be practiced apart from the Law, instead through the *"grace and truth"* that came by Christ (see Rom. 3:20-31; 6:14; 8:3-4; 10:4; Gal. 2:21; 3:11-13).

The Mosaic Law is known better as the Torah, a word derived from the Hebrew, meaning *to teach, to lead out.* This term is eventually applied to all of the Pentateuch since the whole five books reveal the principles by which God leads His people. Technically, though, the Ten Commands are the heart of the Torah, and are the basis for Israel's covenant. Accordingly many scholars divide the law into three groups: Moral, Civil, and Ceremonial.

The Moral Laws are rooted in the Ten Commandments and are the laws that reflect most clearly the character of God. The Civil Laws are those given for the government of Israel as a nation, while the Ceremonial Laws are all those that relate to the ritual of sacrifice and prescribed worship. I have thought there were more precise divisions to the legal codes (in addition to those laws that spring from the creative order) and mention these—but without the presumption that everyone will agree:

- Camp Laws (governing aspects of life in the wilderness)

- National Law (governmental rules for the work and setting up of the nation)

- Settlement Law (the land and provisions for life in Canaan)

- Personal Law (such as applied to kings, etc., but not to the populace)

- Community Law (as with the cities of refuge, etc)

When this whole body of Law is studied, it should be easily observed that not *all of the law* is for *all of the time*, even though we may make some general applications that go beyond a particular time period. The laws of the camp are very specific about body waste and these laws would not be practicable in the settlement of Canaan (Deut. 23:13). They do, however, go with other laws to teach us the importance of cleanliness and concepts of sanitation that are still beneficial today. The laws of war have limitations due to the nature of prey, etc, but they aid in understanding justice and integrity. The result is that we learn from all of the Law *in principle*, although we in no way keep all of the Law *in practice*. We know that no one could ever be saved by keeping it, but we also know there can be great gain in observing the principles it promotes.

Therefore, if we are to apply a particular law in a universal way, not related to a particular time, it must be seen to apply to all people without distinction. Where a law does not reflect this character, it must be studied in the light of its time, intention, persons to whom applied, and historical context. This in no way weakens the legal statements of the Lord—in fact it enriches them and gives them a fuller meaning in the total presentation of truth.

From an understanding of the legal strictures which God wisely gave to His people we will learn more of His will and character, be better taught in all the issues of life, and have a very strong impression of the awfulness of sin. For a fuller reading of the services of the law, the book of Galatians is recommended. But out of all this, as the student comes to the historical sections, he will be able to see the difference between principle and decree, will better apply the former and understand the meaning of the latter.

5. *A general recognition of Types and Symbols:* Mentioned earlier, a type is the use of an entity to both describe and predict the coming of another entity. A good illustration is that of the brazen serpent in Numbers 21. In John 3 we learn that this brazen serpent, which represented healing to all who would look to it, prefigured the death of the Lord Jesus. When also *"lifted up,"* He would give life to all who looked to Him. The Lord makes this identification Himself in John 3, and it is a telling episode.

A type, however, is not just a mere similarity or a coincidental connection. It is an intentional biblical link with both a description of the initial action and a prediction of fulfillment. There was, for example, an intentional link between the lambs offered in the Old Testament and *"the Lamb of God, which taketh away the sin of the world"* (Jn. 1:29). As noted, the terminology is *type* and *antitype.* One must be aware of these occurrences as we read Scripture.

A symbol, on the other hand, is a stand-in of one entity for another. The blood on the door posts in Goshen symbolized the death of the substitute; the pillar of cloud symbolized the real presence of God overshadowing His people; the rod in Moses' hand symbolized his God-given authority to rule. The chief purpose, then, in the symbol is to call visible attention to something spiritual that might otherwise be overlooked.

There is, admittedly, some ambiguity in these matters, and the Bible student must be aware of it. Some see every object as a symbol and some can hardly see any symbols. Others find types on every page and some have difficulty with any but the most obvious ones. The guidelines championed at this point are these: if Scripture calls it a type, that is what it is; if it calls it a symbol the same thing is true. If the predictive character is displayed and the action so fore- seen, it is a type. If it bears a reasonable resemblance to something otherwise unidentified, it is a symbol. The meaning of a passage, however, will often be greatly enriched by the observation of these. And to fail to take note of them will certainly diminish the teaching.

Level Three: THE HISTORICAL SECTIONS

In our arrangement of materials, the progression has been from the most basic needs to the more complicated. The suggestion that one needs to know everything has been discounted as impractical. *Level Three* suggests materials that are very important but not so available or so readily made part of one's study. To the heavily scholastic mind these things are very important, but they are placed at Level Three because a great deal of satisfactory study may be had without them. Three items will be mentioned:

1. *A basic understanding of the Hebrew language:* Hebrew is the language in which the great bulk of the Old Testament is written, a few small portions being in Aramaic, a Hebrew cognate. To gain a mastery of any language, whether ancient or modern, is something that few people can do. Most of those privileged to study the lan- guage may gain a working familiarity with it. That is a great bless- ing, but is not the end of all knowledge. Translations are always lim- ited in exactness of expression, so that is where most of us must do our work. To have an understanding of the original is an asset, espe- cially in the poetry sections of the Old Testament, but we cannot say it is an absolute necessity since many of the greatest scholars con- tinue to differ on even very major points.

There are many programs today that offer help in understanding basic Hebrew idioms. These include *Interlinear* and *Concordant* Bibles, but in all of these cases the non-Hebrew student is still at the mercy of the writer and not able to make evaluations of his own. Excellent works such as the *Theological Wordbook of the Old Testament* are of limited use unless one knows enough Hebrew to understand the alphabet and follow the development of the text.

However, one does not need to know an enormous amount of Hebrew to benefit from this. A knowledge of the alphabet is just about enough for basic reading. But for many students, further language study is not realistic. So we will simply note that Level Three benefits by a good understanding of basic Hebrew, but there are many fine Bible teachers whose Hebrew is little or none. It is not a matter that keeps one from being a detailed Bible student.

2. *Detailed Near Eastern historical knowledge:* This subject might be broadened to the whole Mediterranean area, but the Near East—the territory including Israel and the Fertile Crescent—are, on the whole, more important to the Bible scholar for Old Testament purposes. It is necessary in this regard for one to have a good grip on biblical archaeology and Bible geography (in the BIBLIOGRAPHY several helpful books are suggested). In both cases it is probably as important to have the tools to work with at hand as to have recall learning. These fields are constantly being updated by current research and the Bible student does well to be a subscriber to some modern journal that will help keep abreast of issues. (References in the BIBLIOGRAPHY.)

While written a long time ago, the historical works of Herodotus are still of some help, as are Plutarch's *Lives* and the history writings of Tacitus. While these writings do not go into deep antiquity, they do go into many of the foundational kingdoms and peoples of the Old Testament times. The more background one knows, the better.

Many of the larger Bible dictionaries (*International Standard Bible Encyclopaedia,* for example) carry data in these areas and such tools are helpful. These works will also give insight into the worship practices of some of these civilizations, helping the student to appreciate the dramatic contrasts to the truth given by the Lord. With this more detailed knowledge, the Bible student will watch for those progressive events in history that lead to *"the fullness of time"* and the reality of the Messianic promise spoken of in Galatians 4.

3. *Observing principles in history applicable to other (our) times:* Not much can be said right now of this, but it is a vital aspect. From the study of any historical setting, it is appropriate to ask, "What do we learn from this?" Whatever we think we learn must be corrobo-

rated by Scripture and seen consistent in the historical process. Unfortunately this is a point to which many make impromptu and immature judgments. The Bible scholar will know that the reality of these principles will depend, in the long run, on a careful and complete analysis of all available material. Only then will there be conclusions of lasting meaning.

AN ILLUSTRATIVE STUDY

Putting these concepts to work: the Battle at Ai

It is fitting at this time to look at one of the historical sections to illustrate how these ideas work. Since some of the historical portions cover entire books and others give only a brief enclosed account, we must understand that the larger the selection, generally the greater the work that will be needed.

One of my favorite books for this sort of study is Joshua, where several historical accounts are given in the first few chapters. Each of these may be studied along the suggested lines. In this case, our consideration will be the taking of Ai, related in Joshua 7 and 8.

The first thing we do, of course, is to read the passage. In the case of a short passage like this, I suggest reading it several times, including one reading aloud. You are reading it to get a feel for it and to have an impression of the total passage in your mind.

Then it would be good to make an outline of the passage or a table of events so that you see the sequence in the account. These are items one would do for any study, as mentioned earlier. But to make this lesson as complete as possible, we assume we have read the passage carefully and now observe its content in this order:

7:1-5	the first assault on Ai, and the rout
7:6-9	Joshua's complaint to the Lord
7:10-15	The Lord prescribes an action to rectify matters
7:16-26	Trial and judgment of Achan's family
8:1-2	God's promise for the future
8:3-29	The plan; the battle; the victory; the outcome
8:30	The renewal of the law and the promises

At this point, we think of the things that will help us in our study.

We begin at *Level One*, with the most basic facts. In this category, we should have a broad survey knowledge of Israel's history and
the general details of this book. Do we know the author of the book?
(It is not always possible but, if so, we want to know that.) We should
know the approximate time period covered by the book, the reason
it is written, and those to whom it is given. It should also be known
how the book or historical material relates to the rest of the Bible
(the broad context) and the circumstances that have affected the
writing of the book.

We know why the people are entering Canaan, how Joshua has
come to be the leader, and how the Lord has challenged him. The
knowledge of God's promises to Abraham is available, and the commands given for the conquest should be known.

If any part of this information is forgotten or unclear, the student
must return to discover these basic facts from the Scriptures or from
a study Bible in order to have this clearly understood.

At the same time, it is understood that we are reading of a period
during the Age of Law, and Israel has directives on most things
social, political, and spiritual. Failure in meeting those directives
will not produce success. While it may seem that the knowledge of
the redemptive program does not help us much in this context, the
fact that God is working to establish and bless His people should be
kept in mind.

Of course, the bibliographic material should be at hand. You will
want to read about Ai in one of the dictionaries and find the possible location on a map. The student will want to study to see how the
existence of this town was important to Israel. One should note the
locations of towns close to it and what the strategic significance of
the whole area was. Now the exact location of Ai is still a matter of
archaeological dispute. One must be content with the fact that some
things are not yet fully defined, but the general area is well known.

In the bibliographic material the student will want to identify any
place or persons otherwise unknown, paying special attention to the
mention of the mountains Ebal and Gerizim. These First Level facts
help us with a more comprehensive understanding of the event.

In *Level Two* we recall more exactly the promise of the land to
Abraham and the continuance of that promise through his seed. In

particular, the words given by Moses to Joshua at the conclusion of Deuteronomy are important, and the charge given by the Lord with the attendant promises stated to Joshua. The promise of Joshua 8:1-2 will be noted, as well as the conditional aspect that is implicit.

While there is not much said related to priesthood, the garment taken by Achan has a deep religious significance that alters a good bit of the action in the account. Note as well that the judgment of God on flagrant sin is never to be overlooked, although we do not much enjoy reading about it.[4]

The student will watch for speech figures such as in 7:5, 7:9, 7:10, and 7:25. The clue to a suspected speech figure will generally lie in wording that seems awkward or hard to understand until a speech figure is suggested. APPENDIX 1 has a listing of the more easily recognized speech figures and devices. The identifications are given briefly. The speech figures become more prominent in poetry and prophecy, but they are used elsewhere to enrich the language and give graphic reality to the action.

In this account the legal strictures of the Lord relate to the background battle of Jericho. Note, however, when the sin has been established, justice executed, and the battle won, the immediate act of Joshua is for the renewal of, and understanding of, the law, and *"all"* Israel is summoned to attend to it—the text is very emphatic on this. By careful reading, one notices expressions such as *"unto this day"* (8:28). Such terms do not indicate perpetuity but that the condition existed to the time of writing.

At *Level Three*, the help of Hebrew would be significant. One would appreciate the way the Lord spoke to Joshua—there is really no easy way to put it into English with the same significance without a lot of wording. The devoted or accursed object would be seen or understood more clearly and there are several speech figures in Hebrew that simply do not translate into English. This is especially true with plays on words and emphatic construction.

As noted, a general knowledge of Hebrew is invaluable, but one can have a very fine study without it. The chief liability of limited Hebrew knowledge is that one is dependent on commentators at many points, not being able to make a judgment on critical matters based on one's own study.

A fuller understanding of these Canaanite civilizations is also very helpful as a background for what the Lord is doing. Needless to say, the principle that obedience is what pleases God is true through the ages, and the antagonism of the Lord towards sin and rebellion should fill the people of God with a hatred for such things. Self-willed defiance not only displeases the Lord, but also disturbs His people.

One of my students asked one day, "Why do we have to know all of this? Can't we just read the story and enjoy it?" Of course we can enjoy it just because it is the Word of God, but the fuller our understanding and application of it, the more meaningful our blessing and the greater likelihood that our lives can be lived in alignment with the principles so graphically illustrated.

It goes without saying that the size of the portion one studies will determine how much detail the study requires. For example, if one is going to do a study of Numbers, rather than attempting to get the whole book in one study, it would be best to see it in the divisions that are given in the Bible. When these are studied individually, a pattern will develop to tie the whole together.

If one is simply working on one verse, infinite detail can be paid to every letter, but if one is working on 50 chapters, a less extensive study will probably be utilized.

Remember also that no study is completely final. One will come back to a passage studied years before and wonder how this or that was missed. The total value of the studies is the key thing and all scholars are kept humble by remembering there is something yet to learn both from the Bible and from other Christians who study it.

However, we can conclude that, as with other Scriptures, the historical books come alive when keen and particular study is given to the details and the lessons that flow from these sacred stories.

II
OLD TESTAMENT POETRY

Whereas the study of the Old Testament historical materials could be accomplished by observing all the historical materials as a "mass," the poetry section must be treated differently. The nature of the poetical materials shows great diversity and the approach is developed on two lines: first, our discussion will center on poetry at large in the Old Testament (Section I), and then the study will move to observe the major poetic books and the special hermeneutics, or principles of interpretation, needed for them (Section II). In both areas the "three level" approach will be followed.

AS WE BEGIN OUR POETIC STUDIES

What is poetry, anyway? It is not easily defined for it has many shapes and forms. It is not governed by well-defined rules. Poets do not follow schemes of syntax and grammatical laws—they create them. We learn a language more by the study of its poetry than any other single factor. Consequently the more "poetry" we have to study, the more appreciation we have for the breadth and feeling of a language. For this presentation, poetry is seen as the description of life in the abstract—a symphonic presentation of ideas.

In English, we have many poetic forms. We have those that rhyme and those that do not. We have those that present very simply points of life, and those that wax eloquently into great operatic melodramas. While there is some diversity in historical reporting, there is enormous diversity in poetic expression.

47

This situation is true in Hebrew poetry as well. Thanks to recent archaeological discoveries of other languages and literature in the Semitic family, we know much more about ancient Semitic poetry than we did when we had chiefly the Bible as source material. Some of this material is helpful in our Bible study, some is not. But Hebrew is a beautiful language and even in its prose portions it moves with a fluidity that is attractive to the ear and the tongue. Such a melodic language is bound to spawn a host of poetic expres- sions, and that is exactly the case.

Hebrew poetry does not depend on rhyme; it seems to move more on rhythm and/or cadence. Unfortunately we have no books written in antiquity on the subject (there are plenty of theorizing books writ- ten today, however). The attempt to govern Hebrew poetry by "rules" is a trying experience, for it is governed more by the empa- thy of life and the exultation of experience. Such mystical ideas are hard on the minds of those who are pragmatic, but the fact is that Hebrew poetry must be felt! That may well be true of all poetry, but it certainly is true of Hebrew. Unfortunately many of our readers will not have the advantage of Hebrew so our study will be based on what can be appreciated by all. It will be seen that Hebrew poetry is a very good medium for the truth of the Word.

Among scholars there is considerable disagreement on the his- toric understanding of Hebrew poetry, but fortunately we have nei- ther to resolve that nor to discuss it in detail in this work. In gener- al, however, it may be said that Hebrew poetry is marked by these characteristics:

- considerable repetition: not so much word for word as idea for idea
- stress on nouns and verbs; much less on adjectives and adverbs, but infinitives and participles may have a substantive role as well
- some adherence to cadence, rhythm, or meter
- wide use of speech figures, some of which (assonance, acrostics, etc.) do not translate into English. Special attention will be given to some of these in later discussion.[1]

Some English Bibles do not show the portions of Hebrew poetry in poetic form other than in the Psalms and some obvious passages. More of the modern translations show poetic form wherever it occurs, in the psalms, or in prophets or historic material. In the statements about poetry in this work, poetic forms will be indicated as we go, whether they appear that way in the English Bible or not.

Several varieties of poetry occur in the Old Testament. Among them are:

- triumph songs (Exodus 15)
- laments or dirges (the Book of Lamentations)
- psalms—several varieties
- love songs (Song of Solomon)
- aphorisms—wisdom, advice (Proverbs)
- prophetic narrative (Isaiah 53, *et al*)

In the present study some generalizations are given about poetry in the Old Testament at large, and then more specific materials are given in Section II. The question is: What do we need to know about the poetry of the Old Testament to help us in this study?

SECTION I—SOME GENERAL OBSERVATIONS

Level One: OLD TESTAMENT POETRY

In *Level One*, five items are noted as being basic to the study of poetry and these are considered in the light of the need, as mentioned, to read the text many times and commit ourselves to prayer for the study. The items are:

1. Basic data about authorship (when possible) and the recipients
2. Historic background or occasion for the writing: especially useful for poems in the historical books and the Psalms
3. Relationship in context to similar materials
4. The emotional, pictorial value of poetry
5. Proper bibliographic material at hand

It becomes apparent that these are simple features and may be quickly comprehended, but each adds a new dimension to the understanding of the whole.

1. *Authorship of poetry and recipients (where known):* Remember that human authorship is not the test of canonicity. That test con-

cerns whether it is determined that the work came from God or not. There are several books in the Bible for which authorship is not determined, but the nature of their inspired character was the deciding factor in canonicity. But when the author *is* known, it allows the reader to enter more fully into the nature of the poem.

Psalm 23 is a good example in that we know David was a shepherd. Thus he is transferring his knowledge of the shepherd ideals to the Great Shepherd. The psalm would be a blessing even if its authorship were not known, but the message is greatly enriched by knowing the author and something about him.

It might not seem so important to know the recipients, but the tone of a poem and the force of its content is very much conditioned by the parties addressed. The long poem in Exodus 15 demonstrates this. The triumph over the enemy is written up in song that the people who have experienced this deliverance might rejoice in it day by day, and be guided by the confidence that such a lesson gives.

2. *Historic background or occasion for the writing:* This ties in immediately with the previous point. In the psalter, some psalms are given with superscriptions. (There are many academic arguments about these, incidentally, but that is not the point at this time. They will be noted in Section II where the technicality is better discussed.) The psalm becomes much more meaningful when the historic background is seen. This does not mean it is more inspired; only that the student can grasp the message much more quickly and in a fuller way. This is true in the psalter, of course, but it is equally true when reading poems in the prophetic books and the historical books. Imagine how much less the song of Deborah and Barak would mean if we did not have the background of the warfare! The song not only celebrates a victory, but allows us to see how God did it. And that, ideally, is what a good Scripture song will do.

3. *Relationship in context to similar materials:* Psalm 109 is one of the imprecatory (cursing) psalms and it uses some fierce language on the foes of David. To get a grip on this poetic medium, it is vital to consider the other imprecatory psalms. A study Bible will help one locate these and a more complete picture will give the student an appreciation for holiness and truthfulness that may not be so

easily obtained otherwise. In some ways, however, the key to this sort of information is more a matter of individual Bible reading. The student, being a careful reader of the Bible with a notebook at hand, will want to keep parallel ideas and events under scrutiny.

4. *The emotional, pictorial value of poetry:* Poetry is not a puzzle nor a problem to be solved. But it does have within it the feelings of the author and the emotion of the circumstance. It needs to be read aloud to get the full intonation of this. For example, 1 Chronicles 16:7 is a valuable passage illustrating this. When one reads it out loud, the emotion of the author can be felt, as well as the passion of the listeners. Poetry fails if it does not stir the heart. While students must use their heads, too often the heart is overlooked in the process.

5. *Proper bibliographic material at hand:* A dictionary should be used for those words the student does not recognize, a Bible dictionary for unfamiliar place names, and a good commentary on the portion being studied. There are many more helps, and no attempt is made for a full enumeration. Too often, though, the student is tempted to overlook these things and thereby miss a good part of what is intended for the message.

Level Two: OLD TESTAMENT POETRY

Level Two involves five helpful items, and in this order:

1. The major poetic books and passages
2. Recognition of poetic forms
3. Normative speech figures and poetic devices
4. Basic concepts of parallelism
5. Particular hermeneutics for the individual books

There is some overlapping in these materials and those that will come in Section II, but nothing is contradictory. Similar to building with blocks, the amount of information grows and rests on what has come before.

1. *The major poetic books and passages:* The great books of poetry are Psalms, Proverbs, and Job. Beyond these are the Song of

Solomon, Lamentations, and Ecclesiastes. Much of Isaiah is poetry (the translation by F. C. Jennings[2] attempts to show this) and there is a lot of poetry in the other prophetic books as well. The Songs of Triumph are mostly in the historical materials and the Psalms. Knowing these things simply helps the student to be prepared for the message and for the method in which it will be delivered.

2. Recognition of poetic forms: The student should recognize the aphorism (the maxim), the worship song, the victory song, the teaching song, and other special forms that will be studied in greater detail in Section II. Recognizing the form will enable the student to apply the particular hermeneutics that relate to that form.

It will help to understand why, at some points, the translators have introduced words and phrases not found in the original but needed to make a better understanding of the message.

How will the student recognize the form? You will recall that there are several varieties of Old Testament poetry and, having read the text thoroughly, you will be able to assess to which group it belongs. One will not put Psalm 23 in the triumphant songs, for example. Nor should we look at a song of triumph and think it is narrative history.

3. Normative speech figures and poetic devices: In this case the reader is referred to APPENDIX 1 and the speech figures designated as normative. These do not change materially from the historical materials to the poetic materials. Poetry, however, has many more speech figures and these are listed in the second part of APPENDIX 2 as Extended Speech Figures. This subject is very complicated in its entirety, and better learned in observation than in purely academic endeavor.

A speech figure my be presumed when the language does not seem directly literal, but even in literal language there are figures. A survey of the list in the appendix should prove worthwhile.

4. Basic concepts in parallelism: Hebrew, as noted, is a language that delights in repetition. Parallelism is the speech device by which the writer repeats in particular patterns for emphasis.[3] Although the older ideas in parallelism are being challenged, they may still be observed as having meaning. Here are the basic categories:

Synonymous parallelism—repetition of an idea or a thought with no intention of enriching or enlarging it. Psalm 24:1-3 from the KJV gives an example in each verse:

1 The earth is the Lord's and the fullness thereof
   The world and they that dwell therein
2 For He hath founded it upon the seas
   And established it upon the floods.
3 Who shall ascend unto the hill of the Lord?
   Or who shall stand in His holy place?

Synthetic parallelism—repetition of an idea or a thought, and in the process adding or altering material for greater clarity. Psalm 19:7-9 illustrates this, as the second half of each verse adds a new dimension to the first half of the verse:

7 The law of the Lord is perfect, converting the soul,
   The testimony of the Lord is sure, making wise the simple.
8 The statutes of the Lord are right, rejoicing the heart
   The commandment of the Lord is pure, enlightening the eyes
9 The fear of the Lord is clean, enduring forever.
   The judgments of the Lord are true and righteous altogether.

Antithetical parallelism—repetition of an idea with the presentation of an opposite idea. Psalm 1:6 illustrates how the second half of the verse reverses the first half:

6 For the Lord knoweth the way of the righteous
   But the way of the ungodly shall perish.

More will be said about this in Section II, but it is important to remember that this feature will be seen in many poetic sections, not just in the Psalms.

5. *Particular Hermeneutics:* These will be taken up in greater detail in Section II but the student must be aware of the basic issues involved. Hermeneutics is the science of interpretation and there will be special features to note if we are to correctly interpret many of the poetic passages. It will always be important to have the general concepts of authorship, context,[4] etc., in mind and then other key points may be added to these facts.

Level Three: OLD TESTAMENT POETRY

Level Three contains more complicated materials still. Some of them go far beyond the character of this work, but give the student some goal for which to strive. Five items are included:

1. A knowledge of biblical Hebrew
2. More complex speech figures and organization
3. Further study in metre and accentuation
4. Basic differences in Old and New Testament poetry
5. The Song of Songs—understanding and interpretation

1. *A knowledge of biblical Hebrew:* What an asset it is in reading the poetry of the Old Testament! A surface knowledge is better than none so long as the possessor knows it is only a superficial exposure. The conjunctions, the infinitives, etc., spring to life and the word arrangements, including plays on words and special composition features, become gems. Unfortunately a lot of this learning is for the good of the learner; it is hard to pass it on unless one is sharing with others of equal learning or desire. But for any student to whom the opportunity comes to study the original languages, it is the acquisition of a beautiful tool. It must be known, however, that in spite of many claims today, it is still a work of "blood, sweat, and tears." While the reward is enormous, the work is considerable.

2. *More complex speech figures and organization:* In APPENDIX 1 there is a listing of what are called Normative Speech Figures and Extended Speech Figures. This latter grouping is helpful to observe at this point. This list by no means exhausts the speech figure category, but gives the ones deemed most important in poetry (although it is always dangerous to suggest some are most important while others are of less significance). A total listing of all speech figures known and suspected would be much larger than this book!

The list given in the APPENDIX has illustrative material with the definitions, and, at this level in poetry, the student should survey the list and illustrations to at least be aware of these things as the study continues. Do not, however, expect every speech figure to be found in every passage! Some are rare, others more common—the most common being listed with the "Normative" portion of the APPENDIX.

3. *Further study in metre and accentation:* These are complicated studies and relate to the purer poetical sections—the Psalms and Lamentations—where it is determined that in each Hebrew phrase there are stressed measures and unstressed measures. Some knowledge of Hebrew is mandatory for a conquest in this battle, but the student who has no such knowledge is, at least, able to understand the idea. Oftentimes commentators or translators will amend a line in a translation so that the number of measures (stressed and unstressed) come out to an appropriate number. It is impossible to know if this assessment is really accurate or not, so the student must hold the matter in abeyance until some further help is given. Again, however, it is good to know that this dimension of study exists, underlining the detailed beauty and intricacies of the Word of God.

4. *Basic differences in Old Testament and New Testament poetry:* There is no established or given form for poetry in the New Testament (such as a Pindaric ode or some other form customary to the Greek language). Most of the poetry in the New Testament is suggested exegetically, based on the text. Good examples are 1 Timothy 3:16 and Philippians 2:6-11. It is thought the songs of Elizabeth and Mary approximate a poetic form, as does the singing of the redeemed host in heaven in Revelation 4 and 5. Yet even with the passages suggested in the New Testament, there is relatively little poetry in the New Testament as compared with the Old.

A few other clues for disclosing Old Testament poetry sections might be mentioned, but, to a very large extent, the poetry of the Old Testament is set out in the form of the text. Thus we generally do not have to search for it in an exegetical sense; we see it in a form or written sense. Interestingly, the Septuagint (the Old Testament translated into Greek) does show poetic form for the Psalms, Proverbs, Job, etc., but does not show poetic form for the narrative poetry of the prophets.

5. *The Song of Songs—understanding and interpretation:* In some ways Solomon's Song is the most difficult book in the Old Testament. I have placed this study in Level Three for particular interest and work. In the BIBLIOGRAPHY several titles are suggested as helpful books for this study, and in Section II there are some notes

on particular hermeneutics. A great deal of study is needed for this book, and it is necessary to grasp the Hebrew poetry of love. It presents the biblical ideal of a man and woman reflecting the unity God gives.

AN ILLUSTRATIVE STUDY

Putting these concepts to work: Deborah & Barak

For this study we will use the song of Deborah and Barak as recorded in Judges 5. This is one of the great songs of triumph in the Old Testament. It came at the conclusion of a military conflict which Israel should have lost, but two factors saved the day: the willingness of the people and the intercession of God. Our approach to the account will again utilize the three levels of study.

At *Level One*, it is observed that we do not know who wrote the book. Some think it was Samuel, but no one knows for sure. The song in view is obviously sung by Deborah and Barak, but who wrote it down and included it in the text is a mystery. It is not necessary to know this, since the book is viewed canonically as coming from God.

The historic background shows the early days of settlement in Canaan and the student should be familiar with the "judgeship" cycle in which Israel fell away, went into judgment, turned to God, accepted deliverance—and then allowed the whole process to be repeated. The cycle is seen clearly in chapter 2.

Chapter 4 finds Israel under the harsh control of Jabin, a Canaanite king, who is represented by his military leader, Sisera, a man commanding an army with 900 chariots, a very formidable force in that day. The student will want to read about chariot warfare in a Bible dictionary to get a better picture of it—say, than one might get from reading Ben Hur! In this level the student will ascertain the locations of the places of action and be particularly careful in the study of Mount Tabor and the plain of the River Kishon. Having read the chapter several times, the student will feel the sense of triumph in the song and, if one reads it aloud, may want to parade around the house carrying a victory sign!

1   In the context of the passage, the student will note chapter 4 and
1   see that the provocation has been going on for a long time. The per-
1   son of Heber and the role his family will play in this drama must be
1   studied and the move of Barak (with Deborah) and his army to
1   Mount Tabor in chapter 4 is a key piece in the drama.
1   Note the prediction of Deborah in 4:9 and the challenge of battle.
1   See how the Lord *"discomfitted"* Sisera in verses 15-16, how this
1   unfortunate general fled for his life—to the house of a suspected
1   friend—-and how he met his doom at that place. Eventually the stu-
1   dent will see that Israel not only won this war but continued to press
1   Jabin, the Canaanite king, until he was destroyed (4:24).
1   Whether the song was sung immediately after the battle or after
1   the end of Jabin is not certain, but the song is given—a glorious tri-
1   umph song. Now, with the context and the background clear, the stu-
1   dent may progress to the high poetic concept of the song itself.

2   In *Level Two*, having observed this is a triumph song, one quick-
2   ly meets a host of speech figures. See an apostrophe in verse 3, a
2   metaphor in verse 5, a probable hyperbole in verses 6-7, a rhetorical
2   question in verse 8. This is by no means all of them.
2   The student remembers that when the language is too grand or too
2   impersonal, a speech figure is likely involved. Until they are lodged
2   in one's head, one may search in our appendix to see if anything fits!
2   Note the list of those who helped in the battle. See the sad com-
2   mentary on Reuben (5:15-16) and the speech figures that denotes
2   failure on the part of this family. Observe the repetition of words in
2   verse 12 and determine what speech figure is in use at that point.
2   See what is significant about Zebulon and Naphtali in verse 18.
2   See a synthetic parallelism in verse 22 (not the only one available)
2   and what appears to be another in verse 24. Observe the synony-
2   mous parallelism in verse 27. And be sure to observe the assumed
2   discussions of Sisera's people in verses 28-30. Surely there was no
2   newspaper reporter on the scene but knowing the nature of people
2   allows an understanding of what was thought. As a closing thought,
2   look for antithetical parallelism in verse 31.
2   Regrettably we do not always read the text with such care. The
2   thought is not that it should be made a chore, but when the text is
2   studied, the reality of the action is gripping. How did Barak win the

battle? The Lord is the key, of course, the willingness of the people
is vital, but the geography of the land and the statements of verses
20-21 give the secret to the success. That a man who had a chariot
ran away on foot is also very telling. Chapter 4 gives us the historical material while chapter 5 gives us a wonderful triumph song, and
together they show a great victory for the Lord and His people.

At *Level Three*, if the knowledge of Hebrew were available, it
would open many other avenues of thought.

For example, chapter 4:6 tells us that Deborah challenged Barak
on this mission and the Hebrew makes it plain he had been instructed to do it before, but was just dragging his feet.

There are a number of word plays that enrich the text but they are
not translatable, one in verse 2 and another in verse 12. A good commentary that takes in the original language will usually point out
these things. The apostrophe and aside speech figures are of special
interest (as with the expressions in verses 28-30) and the direct
addresses that are given to the Lord. There does not seem to be any
problem in the nature of the text (with meter or accentuation) and
that aspect of Level Three may wait for some other portion.

This material, presented in general for the poetic books, serves as
an introduction to the whole scope of poetry. One of the most important aspects is that the poetry must be read, read often, and, when
possible, read aloud. When the poetic pieces are felt in the heart,
they are better prepared to be understood in the head.

SECTION II—A LOOK AT SPECIFIC BOOKS

INTRODUCTORY NOTE

The division of this material is due to the dissimilarities in Old
Testament poetry. In Section I, our work was with the general concepts in the poetic studies while Section II is really a development
of Level Two and the matter of particular hermeneutics. It is hoped
this will not be too confusing, but the fact is that the different poetic books use such different forms at times that it seems necessary in
this work to point out these differences.

We will discuss the Psalms, Proverbs, and Job in particular and the other poetic books—Lamentations, Ecclesiastes, Song of Solomon—as a unit. Then we will look at the poetry type that is used most widely in the Prophetic books.

THE POETRY OF THE PSALMS

The psalter as a whole is one of the best known parts of the Old Testament, although we discover that only a few psalms are well known, a few more are roughly familiar, and a great many are rarely used at all. It was Israel's hymn book, and it served a similar purpose for the early Church. It is interesting to note that when the Lord and His disciples had completed the final feast, before leaving for the trials of the night to come, they sang a hymn (Mt. 26:30, *cf.* Mk. 14:26). Some think it was a hymn from the psalter but there is nothing dogmatic to sustain that.

At any rate the psalms have been a favorite source of blessing and comfort. The beauty of the pastoral psalms contrasts with the fury of the imprecatory psalms, but all together they present a great picture of personal relationships with the God of the universe.

Level One: THE PSALMS

Most of this material is fairly general information. As such it is basic to the general understanding of the psalter. The student must remember the principles stated on page 26 of this work—the reading and praying over a passage before it becomes an object of deeper study. In *Level One*, the following items are discussed:

1. Basic data on the psalm (or psalms)
2. The nature of the collection
3. The varieties of psalms
4. The worship character and use of the Psalter
5. The psalm titles
6. The spiritual relationship between the Lord and the writer

1. *The basic data on the psalm or psalms as indicated:* This includes the identification of the author, when possible, as well as determining the historical context in which the psalm was written, when possible. It is well known that not all the psalms are identified

with a writer and many do not have a particular historical point of reference. But where it is possible to discern these things, the information will prove to be of real help.

Along with this, one should also think about the intended recipient by asking if the psalm is addressed to anyone in particular, any group or class of persons identifiable, to the Lord alone, or to any hearer whatsoever. A good commentary on the psalms is helpful for these matters and there are several listed in the BIBLIOGRAPHY.

2. *The nature of the collection:* The Hebrew and Protestant Canon consists of 150 psalms. The Orthodox Canon has an additional psalm (151) and some rearrangements or placements of psalms. There is some evidence that this psalm (151) was known and used at Qumran so it may be that it has more importance than has been thought. Such matters cannot be settled in a work such as this, but the student needs to know that the question does exist and it has not been fully answered. These 150 psalms are organized into five books:

Book I: 1-41
Book II: 42-72
Book III: 73-89
Book IV: 90-106
Book V: 107-150

Some think these five books of the psalter were developed to follow the five books of the Pentateuch, although that is not at all certain. Similarly there are no sharp divisions[5] of material so that one book looks distinctive from the others. The personal opinion of this writer is that the division was made for liturgical purpose and was arbitrary. The Psalms came from the Holy Spirit, the dividing came from worshipping persons who could more easily work with a smaller collection than one that was larger. Of course the scroll could be held more easily. This, too, is a suggestion that is not followed by all.

3. *The varieties of psalms:* The wide variety in the Psalms is amazing. Some are written as simple poems extolling God or an aspect of His character. Others are written as historical reviews, intended to remind the Israelites of their dependence on God and their own poor performance in many situations. Still others are

deeply personal, telling of great trials and great blessings, but having that touch that makes one feel like a diary is being read or that something very confidential is being discussed.

Within these parameters the psalms are categorized in various ways. The following groups are suggested by Bullock[6] (*Introduction to the Old Testament Poetic Books*) and seem to be inclusive enough to cover the whole psalter.

- hymns: formal singing by choirs or congregation (pastoral)
- penitential, e.g., Ps. 51
- wisdom, e.g., 73
- Messianic, e.g., 110
- imprecatory (cursing), e.g., 109
- enthronement (Kingship), e.g., 47
- historical, e.g., 107

Various authors will use other titles and there is no total agreement on terminology. But on the broad concept there is wide acceptance. The student keeps these things in mind so that the reading is directed, and the lessons that are found are appropriate.

4. *The worship character and use of the Psalter:* The psalms were important in Israel's worship, both in the temple in earlier days and in the synagogue as that institution developed. It is apparent that the songs were intended to be sung by a choir (David's choir was a great operation) certainly and most likely by the gathered assembly, as witnessed in the antiphonal psalms of which 136 is the prime example. Certain psalms were used for special occasions and the days of the week were commemorated by key psalms:

- the Sabbath   Psalm 92 (designated in Scripture)
- Day 1   Psalm 24
- Day 2   Psalm 48
- Day 3   Psalm 82
- Day 4   Psalm 94
- Day 5   Psalm 81
- Day 6   Psalm 93

One is reading the very heart of worship when reading the Psalter and it is an deeply moving fact that the student must keep in mind.

5. *The psalm titles:* The psalm titles are important in that they give clues to authorship and historical situations in many cases. This work does not suggest that the student should know them all or put them in the memory bank, but should know of them and thus have a resource for consideration. Some of the titles are patently clear and these are such as define authorship as in Psalm 23. Many English Bibles print this title above the psalm and in small print. But in the Hebrew Bible it is the first line of the psalm. The same is true with psalms assigned to Asaph. Other psalms have an identifying line as to the history or occasion of writing (Psalm 30).

There have been questions about these superscriptions[7] as to whether some of them belong to the previous psalm or the following psalm. (One must look at an ancient Hebrew manuscript to see the nature of this problem) but the view in this work is that the superscription defines the circumstance under which the following psalm is written and that gives added meaning to the understanding of it. Not every psalm is so identified, but when it is, it is a key factor.

In addition to the superscriptions, many psalms are given titles that are not translatable, the meaning of which must be assumed as far as possible. Some of these terms seem to indicate the character of the poem and included in this grouping are: *Mizmor*, (psalm), *shir* (song), *maschil* (a skilful song), *michtam* (a golden song), *Shiggaion* (a loud psalm), *Tehillah* (a prayer), and *hallel* (a praise).

Others given are thought to tell something of the music. These are often accompanied by the phrase *"to the chief musician,"* etc. The student does not need to know all of these, but should have the bibliographic material at hand so that they may be studied for background suggestions.

Two other interesting classifications of psalms are the Songs of Degrees (Psalms 120–134), fifteen psalms apparently arranged in groups of three in which a common theme is observed. The first psalm in each group speaks of distress, while the second tells of trust, and the third speaks of blessing—particularly on the holy city. It is a mystery as to how the psalms got the title but the popular suggestion is that they are written commemorating the ten degrees[8] on the sundial given to indicate that God had heard Hezekiah's address and had granted him 15 more years of life.

The second group is the "Hallelujah collection" featuring Psalms

146–150, songs of praise and worship built around the Hebrew verb *hallel.*

6. *The spiritual relationship between the Lord and the writer:* This is a critical point, although it is not observed so much in explicit statement as in the awareness of the heart of the writer and the proximity of the Lord. The student will see if the writer is primarily addressing the Lord in a worshipful sense, in a petitioning sense, or in a recriminating sense. There is also the matter of determining whether the Lord is being thanked for what has been done or being called upon for some further action. The question arises as to whether the psalmist is showing trust, a resolution of some problem, or just exulting in God. This is not the full run of emotions but it is all that can be noticed at this time.

Level Two: THE PSALMS

In *Level Two,* more difficult matters are approached. These include:

1. Problems in the text
2. Parallelism
3. Additional data on speech figures
4. Dispensational thrust

All of these have been touched on in a very general way, but now they become the focus of direct attention.

1. *Problems in the text:* These matters cannot be dealt with fully unless the Hebrew is understood, but the basic areas of discussion can be seen and the student will feel assured that there is enough sound data to let one read the texts of the psalms with confidence.

Our oldest complete texts in Hebrew are those of the Leningrad Codex and the Aleppo Codex, both dating about 1000 AD. But there are many earlier fragments and considerable material from before the time of Jesus, thanks to the discovery of the Dead Sea Scrolls.

The Greek translation of the Old Testament (the Septuagint) contains the psalms in a few manuscripts in the earlier Christian period and there are many fragments of this also prior to the coming of the

Lord. All in all, it seems that we have a good text foundation for the psalms, and we believe that God who gave the Word has also preserved the Word.

There are some perplexities, however. The duplicated portions are one of these. Psalms 14 and 53 are virtually the same and have the Davidic authorship assignment. There are some minimal changes, some in the Hebrew and some in the translations, but it is hard to understand why this song would be given twice, unless it had some deeper meaning in David's life and so needed repetition.

Similarly Psalm 40:13-17 is the text of Psalm 70—not to the identical words but with many identical words and ideas. One can understand that this might be a common expression in life but one might also wonder if a copyist may have confused a text. Also Psalm 57:7 combined with Psalm 60:5-12 is the message (text) of Psalm 108. It is always possible that the nature of these passages required repetition, but it is perplexing that, while these are stressed, many other passages of great personal importance are not. These questions are not answered in this work but the student needs to be aware that they exist. For the moment, be content with the answer that there are many things we do not know—including these repetitions.

Of keen interest also is the fact that the Hebrew preposition translated "of" may also be translated "to" or "for." This means that a psalm which is identified as a psalm of David could be written to mean a "psalm for David" and this would also be true for the psalms associated with Asaph, etc. Literary technicalities of this sort are not easily answered to the satisfaction of all, but in many cases the context of the psalm, as in Psalm 90, gives the clue as to which translation is proper.

At one time, liberal scholars sought to make the whole psalter a book developed late in Israel's history. But discovery of the literature of other cultures (Ugarit, etc.) has made this untenable. There is no reason for thinking the psalms are anything other than what they profess to be—the spiritual cries of the nation to a redeeming Lord.

2. *Parallelism:* This is a giant subject with many diversions. In this work our attempt is to familiarize the student with the broad ideas so as to increase our perception as we read the Psalms. As noted earlier, the concepts in parallelism grow from the repetitive

nature of the Hebrew language—meaningful repetition so the basic intent is made increasingly plain to the reader. The older ideas about parallelism are being challenged, but there is enough substance to them that there is profit in them so long as the student does not think it is the end of all study. In other words, observe basic parallel constructions but do not build a theology on syntax and grammar alone.

The basic ideas, as mentioned earlier, are summarized in this way:

- *Synonymous parallelism* finds phrase 2 saying the same thing as phrase 1 with different words but no extension of the idea.
- *Synthetic parallelism* finds phrase 2 taking the idea of phrase 1 and enriching or adding to the concept as it repeats the basic thought.
- *Antithetical parallelism* occurs when phrase 2 reverses the action of phrase 1 and actually presents a contrary position.

The term "phrase" is used in this section as a parallel to the Hebrew term *stich*. A stich is a line of poetry which may be very short or somewhat extended. The problem with the word "line" is that one assumes it is something written on one level but a "line" of Hebrew poetry might begin at one level and end at another. So the word "phrase" is used in this work. It is not a perfect term, but usable.

For a fuller understanding of parallelism, Psalm 15 will be used in an exemplary fashion. The psalm is printed from the King James Version of the Bible and marked by phrases as understood in the text and compared with the Hebrew text. There are many other passages that would serve as well, but this is a short psalm and it is easier to work with a short psalm than a long one. At this point in the study the student is probably eager for something that is easier.

PSALM 15 (KJV)

A Psalm of David	Hebrew *mizmor*, a spiritual song
Lord, who shall abide in thy tabernacle?	Phrase 1, an interrogation that will be answered at the conclusion. Note the direct address...

Who shall dwell in thy holy hill?	Phrase 2 is synonymous parallelism. Note the speech figure metonymy in the expression "holy hill."
He that walketh uprightly and worketh righteousness	Phrase 1 of verse 2 as the begining of the answer. The structure of the psalm is the speech device *anabasis,* a gradual ascent in the development of the answer.
And speaketh the truth in his heart	Phrase 2 of verse 2, synthetic parallelism, and it is plain how it stresses the key thought of phrase 1 and adds to it.
He that backbiteth not with his tongue Nor doeth evil to his neighbor, Nor taketh up a reproach against his neighbor	Phrase 1 is an "independent" thought while phrases 2 and 3 are in a synthetic relationship
In whose eyes a vile person is contemned	Phrase 1 of verse 4
but he honoreth them that fear the Lord	Phrase 2 is antithetical parallelism contrasting the vile person with the one honoring the Lord.
He that sweareth to his own hurt and changeth not	In the structure of the *anabasis* device mentioned in verse 2.
He that putteth not out his money for usury Nor taketh reward against the innocent	Most likely a synthetic structure but it could be argued!
He that doeth these *things* shall never be moved.	"things" is italicized to show an *ellipsis*, a word omission that must be supplied by the translator in the proper context[9]

There are several occurrences of ellipsis in the psalm and, as a general rule, if one is reading the King James, the vast majority of italicized words represent these. In any translation there is a necessity to supply "missing words" since the nature of the grammatical expression is never identical. In Hebrew many words will be assumed and the subjects of a verb are often contained in its form while objects (especially indirect objects) are frequently assumed.

The advice in this work is that the student should be aware of the parallelisms and not attempt to make great theological assessments based on the fact that a different word may be used with regard to a common subject. Watch for the ways in which these expressions occur (Psalm 27 is an excellent study area) and enjoy them, but the student should not become a parallelism detective. Nevertheless, without an understanding, it is possible to miss the depth of a verse or the intention of the writer

There are several variations in the parallel ideas and these are summarized nicely by Bulloch in his work, *An Introduction to the Poetical Books of the Old Testament,* as noted in the BIBLIOGRAPHY.

3. *Additional data on speech figures:* APPENDIX 1 lists speech figures and devices. The student may have observed the different figures and can see illustrations of them there. But it must be noted that the total number of figures identified in APPENDIX 1 is only a small portion of the total that may be suggested.

This appendix is divided into three segments. The first deals with "normative" speech figures (the designation in this work) while the second looks at speech figures that are deemed important and are widely used in the poetic works (although also seen in other places). The third division of APPENDIX 1 deals with literary (speech) devices. But those that are given in the second segment are those which I have found to be most common and useful. Of the few hundred that are not mentioned, one who wished to major in this area will find the fuller definitions in Bullinger's *Speech Figures in the Bible.* This is an area where one can know too much; the object of this work is to supply materials that will aid the study and not boggle the mind of the student.

4. *Dispensational thrust:* In the case of Psalm 15, it is probably

clear that it is a "kingdom" psalm, a work belonging to Israel's rule
as the people of God. It is not describing a way to be saved but a way
to live and enjoy the presence of God. Salvation is always by grace
and never by works, but the practical relationship of a believer and
the Lord is governed in a very big way by the character of life. The
life prescription mentions only a handful of things, but they touch on
many aspects of the law, and the worshipper is reminded that one
cannot live and please God without obedience to His Word and will.

Some of the psalms will relate to the millennial age (Psalm 2) and
some to the historical periods of Israel's wandering. The great truths
of Scripture are good for every age, of course, but the local or governmental expressions must be understood in the context in which
they are given. There are not so many conflicts in this area as may
be supposed—especially when the Bible student is careful with the
full interpretation and the teaching of the whole of Scripture. But the
matter must be borne in mind.

We are helped when we see that the picture of the good shepherd
in Psalm 23 is virtually identical to that presented in John 10. But in
the matter of the imprecations (Psalm 109) and other personal experiences of the psalmist, a good deal of study may be needed to see
how the writer is reflecting the truth of God in the context of the age
in which the work is given.

Level Three: THE PSALMS

Level Three involves the most difficult items in our studies and
while they are very important, they become luxury pieces for many
students. It would be good if they, too, were understood from the
beginning, but that requirement would prevent many from becoming
students. In Level Three of the Psalms two things are mentioned:

1. A working knowledge of Hebrew
2. An understanding of some poetic structures

1. *A working knowledge of biblical Hebrew:* The most important
thing in Level Three would be a working knowledge of Hebrew. This
basic knowledge allows the student to see nuances in words and
phrases, and also permits one to see occasions of *assonance, alliteration,* and *acrostic* that are not translatable. While these details do

not seem to have a theological thrust, there is always an interest in them that will enrich the student's appreciation of Scripture's intricacies. Psalm 119 is the classic example of this, although there are several other examples.

One should begin the study of Scripture as soon as one is saved! A student does not have to wait until some level of intelligence or knowledge is reached. The study will deepen with the experience of the student and one will restudy a passage and be amazed at how much was not comprehended at the beginning.

In this book there is no intention of suggesting one cannot begin the study until these items are mastered! No, begin quickly! Then as bits of information here and there are added, we are better able to see the total picture. There are many helpful works in this area today, and the BIBLIOGRAPHY mentions some that may be of interest to those who would like to acquire a working knowledge of biblical Hebrew.

2. *An understanding of some poetic structures:* There are two poetic structure forms that are important and worthy of consideration in Level Three. The first is *alternation.* The idea in this form is that subjects or topics are viewed alternatively in common progression. From the *Companion Bible*[10] the following alternation is seen in Psalm 77, a psalm of Asaph.

1-6	occupation with self and one's problems
7-9	the result is misery (grief)
10-12	occupation with the Lord
13	the result is happiness

Within this psalm are other alternatives. The subject will be mentioned and, following another point, will be mentioned again. That is the idea in alternation. It does not need to cover the whole psalm and, in fact, may only touch on a few verses. But the intent is to force the reader to see a point of truth in the mind of the writer. A student may suspect an alternation any time thoughts are repeated in a regular order.

The other form is *introversion* or the reversing of an order of subjects or the treatment of a subject. Again, the *Companion Bible* helps us with an example in Psalm 82. The arrangement goes like this:

1   God is the righteous judge

2-4   Earthly judges are seen as often wrong

5a   The negative side of their poor judgment

5b   The positive side of their poor judgment

6-7   Earthly judges are condemned

8   God is seen as the righteous judge

This is a simple example of introversion—the subject turned around. In effect, it gives steps 1-2-3 and then reverses the order, 3-2-1. Alternation and introversion are often put together in complicated form and are extensively used in the poetic books

A personal note: this writer has often had students who asked if the people who wrote these things "understood all this" when they wrote it. The reply is that they did not understand it in our terminology—English was unknown—and the modern development of grammatical ideal was not pronounced. But they certainly knew what they were doing. These writers were the masters of Hebrew and communication and while they would not have used the same terms, we are simply describing what they did. When one reads Psalm 119 we cannot believe the arrangement was by accident! Modern students must be careful that they do not force some arbitrary piece of literary skill on an ancient writer but when one finds the ancient writer using it and promoting it, we have reason to define it and watch for other passages where a similar device is used.

INTRODUCTORY NOTE: THE POETRY OF THE PROVERBS

The Book of Proverbs is the great "wisdom" book of the Old Testament. In Proverbs thoughts fly like lightning flashes on a summer night. Many of them are immediately meaningful and clear; some will seem cryptic and mysterious, and some will seem like they came from *Poor Richard's Almanac*, but all are based on life experience and teachings of the Word of God.

Virtually every issue of life comes into view, but the strongest issues are concerned with the importance of being right with God—living a morally healthy life and having good relationships with others. The book is concerned with discipline or order (3:11-12; 13:18; 15:10, etc.) that comes from a proper relationship with God. This relationship is the *"beginning"* of wisdom (1:7; 9:10) and affects the family (10:1; 11:29), business (10:9; 11:1, 18), charity (11:24-25; 14:321), speech (10:19; 21, 32), and many other aspects of daily living. The Lord is depicted as sovereign (16:1, 4, 9, 33: 19:21) and omniscient (15:3, 26; 16:2; 17:3; 20:27) as well as having many attributes clearly identified.

To every category one might add a great many scriptures, but Proverbs is not so much a book of proof texts as a guide that challenges the reader to think and act appropriately. Urging the reader to think and listen, the book delights in contrasts and often does not finish them but allows the reader to complete "the rest of the story." Proverbs is outlined in various ways, depending on the stress given to the identity of individuals in the book. The simplest form is this:

chs. 1-9   Solomon's advice to his "son"
chs. 10-24   Wise sayings of the king
chs. 25-29   Solomon's statements as known to men of Hezekiah
chs. 30-31   Wise saying of identified but unknown sources.

Many scholars bring a division into the outline at 22:17-24:22 and call it the words of the wise and add another section at 24:23-34, further words of the wise. But the simple outlines have always appealed to this writer and this introversion outline has been impressive in looking at the total book:

A. Wisdom personified (1:1–9:18)
    B. Solomon's Proverbs (10:1–22:16)
        C. Sayings of the Wise (22:17–23:14)
        C. Sayings of (other) wise (23:15–24:22)
    B. Solomon's Proverbs (by Hezekiah's men) (25:1–29:27)
A. Wisdom demonstrated (chs. 30–31)

As noted earlier in this work, the student coming to the book of Proverbs will want to give it a prayerful reading whether one is looking at the whole or a part. The student will want to read about the authorship and have in mind a working outline, if none of those suggested are satisfactory.

Proverbs is pure Hebrew poetry and the parallelistic style is seen everywhere. The book may be studied by themes, individual subjects, or simply read for personal advice. But as one comes to the

study of the book, it will help to make some observations. They are
arranged as usual in three levels.

Level One: THE PROVERBS

In *Level One*, the following items are discussed:

1. The nature of the book of Proverbs
2. Aphorisms in general; parallelism in particular
3. Normative speech figures
4. Meanings of key terms: wisdom, knowledge, instruction,
   learning, understanding, etc.

1. *The nature of the book of Proverbs:* The Hebrew word translated as "proverbs" may be understood to mean "wise sayings" or, in
more modern English, "aphorisms" or "maxims," although the latter
term is more limited. Proverbs is a book of practical advice. We must
see it as a book of principles, not promises; a book of advice, not
laws. When Solomon says: *"A soft answer turns away wrath but
grievous words stir up anger,"* he is not saying this will inevitably
happen, but the general principle is that it is most likely to occur.
Therefore the wise person follows the principle and the result is
much more likely to be healthy. But you may find a time when a soft
answer provokes a vicious person and, as in the case of this writer,
one receives a bloody nose (also given comment in Proverbs) as a
return.

Thus the ideas are not intended to be taken in an absolute sense,
as can be seen from the experience of those in the biblical records.
But the principles are founded on the overall teaching of the Word
of God and are productive of better results when followed.

Similarly much of the advice is given in this same order. One
might make a friendship with an angry man and one might go in
company with a furious man and not develop his bad manners for
oneself, but the greater likelihood is that such relationships will have
a detrimental effect. The Proverbs writer urges us not to do them for,
in general, they are contrary paths. But his admonition is not a law
but an observable practice that is useful in general conduct.

The same concepts are true with training up the child in Proverbs
22:6. *"In the way he should go"* does not assume there is one way

that patterns the life of every child. It boldly asserts that he will not depart from the right way when he is older if he is directed in the proper way. But that way may vary from child to child and every parent is obliged to seek the guidance of the Lord in every life decision.

It must be understood, of course, that elsewhere in Scripture there are many absolutes given, such as *"thou shalt not steal."* These need to be taught and obeyed. The total advice for living, however, is not so cut and dried. The great issues of life require discernment based on the truth of God and developed in the practice of living. The Book of Proverbs is given to us to help in such matters.

2. *Aphorisms in general; parallelism in particular:* The Book of Proverbs abounds in parallelisms. The most common form is the "two line" parallelism, as in 22:2, *"The rich and poor meet together: the Lord is the Maker of them all."* The basic idea in parallelism continues to be repetition that is purposed to directly restate the principle, or add something to it, or reverse the nature of the order of things. As in the book of Psalms, the parallelisms follow the ideas of being synonymous, synthetic or antithetical.

Some commentators recognize a fourth variety in parallelism and call it *comparative* parallelism where a principle is stated and then some illustrative material is used to explain it. Adequate discussions of these are found in Bullock (see BIBLIOGRAPHY). The student, in coming to grips with these expressions, simply reads and thinks.

A *synonymous* example may be see in Proverbs 19:5,

> A false witness shall not be unpunished,
>> and he that speaketh lies shall not escape.

In 22:2 (cited above) shows an example of a *synthetic* form. An *antithetic* example may be seen in 12:15,

> The way of a fool is right in his own eyes,
>> but he that hearkeneth unto counsel is wise.

A *comparative* example is seen in 26:11 where the subjects are reversed:

> As a dog returns to his vomit,
>> so a fool returns to his folly.

Here the natural observation of canine life explains why a fool repeats the same errors or makes the same blunders repeatedly.

There are some forms of parallelism that involve more than two lines (remember that *stichs* is the academic term for lines). A four-line example is seen in Psalm 24:3-4:

> Through wisdom is an house builded,
>> and by understanding it is established;
> And by knowledge shall the chambers be filled,
>> with all precious and pleasant riches.

There are a few six- and eight-line parallelisms and they are recognizable by the nature of the material or objects they discuss. In seeing these parallelisms, the student avoids the pitfall of trying to make every line mean something different! Each form calls special attention to the meaning of the passage in view, and the enjoyment of what is written is greatly increased.

3. *Continued work with speech figures:* The speech figures are consistently distributed throughout the Bible but they abound in poetry, as has been previously noted, for poetry is a language of imagery and ideal. The things described or discussed can only rarely be put into absolute or concrete terms.

To recognize the "normative" speech figures (see APPENDIX 1) is a good part of the student's mastery in this area. To see, for example, that *"feet"* in Proverbs 1:16 is a *synechdoche* (a part for the whole) allows one to understand that *"sinners"* (v. 10) are totally given to their error. Once these things are in mind, the understanding and use of them is almost automatic.

Very important in Proverbs is the speech figure of personification. Wisdom, the gem of all important things, is depicted as a feminine person following 1:20, and this designation is made emphatic as wisdom speaks in that role in chapters 8 and 9. Folly is also personified as a woman—the very opposite of wisdom as in 7:5 and many other places—but a low and immoral sort of person. The characterizations are not speaking of any one person in particular but of a class or system of thinking that allows the reader to place himself on the side of right or wrong. The big question is: to which woman does one give one's attention?

4. *Basic meaning of key terms:* Basic meanings are derived from bibliographic help such as dictionaries, lexicons, etc., and by careful observation of the way in which a term is used in the text as it is discussed. *Wisdom* is apparently the ability to take what one knows or what one has been given informatively and apply it to life. *Knowledge* is the acquisition of information while *learning* is the process that develops it. *Instruction* involves hearing and following the advice of a teacher and *understanding* is a matter of knowing what the instruction means and being governed by it.

These are not full definitions but the terms are not synonymous and the writer wants the student to be able to apply all of them in proper perspective. In that connection it is vital to see how the *"fear of the Lord"* enters into these things and such a word as "fear" also needs careful defining as it covers almost everything from deep respect to pure fright! The term *"evil"* is another word whose meaning might seem obvious but actually covers a spectrum of ideas from moral sin to a broken leg! The dictionaries and lexicons are vital tools and the student should not take for granted the understanding of a term based purely on one's own intuition.

Level Two: THE PROVERBS

At *Level Two*, a few items are added to the basic information in Level One. These include:

1. More work with speech figures and devices
2. Discerning themes in Proverbs
3. Relating Proverbs to the Law of God
4. Considering authorship questions more deeply

Some of these items proceed naturally from simply reading the text, but the plan at this time is to see them individually and add the information to the fund of knowledge.

1. *More work with speech figures and devices:* By this time the student should be familiar with APPENDIX 1 where the speech figures are listed alphabetically in categories, designed just for this work. The first category is called "normative" and the second is styled "developed." The chief distinction is in the frequency of use

on the whole. Further work on speech devices will be found in the third part of this APPENDIX. Proverbs makes considerable use of one of these, known as a *numerical collocation*.[11] This is a device in which things are itemized by number to show a progression without indicating much about relative importance.

One of the clear examples is seen in Proverbs 6:16-19 where the text reads: *"These six things doth the Lord hate, yea seven are an abomination unto Him."* The writer proceeds to name six things and concludes with the seventh as the *"sowing of discord among the brethren.."* The collocation (*"six"* and *"seven"*) indicates there are many things the Lord hates and here is a sampling of them. Number seven is not necessarily worse than the first six and it is not the end of what the Lord hates. In verse 12-15 the Lord has warned against the influence of wicked persons and in verse 20*ff* the writer calls his "son" to attend his commandment and follow the instruction given.

In between is the numerical challenge reminding the "son" that the Lord is opposed to anything unrighteous and there is no end to His indignation with evil. More of these collocations will be seen in chapter 30 and some are implicit in the text of the book as well.

2. *Discerning themes in Proverbs:* It is not difficult to discern themes in Proverbs, but having some in mind often puts passages together in a more meaningful way. Certainly the great theme is the fear of the Lord and (when one has defined *"fear"*) following 1:7, the student will track this expression through its 23 occurrences including 9:10; 10:27; 15:33; 16:6; etc., and notice all that is accomplished in life by the *"fear of the Lord."* It becomes obvious in this study that the phrase is a life indicator, not just a slogan! The path of life, however, is traced in the book not by a phrase but by a combination of things that make for life as opposed to those that make for death. Careful reading is needed to observe these concepts.

Right relationships with a neighbor or a family member also show up in the text in numerous occasions and the contrast between industry and slothfulness is a full study by itself. With that one will have a great deal of data showing who is wise and who is foolish; sometimes this is embarrassing when we think of the things that we believe are life's essentials.

The use of a notebook is vital to discern these themes. While one may read a study Bible or track a word with a concordance, there is no substitute for seeing and annotating the theme for oneself.

3. *Relating Proverbs to the Law of God:* This is an important study even if difficult. Proverbs is a book of advice along lines previously noted, but the character of its advice is deeply entrenched in an understanding of the law of God. The initial concept of 1:8 with regard to listening to the teaching of father and mother surely goes back to Deuteronomy 6; this idea is restated several times.

The advice to the son with regard to morality is anchored firmly in the commandments, and the terms that govern industry and business are rooted well in the concepts of *"thou shalt not steal"* as well as the Levitical teachings in Leviticus 19, etc.

Note how simple directions about observing property lines (23:28, etc) are grounded in the Deuteronomic code (Deut. 27:17, etc). The Scripture is one book, as we know, and its parts relate to one another in a non-contradictory fashion. A study at this level in Proverbs helps us to see it more clearly and to be thankful for the unity in the Word which God has given us.

4. *Considering more deeply the questions of authorship:* These are technical questions that enter into higher criticism—the consideration of authorship, integrity, dating, etc. ("Lower criticism" is essentially the study of the text. The terms are merely used to define two areas of Bible study with regard to its origin and preservation.) This study might also be moved to Level Three and, while it is not indispensable, it is also not absolutely required for a fuller understanding of the text.

The related issues cannot be taken up in detail in this work, but one has to think about Agur (ch. 30) and Lemuel's mother (ch. 31). The idea that they were persons of credibility known to Solomon is possible, but we are not sure.

Likewise the work of Hezekiah's men (ch. 25) is vague and we are not certain what their service was. Negative biblical criticism at one time doubted the veracity of a Solomonic authorship for the earlier parts of the book, but comparative literature studies have shown this to have been an unnecessary concession. Aphoristic literature is seen well before the time of Solomon, in earlier civilizations.

Level Three: THE PROVERBS

In *Level Three*, the student meets some familiar ideas, and discovers that there is not much more material of a complicated nature that is needed for the study of Proverbs. Three items are mentioned specifically:

1. Basic understanding of the Hebrew language
2. Comparison with "similar" ancient Near Eastern literature
3. Working with difficult proverbs

1. *Basic understanding of the Hebrew language:* Every part of speech is enriched by Hebrew—right down to the conjunctions "and" as well as "but," etc. One may gain some understanding of these from a Concordant Bible or a study Bible but unless one actually knows what is being discussed it is always tentative. Our point, however,. is that all should study the Bible and if one cannot have the ideal situation, then one works with what is available. Some excellent Bible students and teachers have not had the advantage of the original languages, yet the Lord honored their services as they put themselves at His disposal. In many cases they were able to give excellent Bible pointers to the keen scholars who read all the languages but sometimes missed the key relationships with the Lord that make ministry possible.[12]

2. *Comparison with "similar" ancient Near Eastern literature:* This, too, is a more technical study and the student will need to go to a library to compare the Proverbs work with texts from Ugarit, etc. There is more material available in this line today than when Pritchard edited his *Ancient Near Eastern Texts* (still a very valuable work)—half a century ago. The codes of Hammurabi have often been compared with the Mosaic Law, and the Song of Solomon has been compared/contrasted with the Ras Shamra love poetry, etc.

From this point of view, the Bible is seen to be the supreme piece of literature. What we learn from these other works is chiefly in the role of apologetics, indicating that the Bible is a faithful representative of that age which it claims.

The ancient world was much more literature-minded than scholars at one time thought, and the Bible was not produced in a literature vacuum but from a world that appreciated literature. God gave this work to His people for their edification and direction in life.

3. *Working with difficult proverbs:* As noted earlier, some proverbs are cryptic, and a special study is needed for these. The most important feature is to read them carefully and, where possible, understand them in the context available. Two such segments are cited as examples of proverbs in this category. Note Proverbs 26:4-5, where the text reads:

> Answer not a fool according to his folly, lest thou be like unto him.
> Answer a fool according to his folly, let he be wise in his own conceits.

The general context in 26:1-12 concerns the character and actions of *"fools."* There are five Hebrew words translated *"fool,"* although the most common one is the term used in these verses. The student has available in any of the major concordances the information that will show this definition. It is important for this "fool" is not the "fool"[13] of Psalm 14:1. The "fool" under view in this passage is someone who is self-confident or conceited and presumes to know a lot more than he really knows. He is a fool due to an inability to admit the need of other's advice, the counsel of those who are wiser.

Similarly the word "folly" needs identification. There are several words given this translation, but this is the primary one in Proverbs. It means simply the mistake that the "fool" is making in his poor judgment. The text is talking about an arrogant, self-important and confidant person to whom the advice of the wise is nothing.

The verses are framed in an antithetical parallelism, and one is first advised not to answer a fool according to his folly. The negative is not an absolute negative but a reasoning negative, meaning you should not do it, but you are not emphatically commanded not to do it. It is not reasonable that one should answer a fool according to his folly, for in doing so one may become like the fool (a *simile* in the speech figures) and thereby assume that one knows a great deal more than one really knows!

But in the following verses one *should* answer a fool according to his folly so that the fool will know he is ignoring the advice that is right. The thrust is that Proverbs is saying: "Don't become a fool to rebuke a fool, but don't allow a fool to think he knows it all." The proverbs then make perfect sense if understood in that light.

Another proverb that sometimes perplexes the student is the "gift" proverb of 18:16, *"A man's gift maketh room for him, and bringeth him before great men."* (This is by some connected with 21:14: *"A gift in secret pacifieth anger and a reward in the bosom strong wrath"*). The question coming from the verse is this: what is a gift? There is no clue in our bibliographic helps. The word is a substantive derived from the verb "give" (used innumerable times) and does not indicate what sort of gift it is. It could be a bribe! or a present! or an ability of unusual force, although the latter is the least likely.

A bribe would seem inconsistent with the integrity ideas in Proverbs, but the thought of a useful present not directly associated with any personal gain would be acceptable. And, if the term is tied to 21:14, it might simply indicate that one shows a kindness to another who has a cause to be angry and the gift reestablished friendship and confidence. In the case of this proverb, the context is not significant (as thought here) although the following verses discuss relationships that are on the harder side of things. One is left with the conclusion that the gift is an honorable thing that states a concern, a yieldedness, a general interest in the welfare of others.

In the BIBLIOGRAPHY several books are mentioned that help in the interpretation of Proverbs on the whole and individual segments as well. In the case of the understanding given for this proverb, there is not total agreement but the authors concur generally.

A fuller study of wisdom as noted in Proverbs would be useful, and for family matters the study of a wise son and of parental responsibility would be meaningful. No amount of time spent in this book is lost. Its evenness and consistent justice shows how superior it is to the wisest of human thinking. The student may commit to a life study of this book and quickly discover that it will show you something new every day—even when one thinks it is mastered.

INTRODUCTORY NOTE: THE POETRY OF JOB

Job is the second of the "Wisdom" books, following Proverbs and preceding Ecclesiastes. Job differs from the others in its format as it is a book of monologues that are intended to teach the listeners. The book begins with a prose prologue and concludes with a prose epilogue. In the passages between, an occasional prose phrase occurs, but the great bulk of the book is poetry. It is an enormously personal book and one in which it is not hard to empathize with the central character. But at times it is difficult to keep up with the arguments that are offered. Job is generally outlined on this order:

> I. Introduction: 1:1-5
> II. Job's misfortunes: 1:6-2:13
> III. The Speeches: 3—37
> IV. The Lord and Job: 38-42:6
> V. Conclusion: 42:7-17

Part III may be subdivided into the speeches of Job and his friends, but those who prefer very simple outlines will find this one functional.

In theological analysis, the book of Job is neither a protest against the theology of Job and his three friends—that the wicked perish while the righteous prosper—nor is it an examination of the question: why do the righteous suffer?

Instead, the book is a study of the nature and person of the Lord, being a protest against the idea that God can be fully understood and so have His actions predicted. Job seeks an answer to the question: "Why has God not acted as theory and previous experience tell me that He should?" Then, in the course of the dialoguing, Job looks for a mediator to plead his case (9:32-35) and to represent him before God in court. Job does not predict or prophesy such a mediator—he only expresses his need and hope for such a person.

Job does express a firm belief in the hope for a future life in fellowship with the Lord (14:13; 19:23-27). This seems to have been a personal hope, not a community or national expression. But it does show that his belief was in a life beyond this life and a divine judgment that would face mankind.

The burden of the book is that human problems and suffering pale into the realm of insignificance when put into the perspective of God's omniscience and omnipotence. Job desires to meet God that he might defend himself, but does not know where to find Him (23:1-12). But when the Lord reveals Himself, it is not with an answer to Job's questions but with a revelation of His wisdom, power and might that fully satisfies Job (42:1-6).

In preparing to study this book, the same essential procedures will be followed. It is hoped the student will have read Job a number of times. Perhaps a more effective way is to have others read the speeches of the other characters so that the development of the ideas of different persons may be traced.

This text, as others, needs the help of the Spirit of God in determining the full sweep of its revealed truth, so the wise student approaches it with an attitude of prayer and dependence on the Lord.

Level One: JOB

Some of the material suggested in Level One may be assumed to be done for all of our studies, but in this case it becomes increasingly important since the text itself tells us rather little. The following items are listed:

1. Gathering the basic data
2. Determining the nature of Job's complaint
3. Learn what is available about the moves of the adversary
4. See what may be learned about Job's wife and family

1. *Gathering the basic data:* In the bibliographic materials the student has available the matters of authorship, date of writing, and the identification of places and persons to be studied. Not a lot is "known" but much is suggested.

The student is encouraged to use competent works that honor the Bible as the Word of God in this pursuit. You will discover that a number of encyclopaedias, etc., spend much time finding fault with the Bible and little time seeing the true value of it.

In this reading one will encounter discussions of the problems of date and composition or compilation; it should be remembered that the work is accepted as coming from the Lord even if many aspects are unknown. The student will take an interest in Job's friends, reading what is available about them and trying to analyze their conduct.

2. *Determining the nature of Job's complaint:* This is done by a careful reading of the book. One discovers in the early chapters that Job can accept adversity better than most of us. He is annoyed with his friends and frequently allows his annoyance to be seen, and he is

very disappointed that he has sunk to a level very inferior to the one he has held most recently. These are superficial aspects of his complaint, as is the whole nature of his suffering. When one has a grip on his true complaint, much of the argumentation and debate in the book is understood more clearly.

3. *Learn about the moves of the adversary:* With the help of a concordance or a study Bible, observe as carefully as possible the ways in which Satan works in his attempts to frustrate the purposes of God. The logic in the approach of the enemy should be analyzed and the claims made by him to the Lord considered.

As a potential parallel, one should see the moves of the enemy in Zechariah 3 and understand that the devices used in antiquity are still around. They may occur to us in different forms (not many have herds of camels today) but with equally disastrous results.

That the enemy does not appear in any personal way following chapter 2 should also come to the attention of the student.

4. *See what may be learned of Job's wife and other members of the family:* This must be followed through the book to the conclusion in chapter 42. Job's wife does not seem to show much compassion in the early chapters, but one needs to study this in detail. In many Bible commentaries there will be notes as to how these passages[14] read in the Greek Old Testament (the Septuagint).

Level Two: JOB

In *Level Two*, a number of points are dependent on the reading of the book and thinking through its message. As noted earlier, the book of Job is somewhat different in format from our other books. This calls for a deeper searching of the text as we are able. In a practical way, the student actually finds the tools that help in a fuller understanding of the message. The following items are discussed:

1. The relationship of the Prologue and Epilogue to the message
2. Assertions of theological error: God's judgment on the friends
3. Analysis of the friends' speeches
4. Textual matters

1. *The relationship of the Prologue and Epilogue to the message:* The Prologue (chs. 1–2) sets the stage for the events of the book in telling us who Job was, what his circumstances were, what problems befell him, how he reacted to them, and how his family and companions came to regard him. Behind the scenes it shows us a "contest" between the Lord and the adversary and we are allowed to see certain aspects in the development of trials that might have been overlooked otherwise. As the book progresses and the speeches of Job's friends become increasingly hostile, one can see how their envy and resentment of Job have materialized, and how his situation is perceived by them.

The Epilogue (42:7-17) is necessary to complete the narrative and to show the vindication of Job and the greatness of his character. The Epilogue enables us to see the errors of his companions and to warn present observers about such presumptuous opinions.

Somehow the reader feels very gratified at the justice and mercy of the Lord when the book comes to completion.

2. *Assertions of theological error—God's judgment on the three friends:* The reader of Job always suspects the three friends are faulty in their determination, but it is the pronouncement of the Lord in 42:7 that seals the matter. He says, *"You have not spoken of Me....right as My servant Job hath."* The fact is that their speeches contain both truth and falsehood, and the student must read with proper discernment.

Where their ideas conflict with the biblical revelation, they are wrong, but there are times when they speak the truth. Eliphaz is quoted in 1 Corinthians, and in many cases their philosophical ideas may neither be refuted nor sustained. The Bible is an inspired book, infallible, and part of the proof of its integrity is in the fact that incorrect sources (the words of Satan, etc.) are quoted correctly. The messages of the friends are often wrong, but they are reported to us accurately that we might profit by contrasting truth with error.

To get a grip on the positional understanding of the three friends, try 5:8-28, for Eliphaz; 8:2-10 for Bildad; and 11:11-15 for Zophar.

3. *An analysis of the friends' speeches:* Eliphaz and Bildad have three speeches; Zophar has but two. The student should study these

to determine the emphasis and the effect they had on Job. The interchanges between Job and these men in their personal relationships are also very interesting, and it is surprising how often we will hear people today talking as they talked.

Elihu is in a different class, but the student should analyze his long speech. That he was younger and held his peace until the older ones ran out of steam is commendable. That he does not fall into their line of thinking is also good, but the student should read his words carefully to see what impact they would have had on Job.

Eventually the Lord will speak, and the reply of the Lord to Job's questions constitutes Hebrew poetry of epic proportions.

4. *Textual matters:* These cannot be pursued in depth. However one matter of importance should be pointed out. In Job 1:5, 11, etc., the word *"curse"* is found in our English text, although the term in the Hebrew Bible is the verb "to bless." It has been understood that an ancient group of Hebrew scholars (the *Sopherim*) before the time of our Lord, introduced the word "bless" instead of the word "curse" for it was offensive in the context[15] to think that one would "curse the Lord." When one reads the text and sees the word "curse," an understanding of the passage seems obvious, until the Hebrew text is read and one sees the word "bless."

There are six of these word changes in Job, but not all are with these terms as used in the first two chapters.

In a different line, the Greek text of the Septuagint shows a longer text for the book of Job and a considerably longer speech for Job's wife in chapter 2. Her reasoning seems less severe and while Job's response is in the same character, we come away thinking a little better of her. (A translation of this passage is given in APPENDIX 3.)

3 Level Three: JOB

Now in *Level Three*, in seeking a more advanced study of the book of Job, these things are mentioned:

1. A knowledge of Hebrew
2. An appreciation of text problems
3. A comparison of Job and other ancient literature on this line.

1. *A knowledge of Hebrew:* Job is, on the whole, very difficult Hebrew. The Prologue and Epilogue are fairly normative, but the poetic sections are more complex. A general knowledge does not help much. The poetry is beautiful and many times in reading it the student is overwhelmed by the character of the language. However the student is urged to take advantage of the helps given by study Bibles, etc., to enjoy some of the suggestive comments on the text.

2. *An appreciation of text problems:* This becomes necessary as one reads the commentaries. Many references and variant readings will be noted. On the whole they are not major and the text of the Hebrew Bible is well understood. But this is an old book. Since some copies of it are also very old, total agreement in the texts is not realistic. The student may view these things as matters not fully settled, but to be settled nonetheless in his confidence in the Word.

3. *A comparison of Job and other ancient literature:* "Suffering" literature is rather common in most societies, and it was so in the ancient world. Job stands alone in the totality of the treatment of the subject, but there are some narratives of antiquity that are of considerable interest. D. Winton Thomas's *Documents from Old Testament Times* offers a good presentation of these.

There are many parts of Job that are beautiful and instructive. One of the most meaningful of these is the poem of wisdom in Job 28:12-28 with a conclusion that is very like Proverbs. Job's plea for mercy and grace in chapter 19 is heart rending, and his response to the Lord in chapter 42 shows the great love and compassion in his heart.

This book is to be studied for a strong picture of the Lord. The texts must be read carefully so we do not fall into errors like his friends. It is a very rewarding study in the appreciation it gives us for the greatness of God and the necessity of our dependence on Him. On this line there is a note in the *New Scofield Reference Bible* on Job 14:14 that every student should read and understand.

INTRODUCTION: THE POETRY OF ECCLESIASTES

This is the third of the "wisdom" books and in some ways the most perplexing[16] of all. The curious nature of the book and its view of life has allowed many students to assume the book is purely man's wisdom and thereby not dependable. This view is seen in many study Bibles and reveals a misunderstanding of what the wisdom of Ecclesiastes is intended to portray. The canonicity and inspired character of this book, however, cannot be doubted without throwing the whole question of inspiration into the doldrums.

The book is best characterized as one that demonstrates intense human experimentation in the affairs of life with a rational view—a reasoned conclusion logically drawn and inferred. This is combined with practical earthy language that "tells it like it is." The factual character of the book has sometimes allowed it to be called *pessimistic* or *fatalistic*, but when the themes are closely examined, it will be seen that the proper term is *realistic*.

The aim of the book is undoubtedly to show the emptiness of life as it is lived without the oversight of the Lord. All pursuits and achievements are empty if the Lord is not in them!

The Hebrew title is *Coheleth*, a noun meaning one who assembles, gathers, or calls together. The term in the English Bible is indebted to the Latin Bible and the term that is sometimes seen—the Preacher—is derived from what an assembler would do. The term *Coheleth* easily agrees with the purpose of the writer as given in chapter 12: to pass on to others words of truth.

The authorship is traditionally given to Solomon, based on Hebrew tradition. His name does not occur in the book, however, and there are several other authorship suggestions. The book has a Jerusalem background and in this opinion must be dated before the Babylonian Captivity. It is not easily outlined, but the following suggestion seems to be reasonable.

I. Prologue: 1-11
II. First Discourse 1:12-2
III. Second Discourse 3:1-5
IV. Third Discourse 6:1-8:15
V. Fourth Discourse 8:15-12:7
VI. Epilogue 12:8-14

The Prologue and Epilogue correlate with one another to give a completed account. The author apparently wrote from a "hidden-

agenda," the purpose being to write from the standpoint of others in
such a way as to demonstrate to them the utter pointlessness and
hopelessness of their lives without God at the center of all things.

Thus being understood, the book becomes a tract to draw people
to God through their despair. It is not a demonstration of sinful
human reasoning for it presses for the necessity of the Lord in our
lives and our needed dependence on Him—His revelation and will.
All men are sinners (7:20) and apart from the Lord everything is
empty, meaningless, vanity.

The key to the book is to discover what *"vanity"* means and how
it expresses itself in areas of life such as learning, material possessions, popularity, and success. The continuing contrast of wisdom
and foolishness from Proverbs is also apparent, and if this study is
pursued (who is wise, who is foolish), it helps unlock the book.

It must be seen that *"death"* in Ecclesiastes is the cessation of all
our normal and human activity—not the end of existence! Therefore
we understand the book better if we realize that it is forewarning us
of the finality of death, the end of all human projects, and the loss
of temporal pleasures in that day.

It is especially helpful to read Ecclesiastes in several translations;
there are so many nuances to key words that comparative reading
awakens to the student's understanding. A prayerful and careful
reading of the book, therefore, will direct us as we prepare to study.

Level One: ECCLESIASTES

Many of the items needed for a study of Ecclesiastes are gleaned
from the book itself. In a sense, then, we study the book in order to
study the book! The following items are treated in *Level One*.

1. Defining key terms
2. Determining the purpose for the writing of the book
3. Observing the author's methods that lead to his deductions
4. Determining the intended sphere of readership (influence)

1. *Defining key terms:* Reading through Ecclesiastes, we see several terms that need definition. Among these is *"vanity."* This is not
our modern concept of vanity but the idea of nothingness—empti-

ness. An English dictionary will not help much with this term, but a Bible dictionary will suffice. Similarly we must grasp the root meaning of words like *"vexation of spirit," "labor,"* and *"travail,"* etc. It is helpful for the student, while reading a book, to keep a list of words that may seem overused. Such are often key words and need careful definition. Watch also for speech figures—metonymy, euphemism, etc. A commentary may prove helpful to the student in this area (APPENDIX III contains appropriate bibliography material).

2. *Determining the purpose for the writing of the book:* Study Bibles and commentaries will help with this, but the student is better served if he can discover this in the reading of the text. Read the Epilogue (12:8ff) and think through the stated aim of the writer.

This may be joined to the Prologue in which the writer is not teaching a cosmogeny (his view of the origins of the universe) but is stressing the constancy of the world as we know it in contrast with the transiency of man and his life and activities. The rhythm of the seasons, the precipitation and evaporation of the water cycle, the passage of day and night, all are silent spectators to generation after generation crawling onto, and then soon shuffling off, the planet.

The student should read the book carefully and note the passages that speak definitively of something the Lord does, or some instruction the Lord gives. Carefully observe the details in the striking differences between those who are the Lord's and those who are not.

3. *Observing the author's methods that lead to his deductions:* What did the author do to enable himself to come to the conclusions he eventually presents? What was his capacity for living and for taking advantage of the circumstances of life? How did he watch others to glean the nature of their responses to the situation of living? How did the behavior of others give him clues as to what one should expect in the performance of life?

All these are questions that enable the student to see how extensive the examining processes of the author were, how complete his inductions and how firm his resolutions. In establishing this point, the student is prepared to see what the real end of man is, and how the inventions he has made on the pathway do not do him nearly as much good as he would like.

4. *Determining the intended sphere of readership (audience):* To whom is this book written? Why does the writer speak so much of the end of life? Why is there so much in the area of challenge about material goods and the possessions that are intended to enrich life? Why is there so little mention of the formal services of religion? These questions are answered in the reading of the book and they help us see that the message is for all of us but especially for all who think that their attainments in life are the *summum bonum* of existence. Every culture is equally warned by the author of this work and it is certainly timely in the materialistic age in which we are living.

Level Two: ECCLESIASTES

In this Wisdom Book will be found the same materials on speech figures, etc., that have been mentioned previously. No special study of them is needed for the present subject so long as the general character of these language qualifiers is recognized. *Level Two* will concentrate on the following:

1. An understanding of Solomon's life and times
2. Authorship questions
3. Consideration of ideas raised in the book
4. Appreciation for the conclusion

1. *An understanding of Solomon's life and times:* Although the authorship of the book is not unanimously assigned to Solomon, there is enough suggestion of the work to be his that one does well to review the Solomonic kingship. The primary Scriptures are 1 Kings 1-11 and 1 Chronicles 29 through 2 Chronicles 9. Make careful note as to how his rule developed and how his own personality changed with time and success. That the kingdom of Israel attained its greatest growth under his rule is obvious, whether one studies it in terms of military power, political expansion, or economic success.

That difficulties arose during this outward success becomes apparent, and the last few recorded events of his life are not happy ones. Considering the great wisdom he possessed and the divine favor that was on him, readers often are mystified by the conduct that marked him in later days. A study of his life is a clue to

Ecclesiastes as we compare the things done by the author of the book and the satisfaction they brought to him. How often do the things we earnestly desire not bring us the end we desire!

2. *Authorship questions:* It is not necessary to solve all the problems involved in this but it is important that the student be aware of them. Solomon's name does not occur in the book although the statements about being king in Jerusalem would seem to fit no one else. Help in this matter will be found in the Encyclopaedias and Bible Dictionaries, but the student must be careful not to become so involved in details as to lose sight of the fact that the Holy Spirit is the real author of all these works.

Jewish tradition has honored Solomon with the authorship role and has attributed it to his old age, written when he finally realized that he had erred in the disruptive judgments that came with too much power and authority. The occurrence of foreign words suggest a later date and some comparison with Greek Stoicism has made some scholars think the book shows "later" ideas[17] than those current in Solomon's day. These ideas are discussed in most of the commentaries on the book as well, and the student will keep them in mind and remember that we cannot know everything. What *can* be known must be accepted: the book is a key part of the Word of God.

3. *Consideration of ideas raised in the book:* What does the book teach us about the reality of death? Do all go to one place? Does the same fate meet the rich and the poor? What has God done to make us conscious of time? How should we handle the matter of vows? What is the proper use of one's life, and what is it to remember the Lord in the days of your youth? Finally, what are the really important things in life and how can we maximize them? All of these questions (and many more) are raised in Ecclesiastes, and most of them are answered as well. The significance of the book will be better understood when these aspects are kept in mind.

4. *Appreciation for the conclusion:* "*Fear God, and keep His commandments: for this is the whole duty of man*" (12:13). Some of the study Bibles have objected to this short treatise because in its brevity it does not touch on every aspect of salvation. The student

will need to survey this and, in the context of the book, determine if
it is suggesting a works way of being saved. In meeting this challenge one will need to know what "fear God" means as well as what
His commandments are—not as totally self-apparent as may be
thought. Furthermore in the understanding of the whole one will
find a disparity between the books of men and the wisdom of God.

Level Three: ECCLESIASTES

At this third level, the following are noted:

1. A general understanding of Hebrew
2. Comparing Ecclesiastes with other ancient wisdom literature
3. Extended imagery or speech figures
4. Dealing with rhetorical questions

1. *A general understanding of the Hebrew language:* Although
this book has a number of perplexities, the Hebrew is much less
complicated than that of Job. No more need be said about that.

2. *Comparing Ecclesiastes with other ancient wisdom literature:*
As mentioned earlier, the ancient world was more literate than one
might suppose. The compilations of this literature in the works of
Pritchard as well as that of Winton-Thomas[18] are adequate for this
comparison (detailed information is in the BIBLIOGRAPHY). In this
work there is some prejudice in favor of the Bible but it is hard for
anyone to read the accounts and not see the superiority of the biblical data.

The comparison of the ideals in Ecclesiastes with Greek Stoic
philosophy come at a later stage. But it should be noted in the reading of Ecclesiastes that the constant emphasis on the role of God in
a personal, interceding way is something not seen in the fatalistic
Stoic style of thinking. At any rate, great thinkers in all ages have
had some thoughts in common so it should not be surprising if biblical ideals were seen in other literature as well.

3. *Extended imagery or speech figures:* Note these well in
Ecclesiastes. Two of the most notable are the poems of time (ch. 3)

and old age (ch. 12). The poem of time stresses the role of the Lord in the lives of men by giving them the time and opportunity to know of Him and His universe. The author drives home his main point: that there is time for everything if man uses the time he has for a particular task. The peculiar parallelisms in this song are worth comparative study.

The poem of old age speaks of the wear and tear of the body as one approaches the time when the silver thread will be broken and men return to their maker. We bury the body, the spirit returns to God who gave it. This poem is really an allegory in which the human faculties are described in terms of physical things in buildings and cities. It is a remarkable poem and the reality of its picture is painfully known in the aging process as human life runs its course.

There are other extended speech figures in Ecclesiastes and the student will want to observe them for the colorful presentation they make of life and the way in which they draw the interest of the reader to a central idea.

Concluding Note: Ecclesiastes offers a compact study in values. Its message should be a vital part in our thinking. If one forgets, or does not allow for God, no other attainment has meaning. Knowledge alone will make one more miserable, popularity makes one the subject of envy and strife, material goods simply become something to pass on to others who often do not use them wisely, and the experience of living is always overshadowed by the fact that one thing comes to them all. But this whole picture is changed if the Lord is honored for, as the writer says, *"it shall be well with them that fear God, with them that fear before Him"* (8:12).

INTRODUCTORY NOTE: THE SONG OF SOLOMON

This beautiful song has been the subject of much discussion in the area of biblical hermeneutics for many centuries. It has been attributed to Solomon due to the inclusion of his name. Although the preposition may mean "to" or "for" as well as "of," all forms point to Solomon as the author or the recipient. Many modern scholars have looked for another author but, in terms of biblical simplicity, Solomon seems just right!

The books shares some of the same problems that perplex us in

Ecclesiastes. There is a lack of historical background, some obscure language, loan words that seem to belong to a later time, and the mention of Solomon in the third person as in 1:5, 3:9 as well as in the second person in 8:12.

The Song of Solomon seems best understood as a lyric poem, although there is also a tendency to treat it as a drama. It has been widely interpreted as an allegory, although in recent years there has been a resurgence of literal interpretation for the book. It is hardly the collection of love poems used at a wedding as some modern scholars insist, and is better understood as a work that shows an idyllic relationship between a man and a woman after the pattern given in creation.

We are not certain of the date of writing or even the occasion, but keeping it in the Solomonic era gives us an approximate time setting and, remembering Solomon's proclivity toward marriage, it is not hard to see it in some historical setting of his day.

A classical outline for this book is the following:

I.   The bride longs for the groom (1:1–2:7)
II. Their love increases (2:8–3:5)
III. Espousal: praise of the king and his bride (3:6–5:1)
IV. The bride Longs for the Groom (5:2–6:9)
V.   The beauty of the bride (6:10–8:4)
VI. The permanence of true love (8:5-14)

There are many other outline suggestions, and, for general interest, here is the outline[19] of the Reformation theologian, Cocceius, as he used the Song of Solomon to outline the history of the Church (a typological interpretation with allegory).

I.   The gospel preached to Jews and Gentiles (chs. 1–2)
II. Growth of the Church and persecution (chs. 3–4)
III. Peace within, danger without (5:1–6:8)
IV. Reformation (6:9–7:10)
V.   Unsettled estate following the Reformation (7:11–8:3)
VI. Persecution (8:4-6)
VII. Rest after suffering, longing for the gospel (8:7-14)

If anyone should ask how he derived this sort of thinking, the answer is that when one moves into broad and unspecified typology anything is possible—and likely. He was a godly man and if one were to examine all the schemes to outline and analyze this book, one would think this one rather normal.

The Song is rich in language and in description. It makes great use of speech figures and devices as well as poetic conceits. (When many superlative speech figures are assembled as a unit, the term "conceit" is used, the idea being that a perfect picture is presented, showing the designated party in an unparalleled distinction.). It describes flora in the Near Eastern world in some detail, and is an encyclopaedia on that subject. The name of God does not appear directly but is found in a cryptogram in 8:6.

Undoubtedly the overriding theme of the book is that of 6:3, *"I am my beloved's and he is mine."*

1 Level One: THE SONG OF SOLOMON

Our approach to the study of the book follows the three-level pattern. In *Level One* are a few things that require both thought and research. The particular items are:

1. Basic identifications
2. Become familiar with the various interpretations
3. Identify speech figures as they are descriptive of persons
4. Browse, if possible, Ironside's commentary on the book
    (Data in the BIBLIOGRAPHY)

1. *Study the identification of the Shulamite and others:* Obviously she is a a key player in the book, and the student will turn to the Bible dictionary or any biographical work related to the subject to research her identity. In reading the Song, watch for statements that might be significant about the character and identity of this person. The student should not feel frustrated if not too much is learned, but should be aware of all that is available. With this study the student will also want to keep in mind the character of Solomon and the extensive nature of his holdings. Learn what is available about the "daughters of Jerusalem" and about any other persons mentioned in the Song. Since it is a lyric poem (or a dramatic lyric poem) the identification of persons is important.

2. *Become familiar with the various interpretations:* A commentary or a study Bible will help. The work of Bullock (noted in the BIBLIOGRAPHY) gives good help in this area.

The literal school sees the Song as a real affair between two lovers—and there are several interpretations regarding who they are and how they relate.

The allegorical school sees the parties representing other entities: the Jewish allegorizers thought the parties were Jehovah and Israel; many Christian allegorizers think they are Christ and the Church. There are some mystical thinkers among the allegorizers who think that "body" and "spirit" may be the parties. Those who see a typology as the main interpretation will think the Song predicts the coming of the Christian age and even the cataclysm that will come at the end of that time. The student does not have to resolve this matter or become an expert on the different schools, but should be aware of them, evaluating of the better and poorer points of each.

3. *Identify speech figures as they are descriptive of persons:* The Song abounds in speech figures. The chief talks by the parties involved are built around them. The student should see what figures are used and how they depict the person. Watch for the passages that contain conceits, places where many superlative speech figures are assembled as a unit (as explained on the previous page). Note that if the speech figures are not understood, some pretty gruesome things are said! The points of comparison are vital in this and one may learn a lot about giving compliments from this book.

4. *Browse, if possible, Dr. Ironside's Commentary*[20] *on the Song:* This is suggested because it is an open treatment that is easy to follow and sensible in emphasis. The author gives enough background material to help, but the style is uncomplicated and consistent. The Bible is more important than the commentaries, of course, but the commentaries are written by scholars concerned with text and message. Total agreement with a commentary is not possible but it serves as a guideline in thinking and, in so doing, offers help in the assimilation of the work. (Dr. Ironside's interpretation is not necessarily the view of this work. It is a recommendation of an interesting work that can be taken in hand and surveyed easily.)

2 Level Two: THE SONG OF SOLOMON

With the basic work of Level One complete, the student has already been in the study of the book and is now prepared for a more detailed analysis. *Level Two* calls the student to the text and wants attention to the following matters:

1. Who is speaking and to whom are the addresses made?
2. How do the two parties respond to difficulty?
3. What is the role of the "daughters of Jerusalem"?

1. *Who is speaking and to whom are the addresses made?* One may determine some of this by watching the gender changes in the talks and recognition of parties. It is really, however, a matter of separating the speeches and categorizing them as to what is being requested or conferred on another. The point that will come to the student is that of proper speech and reaction to stressed areas of life —at least it is hoped that is the point that will present itself. We learn to talk to others by hearing how others have talked and since communication is a very big part of our world, whatever we learn about it is an enrichment of life.

2. *How do the two parties respond to difficulty?* Having sorted the speeches, the student should be able to meet this challenge openly. The manuals that are to teach us these things pale beside the corrective action of the persons defined in the Word of God.

3. *What is the role of the "daughters of Jerusalem"?* A certain amount of imagination must be in the student's pocket. This is a thinking proposition and there may be no direct answer. If the Song is a drama, we can hear this group singing as a chorus. If it is a recounting of romantic episodes in the lives of the parties then we can see a speech figure in place. But in taking these persons into account, the student is completing the background information for the study.

Whatever their identity, they are a device that provides a sympathetic audience to listen attentively to the descriptions of the lovers throughout the book.

Level Three: THE SONG OF SOLOMON

To what has been said in other studies in this book, these concepts of student preparation are now reconsidered:

1. A general understanding of biblical Hebrew
2. A comparison with other Love Poetry of the ancient Near East.

1. *A general understanding of biblical Hebrew:* Following the Hebrew is very helpful in this book. For example, without it one would never see the name of God in chapter 8, and the gender inflections needed in the speeches would be much less clear. This helps to determine who is speaking at a particular time.

The actual Hebrew grammar is casual, but the vocabulary is complex. The vocabulary is not easy in that it includes many terms that are rarely used in the Scripture—especially terms botanical and practical. The present writer was told by another party that every botanical item mentioned in the Bible is also mentioned in the Song. This was never determined in finality, but it was quickly seen that there are many terms that occur in this Song that are rare throughout the Bible.

2. *A comparison with other Love Poetry of the ancient Near East:* This is a study that may be pursued leisurely, and the student will find suggested materials in the BIBLIOGRAPHY. The great value of it is to see that this sort of poetic expression was known in and before the time of Solomon. Therefore there is no reason to believe it originated or was fabricated at some later date.

On the other hand, the poetry of the ancients does not help us understand this work in any significant way. The services provided are auxiliary and come as extra benefits to the whole.

This work is not intended to be a commentary on these books of the Bible and no attempt is made to politicize the ideas. But the present writer cannot help but state that if the ideals shown in the Song of Solomon were practiced in the home lives of our present population, a lot of the domestic problems would be solved and many a troubled home would become one marked by happiness.

A INTRODUCTION: THE POETRY OF THE LAMENTATIONS

The final book in Section II of our poetry work is the little book containing the laments of Jeremiah. It is the shortest and probably the one where the least help is available in commentaries and dictionaries. It is a sad book, but has some spiritual highlights in it to brighten the day. Jeremiah is the author and it is written against the background of the fall of Jerusalem to Nebuchadnezzar.

The Hebrew title is simply "HOW!" and the point is to see what has happened to the people of God and their kingdom and one puts one's hand to one's mouth and says, "How!" (This is a speech figure discussed in APPENDIX I)

Lamentations has many parallels to Jeremiah's book both in style and content. This may be seen in 1:15 compared with Jeremiah 8:21, 4:1 compared with Jeremiah 49:12, etc. The content makes it plain that the author witnessed the destruction of Jerusalem and has first hand information. Jeremiah had predicted it and lived through it.

The book is written in a curious style or metre, sometimes called *quineh* or "dirge," and to understand this one has to read it aloud with an 1-2-3, pause, 1, 2 sort of rhythm. It might not seem like much, but after many verses it becomes a despairing rhythm and fits the mood of the book.

The structure is unique in another way. There are five chapters and chapters 1-4 are all done in an acrostic pattern. In chapters 1 and 2, each successive verse begins with the next letter of the Hebrew alphabet and consists of three lines. Chapter 4 also has the acrostic pattern but each verse contains only two lines. In these chapters the first line carries the acrostic letter, giving each chapter 22 verses.

Chapter 3 follows the acrostic pattern as well, but each verse has only one line and the acrostic letter begins every third line. Therefore in chapter 3 there are 22 acrostics but 66 verses.

This means that chapters 1-3 have the same number of lines and follow a similar acrostic arrangement. Chapter 4 also has the acrostic pattern, but has only two lines per verse and chapter 5 has 22 one line verses without the acrostics.

Perhaps a chart would be easier to see this ingenious arrangement:

1	2	3	4	5
22 verses 3 lines each acrostic on 1st line	Just like chapter 1	66 verses, 1 line each acrostic on three successive lines	22 verses 2 lines each acrostic on 1st line	22 verses 2 lines each no acrostic

It is a work of art! No one knows exactly why it is done this way but it is not accidental. Perhaps Jeremiah will tell us in eternity. A student once offered the opinion that Jeremiah probably had a lot of time on his hands and this was better than working puzzles, but the class did him no credence.

Lamentations is outlined in this way:

    I.   The conditions of the fallen city (1:1-11)
    II. The prophet's complaint (1:12-22)
    III. The Lord's judgment (2:1-22)
    IV. The prophetic lament (3:1-66)
        A. The problem (vv. 1-17)
        B. The song of hope (vv. 18-36)
        C. The song of confession (vv. 37-54)
        D. The song of trust (vv. 55-66)
    V.   Results of judgment (4:1-22)
    VI. Prayer and call for redress (5:1-22)

The overall complaint that grows in this book is the feeling of deep sorrow for Jerusalem and regret at the severity of the judgment of the Lord, even while the propriety of that judgment is recognized as just. Chapter 3 contains a moving section on God's mercy and restates the reality of His covenantal love. But the price of sin and rebellion is high. The evidence of the ruined city before him is proof it has been paid. Yet the heart of the godly is filled with sorrow and takes no glee in the punishment of the wicked.

In moving to a study of Lamentations, the three levels are before us and they are correspondingly brief in keeping with the nature of the book.

Level One: THE LAMENTATIONS

The following are basic to the study of this book:

1. The ministry of Jeremiah .
2. The fall of Jerusalem

1. *The ministry of Jeremiah:* One need not review his whole life, but it would be helpful to read a comprehensive overview of his ministry in a Bible dictionary, for example. Certainly the information in Jeremiah 39–52 would be a good foundation, and the student should familiarize himself with it.

The pleading of Jeremiah for reform and the weakness of the kings with whom he had to deal is a lesson in his faithfulness and the futility of those who forget the program of God. Every lament in this book is conditioned by these factors.

2. *The fall of Jerusalem*[21]: Described vigorously in Jeremiah and Chronicles, one should study this in one of the credible encyclopaedias and in the realm of ancient history. The biblical picture is enough to give us the feeling of horror, but the total collapse seen historically enables us to feel the doom and depression of the godly man who witnessed the event and consequently wrote these laments.

Level Two: THE LAMENTATIONS

At this level there are two important things for consideration:

1. The character of the Lord in judgment
2. The role of the prophet in worship and service

1. *The character of the Lord in judgment:* Of course this is a theological matter gleaned from the law given at the time when God established His covenant and made promises and threats to His people. These warnings are repeated throughout the ongoing history of Judah and Israel as they sought their own will, not His. The fierce nature of the judgment reminds us of the awfulness of sin and the price that is paid for rebellion and treachery. When the careful read-

er sees that God is just in keeping His Word and enacting what He has said, then the book of Lamentations becomes a true expression of grief, not one in which God is blamed or found culpable.

2. *The role of the prophet in worship and service:* This, too, stands out very clearly, and easily challenges the believer to an account-ability with one's own life. God is served and worshiped when we honor His Word. His people are served well by a faithful servant who gives them "the truth, the whole truth, and nothing but the truth." Jeremiah becomes a model for us in both areas and we, as he did, will lament over the lost but will never feel that God is at fault.

Level Three: THE LAMENTATIONS

The services of biblical Hebrew: For this book, the parting note for study would be an understanding of many nuances of meaning that are available to those who have some exposure to Hebrew.

Lamentations 3:18 (KJV) offers an example when the conjunction that opens the verse is studied and some attention is paid to the idea that it might be translated "but:" rather than "and." It opens a new vista on the material and the subsequent ideas.

IN CONCLUSION

There is a great deal of poetry in the prophetic literature, but it may all be treated on the general lines established in Section I. The same is true for the historic materials where our studies have already been done. The study of poetry has an emotional side to it and the student should not overlook this. It is not a matter "cut and dried" but a matter lived and felt.

III
OLD TESTAMENT PROPHECY

A INTRODUCTORY NOTE

And beginning at Moses and all the prophets, He expounded unto them in all the Scriptures the things concerning Himself (Lk. 24:27).

For had ye believed Moses, ye would have believed Me: for he wrote of Me (Jn. 5:46).

For the prophecy came not in old time by the will of man, but holy men of God spake as they were moved by the Holy Ghost (2 Pet. 1:21).

These foundational Scriptures give us the basis for our study of the Old Testament prophetical materials by assuring us of the importance of the writings as they focused on the coming Messiah and as they were given by the Holy Spirit. The study of prophecy is an enchanting study and vital to every age, but one that must be pursued carefully so as to avoid excesses or the oversight of other biblical materials. In this portion of our work the material is divided into two sections—as was done with the poetry—to first see the materials needed for the study in a general sense and then have some concepts on the particular spheres of prophecy.

The prophetic canon is divided into two parts: the former prophets and the latter prophets. Included in the former segment are Joshua, Judges, Samuel and Kings, and the other section encompasses the Major Prophets (Isaiah, Jeremiah, Ezekiel) and the Minor Prophets: the "Book of the Twelve."

There are, of course, many prophecies in the other portions of the Old Testament and these may be treated along the general lines[1] that

will be suggested. (Daniel, although a great prophetic book, is not in
the prophetic canon, but included with the sacred Writings.)

SECTION I—BASIC PROPHETIC CONCEPTS

Section I prescribes materials that will relate to all the prophetic
books and prophetic portions in the Old Testament. Fundamental
concepts in Bible studies as noted on pages 19-26 will continue to
apply.

Level One: OLD TESTAMENT PROPHECY

In *Level One* of this study, a number of basic items are discussed.
It is important the student not simply take these as logical assump-
tions, but will actually collect the pertinent information. These items
include:

1. What is prophecy?
2. Who is a prophet?
3. How are the prophets recognized?
4. How are the prophets called?

1. *What is prophecy?* Prophecy is a message or a word given by
one party as a spokesperson for another. It may involve prediction or
it may not. The messages of the prophets involved both foretelling
(prediction) and forth-telling (practical advice). In most cases they
gave more of the latter than the former, acting as spokespeople for
God. Their words carried divine authority and the prophecy included the total message. This is seen very well in the Old Testament. A
prophet would develop a reputation for knowing and declaring a
variety of things: from helping someone find his lost livestock (in
the case of Saul, 1 Sam. 9:6, etc.) to foretelling the conditions of the
life of a child who was ill (1 Ki. 14:12, etc.)

Prophesying is the act of giving these prophetic messages, of
course, and while this is a primary part of the work of a prophet, it
is not the only task given to that class of servants.

2. *Who is a prophet?* A prophet is a man or woman who speaks

for God. This is not just a form of testimony or public witness but someone commissioned to bring the truth of God to another party. The prophets came from no particular tribe, and had no designated social status, no official "prophet" position in the court of the kings. They did not have any of the requirements, for example, of the Levitical priests. The prophet was not a professional person and in most cases seemed to serve the community in some normal role. The reputation one received, of course, might put one in a special class as far as the recognition of the community was concerned.

A prophet might be blind (Ahijah), young or old (1 Ki. 13), obscure and relatively unknown or active and vigorous like Elijah. Women serve at times in this position (Huldah) although most of the prophets named are men. Some were also in the priestly line and David, in particular, was king.

They had no special training, although some (Elisha, for example) underwent an apprenticeship. What the apprentice did, however, was not practicing prophesying, but fulfilling the sometimes mundane needs of the person that was served (Elisha is remembered for *"pouring water"* on the hands of Elijah.)

At the same time they were not super-heroes. They made mistakes (Nathan in the original temple building plans of David) and were sometimes frustrated by the work of wicked men to the point of utter despair (Jer. 20). They were afflicted with the trials of life (Elijah, 1 Ki. 19) and bothered by the inconsistencies they saw in the people of God about them.

They were marked by commitment and obedience even to the point of doing the will of God when it might seem absolutely absurd (Ezekiel). Many in particular and all in general are memorialized in Hebrews 11 with the notation that the world was not worthy of them (11:38). Some worked miracles and some only appeared as shadow figures who passed by so quickly their names are not known to us.

As the student comes to study the prophecy material in the Old Testament, he needs to remember the character and service of these people of God and find in his own heart a growing dedication to the worship and witness of the Lord.

3. *How are the prophets recognized?* Since the prophets had no official badge of recognition, and since anyone could claim to be

one, it was necessary that there be some responsible way of recognizing a prophet. The essential tests are given in Deuteronomy 13:1-3 and 18:20-22. When one came claiming to be a prophet, he was recognized as a true prophet if he spoke for the Lord alone, if the message agreed with what the Lord had given previously, and if his word came to pass as stated. If his message did not come to pass (the predictions were not fulfilled), or if they did came to pass and he moved to serve another deity, or if the message conflicted with the Torah, he was a false prophet, not to be feared, not to receive a good listening, nor to be allowed the privilege of the community.

But there were times when the prediction was a long range affair. One could not wait 500 years to discern the truthfulness of a prophet. In such cases the prophets usually give a prediction that would be fulfilled soon and the fulfillment of that indicated the accuracy of the messenger.

A good example is seen in Isaiah 7 where the promise of the virgin birth is given. That would not happen for a long time, but there was one prediction that would be fulfilled[2] in a few months, another in about sixty years, etc. The credibility of the prophet was established as the messages were fulfilled as given.

Among those who were false prophets were the ones who served pagan deities. They were supplemented by some imposters who claimed to speak for the Lord but had no credentials for doing so and were demonstrated to be false by divine imposition. A good example of that is Hananiah in Jeremiah 28.

There also seem to have been some deluded persons (Zedekiah, for example, in 1 Kings 22) who did not intentionally work against the Lord's work but the fact is that wherever truth is seen error will not be far away. The claims of the false prophets were often excessive when the true servants showed them up by their own reality.

Many of the Old Testament prophets are unnamed. They are known to God personally and known to us through the recognition of their services rendered. They are prophets in the declaration of the Word of God; otherwise they are persons. As noted, there seems to be no official office of prophet (this is disputed among Old Testament students), and whether a person spoke once or often seems to have made little difference. That individual was a prophet when speaking for God. While he might have developed a respected reputation, he was still only a man[3] who was not exempt from the everyday struggles of life.

A prophet known for truth might make a mistake, as in Nathan's early advice to David on the temple building or may err intentionally for some personal reason. A good example of this is seen in the "old prophet" of 1 Kings 13 who so desired the fellowship of a younger prophet that he lied to him and led the younger prophet out of the will of God. The older prophet repented, but the younger prophet forfeited his life in the process. The lesson for all of us is clear: the servants of God must listen to Him and be wary of any human advice that is contrary to what God has revealed.

As with Hananiah (Jer. 28), false prophets may speak with great assurance, but God's people must be guided by what He has said. God does not contradict Himself and a prophetic message that contradicts the law or the revealed plan of God is a false message.

4. *How were the prophets called?* This was a matter of divine order. Jeremiah was appointed to be a prophet before he was born (Jer. 1). Elijah was told to anoint Elisha a prophet in his stead before Elisha knew anything about it. Amos was a herdsman when the Lord told him to go to Israel and rebuke the idolatry of the court of Jeroboam II. That God spoke to these men in some definitive way is clear, but we do not know all the details in such a call. The motivation for their service, however, never seems to come from the surrounding circumstances but always from the Lord.

We recognize the possibility of fraud in this, but when the tests of the prophets are applied, the nature of the true prophets is distinguished from the false. Their calling was certainly to make God's will known to His people, and to rebuke them in the case of error.

These four items are basic in our work, but further information may be gathered in the works cited in the BIBLIOGRAPHY. The student must remember that in all these studies, a prayerful reading of the Scripture is vital as well as putting together the important concepts of authorship and related matters mentioned earlier. A good procedure is to determine what one is going to study—whether a book, a passage or an individual prophecy—then to note the context and historical background and make sure all terms used are understood. When all that is in hand, one is ready to move forward.

Level Two: OLD TESTAMENT PROPHECY

Coming to *Level Two* in this work, the following items are discussed as helpful for the further study of the Word of God.

1. The purposes of prophecy
2. The role of prediction in prophecy
3. The language of prophecy
4. Problems in interpreting prophecy
5. New Testament use of the prophetic literature
6. Establishing a procedure for study

1. *The purposes of prophecy:* The purposes of prophecy are induced by reading the prophetic books. As we see the burdens of the writers and the declarations by individual prophets in the historic—and poetic—materials, we are able to observe the purposes that give foundation to the utterances. These purposes may be summarized in this manner:

- to inform others to prepare for a particular action at a given time
- to convince others in the matter of sin or action to be taken
- to judge an action or a person by illuminating the activity
- to encourage obedience and trust in an omniscient Lord
- to authenticate a messenger or action beforehand
- to initiate a program or encourage an existing effort

No doubt others could be added, but all of this is in the scope of the prophetic utterance. It will be noticed again that the prophet is very much concerned with performance—more likely than with information of things to come. When one comes to read a prophetic passage, the question that arises immediately is: What does the prophet hope to achieve in this prophecy? Discerning this, the student is better able to bring the message of the prophecy into focus.

2. *The role of prediction in prophecy:* Prediction is fascinating. Our world yearns for it in everything from stock market reports to the weather information on television. One who can accurately foretell what is going to happen will have a following no matter what

field of service. Clear prediction with its accurate fulfillment validates the spokesperson.

This is especially true with biblical prophecy. It strengthens each of the purposes of prophecy (listed on p. 108) because it indicates a higher power of intelligence, and this gives force to the utterance. To some modern apologists prediction and fulfillment is one of the great proofs of the integrity of the Bible.

It must be remembered that predictive and declarative elements are mingled in the prophecy and these are sometimes easily confused. Fulfillment must be more than a general resemblance of similarities. Biblical fulfillment needs the completion of details more than generalities.

Note the passage in Micah 5:2 where the coming Messiah is prophesied to be born in Bethlehem. Considering the date of the prophecy, the likelihood of a small town such as Bethlehem continuing to exist 700 years later is no small thing. But this tiny piece of information is given as a specific detail so that when the prophecy is fulfilled there will be no doubt as to the truthfulness of the prophet or of the God who revealed it to him.

Some prophecies are, however, used in a general sense beyond a specific fulfillment. An example of such is seen in Acts 15 at the Jerusalem council. James offers a decision based on the prophecy of Amos 9. The conversion of the Gentiles is not the specific prediction of Amos but the fact of it (the conversion) "agrees with the words of the prophets." In other words, the prophets speak generally of a time when the Gentiles will come to the light of Israel and what is seen in the Acts report is in agreement with that concept of the prophets. James does not say that the prophecy of Amos is fulfilled but that what is happening is in agreement with something the prophets foretold; Amos is cited as spokesman for the group. The conversion of the Gentiles harmonizes with the teachings of the prophets, therefore the new Church should welcome this activity as clearly from God.

In regard to this, the student should note carefully the item in this level about the New Testament use of the prophetic literature.

3. *The language of prophecy:* Previously discussed in the poetry section, it is important to note that the language of prophecy is one

of the argument areas in theology. People often understand the same words in different senses and it raises the question as to how a particular item is to be interpreted.

Basically language may be seen as:

- literal: there is an entity representation between the word used and the thing described
- figurative: a speech figure dominates the structure
- allegorical (spiritualized): the term used has a secondary meaning or a hidden sense of meaning beyond the term or object itself
- typical: that used to take one entity and predict or describe another. It is also figurative, but *pre*figures something or someone yet to come.
- letteristic: whatever word is used is an exact fixation of what is described

When Isaiah says: *"They shall not hurt nor destroy in all My holy mountain: for the earth shall be full of the knowledge of the Lord, as waters cover the sea"* (Isa. 11:9), the literalist says: "There is a time coming of universal peace when the knowledge of the Lord will be worldwide and violence will be ended."

The spiritualist says: "Holy mountain is a speech figure for the church, and the prophecy indicates that people of every sort will be able to be at peace in the church, the waters covering the sea being the blessing of the Spirit on the Gentiles."

Speech figures are admitted by all, but in this case the literalist[4] sees them as predicting a time of external peace and safety, while the spiritualist (allegorizer) sees them as predicting the peace of the church and the many nations that comprise it.

Our underlying premise in this work is this: language is to be taken literally unless the context plainly states otherwise or the literal usage introduces a conflict or contradiction in biblical ideas, thus showing that another meaning is intended.

The question centers on whether the prophet is describing something in a concrete or abstract way. Abstractionism is often obscure, frequently difficult, and occasionally oracular, although it is used. Thus the possibility of identifying a prophecy this way should not be set aside entirely. Literal interpretation is preferred since, as a rule, gives sound names that refer to given items or characteristics and therefore identifying both the prediction and fulfillment is more apparent.

There is some basis for occasional spiritualization or allegorization as there are points used this way in the Bible with obvious secondary meaning (the reference to the king of Judah as a cedar tree by Ezekiel, for example).

Of course speech figures occur in all forms of language and the student should recognize them (APPENDIX I) and understand what they mean in the context of the passage.

4. *Problems in interpreting prophecy:* The student needs to keep these in mind as the work continues because these factors will condition our understanding of a prophetic passage. Note the following:

• the matter of *language*, as previously discussed

• determine *historic* (declarative) and *predictive* elements in the prophecy. Part of the communication may be immediate advice related only to the circumstances at that time. Part may be predictive, and discernment must be used to see these things. In Isaiah 7:4, when the prophet meets Ahaz at the fuller's field, he is told to tell him the message contained in that verse. It is immediate advice, and a predictive piece will follow. A great amount of predictive material is intended to calm us where we are and prepare us for what is to come.

• discerning *immediate* and *mediate* parts of the prophecy— things that will happen quickly and those that may be deferred for some time. The passage in Isaiah 7 will display this. Immediately the threat to Judah will be blunted. In time, many things will happen and the deliverer will come.

• gaining the *perspective* of the prophecy. Items in a prophecy may not be lined up in exact order or in a a chronological pattern. The student must learn to discern things that are near and things that are far. A distant fulfillment may appear to be occurring before a near fulfillment. For this setting, it is important that the student have a grasp of the total prophetic picture.

• noting **conditional** and **unconditional** items in the prophecy. Time is often a condition of the prophecy, as in the case of Jonah. Nineveh was informed it would be destroyed, but when the people repented and sought God, the destruction was suspended for at least one hundred years. Almost all prophecies of judgment have a time condition. Generally other conditions are made explicit, but a failure to note them may make the prophecy appear to fit a situation for which it was never intended.

• the question of **double fulfillment** cannot be answered in this work but must be kept in mind. This is the idea that a circumstance may be repeated in broad detail and a given prophecy repeated in time. The expression regarding the Lord's return from Egypt (Mt. 2:15) is often thought of in this light, as the earlier citation (Hos. 11:1) spoke of Israel's deliverance from Egypt. There is much debate on this subject among prophetic scholars and the student may keep it in mind without taking a side.

The student will likely become aware of many more problems in his reading, but these are the ones most important at this level.

5. *The New Testament use of the Old Testament prophecies:* The New Testament in general makes great use of the Old Testament throughout its entire content. In the matter of prophecy, it often shows prophetic themes or items that are fulfilled. In general, it does this with three Greek phrases which are translated in the following ways:

• *"in order that it might be fulfilled."* This is very specific and fulfillment is always in mind, although it must be recalled that the fulfillment might be of a specific thing or a general circumstance.

• *"for it is written."* This often shows fulfillment but it is not limited to that, and sometimes is merely a confirmatory point of law or illustration.

• *"it has been said."* The phrase does not mean fulfillment necessarily and is more general that the previous note. It is more often likely to have historical perspective in view.

Actual fulfillment is not limited to these phrases, of course, but they are good indicators of some thinking in the area of fulfillment. Much fulfillment is treated in the historic discussions of a passage and that must be observed as well.

6. *Establish a procedure for study:* The importance of this step may not be overestimated. It has been mentioned before and probably does not need a lot of enforcement. But study in an orderly procedure gives more finished and assured results. A prophetic book may be studied as a whole but in the case of the major prophets (due to size) it is better to divide them into segments. To study the whole at once is a huge task.

The danger in dividing a work into parts, on the other hand, is that something very important may be overlooked or the number of segments may confuse the student. At any rate, select the passage, read it prayerfully, understand the context, the authorship, and the intended audience, then go to work with confidence in the Spirit's guidance. The study of any part of the Bible is enormously rewarding and prophecy is surely no exception to that.

Level Three: OLD TESTAMENT PROPHECY

In *Level Three* we meet some old friends, and two of these are mentioned briefly:

1. An understanding of biblical Hebrew
2. A study of the social structures of the Old Testament

1. *An understanding of biblical Hebrew:* The prophecies in the Old Testament occur in all forms of Old Testament literature. Much of the work is in poetic form and much in prose. Hebrew opens areas of understanding in verbal expressions and constructions, many of which are not translatable. They enrich our understanding, however, when understood. Some of these are included in APPENDIX III in the hope of encouraging study in this area. But with the many helps that are available today, a student can have fair understanding of these things based on the observation of others. There is no substitute for a primary knowledge of one's own but there is plenty of help.

2. *A study of the social structures of the Old Testament:* This is suggested in light of the ways in which the prophets influenced the people and the leaders of the land. The organization of the nation and the development of the kingdom are important themes in the Old Testament, and the services of the prophets are seen in both. One might wonder how a prophet could approach a competent warrior, take away his cloak with impunity, and tear it into twelve pieces (Ahijah and Jeroboam, 1 Kings 11:30*ff*), or how Elijah could order the execution of the Baalite prophets (1 Ki. 18) but when the total structure of the social and religious society is seen, it becomes understandable.

AN ILLUSTRATIVE STUDY

Putting these concepts to work: 1 Kings 22

The items mentioned allow us the opportunity to take them to a prophetic passage for consideration. Following is the study of a prophecy with text printed from the King James Version of the Bible. The aspects of study will be about the same in any Bible but the wording is somewhat different and if one prefers another Bible, probably the same lines of thought can be followed.

The passage for consideration is 1 Kings 22. The time is that of the reign of Jehoshaphat in Judah and Ahab in Israel. Since this is the last year of Ahab's rule, the year is about 852 BC. The student will want to review the history of Ahab[5] and the enormous apostasy of his rule, as well as the rule of Jehoshaphat, Ahab's contemporary in the kingdom of Judah. Ahab is determined to wage war on Syria in the hopes of recovering territory lost some years before (Middle Eastern conflicts are not new!) and he enlists the help of Jehoshaphat, pleading that the territory taken by Syria is really "theirs" and, with the help of Jehoshaphat, it is recoverable.

The plan is set in motion in verse 4, but for some reason Jehoshaphat would like the assurance of the the Lord's mind in this matter and he inquires of Ahab in verse 5.

5 And Jehoshaphat said unto the king of Israel, "Inquire, I pray thee, at the Word of the Lord today."

6 Then the king of Israel gathered the prophets together, about four hundred men, and said unto them, "Shall I go against Ramoth-Gilead to battle, or shall I forbear?" And they said, "Go up; for the Lord shall deliver it into the hand of the king."

Four hundred prophets is certainly an impressive number, and the prediction is with one voice: *"Go up."* The form is imperative, meaning that there is every reason to go. The term *"Lord"* is the common word for Lord, not Jehovah. But Jehoshaphat is suspicious.

7 And Jehoshaphat said: "Is there not here a prophet of the LORD besides, that we might inquire of him?"
8 And the king of Israel said unto Jehoshaphat, "There is yet one man, Micaiah the son of Imlah, by whom we may inquire of the LORD: but I hate him; for he doth not prophesy good concerning me, but evil." And Jehoshaphat said. "Let the king not say so."

In these verses in both cases the expression *"is there"* and *"there is"* is the speech figure *ellipsis*. The proper name for Lord is now given (Jehovah). One gets the feeling that Micaiah is not high on the list of the king, and that he is one vs. four hundred is telling. The student will look him up in the Bible Dictionary for fuller study.

The response of Jehoshaphat is somewhat anti-climactic and the negation is a *jussive negation* in Hebrew, meaning something like "Oh, you shouldn't say that!" It is by no means a rebuke.

9 Then the king of Israel called an officer, and said, "Hasten hither Micaiah the son of Imlah."
10 And the king of Israel and Jehoshaphat sat each on his throne, having put on their robes, in a void place in the entrance of the gate of Samaria; and all the prophets prophesied before them.

From verse 9 the clear impression is that Micaiah was in prison. The "void" place in v. 10 indicates a clear or open space. There is a textual problem on this word but it does not affect the meaning of the verse. That the meeting was in Samaria suggests that Jehoshaphat had already agreed to the campaign. Otherwise why would he go up when Ahab should have come down?

11 And Zedekiah the son of Chenanah, made him horns of iron, and he said, "Thus saith the LORD, With these shalt thou push the Syrians until thou has consumed them.
12 And all the prophets prophesied so, saying "Go up to Ramoth-Gilead and prosper: for the LORD shall deliver it into the king's hand."

Observe the boldness of these prophets now to use the Divine name. It is hard to tell how Zedekiah fits into the picture, but Jehoshaphat had not recognized him previously. His dramatic action seems to carry the day.

13 And the messenger that was gone to call Micaiah spake unto him saying, "Behold now, the words of the prophets *declare* good unto the king with one mouth: let thy word, I pray thee, be like the word of one of them, and speak *that which is* good."
14 And Micaiah said, "As the LORD liveth, what the LORD saith unto me, that will I speak."

This shows the determination of the prophet to be faithful in what he has to do. The facts of his situation or the pressures of conformity mean nothing to him at the moment. In the KJV, the italicized words usually indicate an ellipsis, and it is so in these verses. "One mouth" is metaphoric in figurative speech.

15 So he came to the king and the king, and the king said unto him, "Micaiah, shall we go against Ramoth-Gilead to battle or shall we forbear?" And he answered him, "Go, and prosper, for the Lord shall deliver it into the hand of the king."
16 And the king said unto him, "How many times shall I adjure thee that thou tell me nothing but *that which is* true in the name of the Lord?"

That Micaiah spoke with a sense of irony or cynicism is obvious from the response of the king. However, as he said it, the king picked up a tone of insincerity and now has the nerve to speak to the prophet in a reproving manner. Micaiah now responds:

17 And he said, "I saw all Israel scattered upon the hills, as sheep that have not a shepherd: and the LORD said, These have no master: let them

return every man to his house in peace."

18 And the king of Israel said unto Jehoshaphat, "Did not I tell thee that he would prophesy no good concerning me but evil?"

The prediction is simple: the people will soon have no king. Ahab will be destroyed. The total picture of the prophecy is of a people left without a shepherd but able to return in peace...the Syrians will not counter attack at this time at least.

19 And he said, "Hear thou therefore the word of the LORD: I saw the LORD sitting on His throne, and all the host of heaven standing by Him on His right hand and on His left.

20 And the LORD said "Who shall persuade Ahab, that he may go up and fall at Ramoth Gilead?" And one said on this manner and another said on that manner.

21 And there came a spirit and stood before the LORD and said, "I will persuade him."

22 And the LORD said unto him, "Wherewith?" And he said, "I will go forth, and I will be a lying spirit in the mouth of all his prophets." And He said, "Thou shalt persuade him and prevail also: go forth and do so."

The heavenly scene is likely a picture in the mind of the prophet; this dramatic presentation is probably not to be thought of as an actual occurrence. It is picturesque speech to make the point.

23 "Now, therefore, behold the LORD hath put a lying spirit in the mouth of all these thy prophets, and the LORD hath spoken evil concerning thee."

24 But Zedekiah the son of Chenaanah went near, and smote Micaiah on the cheek, and said, "Which way went the spirit of the LORD from me to speak to thee?"

25 And Micaiah said, "Behold, thou shalt see in that day, when thou shalt go into an inner chamber to hide thyself."

26 And the king of Israel said, "Take Micaiah and carry him back unto Amon the governor of the city, and to Joash the king's son;

27 "And say, 'Thus saith the king: "Put this fellow in the prison, and feed him with bread of affliction and with water of affliction, until I come in peace."

28 And Micaiah said, "If thou return at all in peace, the LORD hath not spoken by me." And he said: "Hearken, O people every one of you."

It is a dramatic encounter. The prophecy contains several factors: that the king will not prosper and not return in peace, the people will be scattered, there will be no pursuit by the Assyrians, and the historic declaration that all the people will hear and listen to the Lord.

By now the student should have located Samaria and Ramoth-Gilead on a map. They are not close. But the king will die in the evening of the battle, struck by an arrow shot "by chance" and he will die in his chariot. Furthermore, the chariot was taken to Samaria the following day, where Ahab's blood was washed in the water from the pool of Samaria while dogs licked the blood from the accouterments, thus fulfilling a prophecy of Elijah in 1 Kings 21:19.

We wish we knew what happened eventually to Micaiah. We do not know, but the truthfulness of his prophecy is seen in the outcome of the battle, a battle in which the king of Israel disguised himself and allowed Jehoshaphat to be endangered as the leading warrior. In spite of his disguise, an unknown archer drew an arrow and fired *"at a venture."* That venture brought the judgment of God on this wicked king. Though the prophet did not go into details on the king's death, the threefold prediction he made and the fulfillment of it showed the inspiration of God. As for his vision of the scene in heaven, the student is left to work out that detail on his own.

Jehoshaphat, of course, should never have been part of this scene but in the providence of God he was a part and played an almost unwitting role in the end of Ahab's wicked career.

SECTION II—THE VARIOUS CLASSES OF PROPHECY

Whereas in Section I the materials needed for general study were discussed, in Section II the attention is given to classes of prophecies. The nature of the prophetic books is such that there is no immediate need to look at the individual books, but there is a need to see the matters needed in the study of particular prophecies. In this section the treatment will concern Messianic, Israelite, Kingdom, Situation, Personal, and International prophecies.

MESSIANIC PROPHECIES

The prophecies in this section concern the coming Messiah. They variously will relate to His Person, role, or ministry, or else to the simple facts concerning the promised leader of the people. Some will relate to different aspects of His coming but all will have as a central thrust the Messiah, the Anointed One, who will fulfill the redemptive purposes of the Lord. That there are many of these is no mystery, for the prophecies are found throughout the Old Testament—from Genesis to Malachi—and while they may not be in every book, they are certainly in every part of the canon.

The purpose in this section is not to study each prophecy, but to underline the materials needed for the study of the prophecies as they occur. The student initially will want to determine the passage, study the word "Messiah," and bear in mind the items mentioned in Section I. These are happy studies for they concentrate on our Redeemer and whatever directs us to Him is good guidance. There are many books to help us in this area and the BIBLIOGRAPHY will direct the student in selecting good textbooks to help.

Level One: MESSIANIC PROPHECIES

Some points will be true for every sort of prophecy and will be repeated in these notes; other points will apply just to one sort of prophecy or another. Remember that prophecy is the utterance of the prophet and it will contain both predictive and directive elements. In fact, the directive elements will outnumber the predictive ones when the whole body of prophecy is studied. The predictive elements, however, always receive great attention, for the future somehow is more exciting than the past or the present. But in the study of a Messianic prophecy, the following items are needed in *Level One*.

1. The historic background of the account, including the social, political and economic conditions
2. The personnel involved: who is speaking and to whom are the messages addressed?
3. Under what circumstances was the prophecy given?
4. Observe the speech figures, devices, etc., that are used

1. *The historic background of the account:* Prophecies are not given in a vacuum. Whether it is in Genesis 3 or Isaiah 7, the historic situation helps us understand the prophecy. For this information one needs a general understanding of the historical background of the Old Testament, including the periods of Israel's history in the Wilderness, the time of the Conquest, the age of the Judgeship government, and the times of the United and Divided Kingdoms, as well as the events following the Babylonian Captivity. Texts on Old Testament Survey will supply this material and there are many helpful charts, etc., available to make the whole affair more simply grasped.

What makes this important is that very often the point of the Messianic prophecy is sparked by the historic situation. When one has this particular knowledge it becomes more obvious how to apply the total prophecy. It is interesting that many of the best known Messianic prophecies emerge in times of greatest trial. The hope of the Messiah seems to be a palliative in the face of disaster.

2. *The personnel involved:* These need to be identified, making a particular note of the person giving the message and to whom it is given. The prophets are not always named and in such cases little research is possible above reading a commentary on the passage. When the prophets are named, it is good to see where they have been serving in the prophetic community and what their relationships have been with the people. There are times when it is apparent that the prophet is speaking beyond the immediate audience or individual. The student will watch for this and understand that the message is given to a much wider audience than might be initially noted.

It is true that all of the Bible is intended for all of the people, but this is in a general learning sense, not a specific action in all times or cases. The specific action may belong just to the person addressed or to the community involved, and the student must see this to keep us from assuming that God has given us something to do when, in reality, it was only given to a certain party at a certain time.

3. *Under what circumstances was the prophecy given?* Is the prophecy given in a time of stress, economic trials, at the order of a king or prominent person? Is it given with almost no clue as to why

it is being given? Such points must be discerned by the text, but many prophecies are better understood when the circumstances calling for them are clear. This was the case in 1 Kings 22 and the ministry of Micaiah, as noted in the portion of this study in Section I. Micaiah's prophecy would make little sense if the circumstances were not known.

4. *Note the speech figures and character of the language:* It is a mistake to hunt speech figures merely for academic reasons but when they occur they add to the meaning of a passage. The prophets use many speech figures (APPENDIX 1) and a great deal of picturesque speech.

Determine whether the language is literal or figurative, whether it is intended to be understood in a concrete or in an allegorical way. The simplest way to do this is to determine if the message is sensible in a literal expression. If it is, then that is most likely the intention of the prophet. If it is not, then some secondary meaning must be the intention. There are large debates in this area, and each student will have to consider the matter and determine one's feeling about it. It is sufficiently complicated that great and godly scholars do not always agree.

Level Two: MESSIANIC PROPHECIES

In *Level Two* the student is concerned with a number of aspects about the prophecy along these lines:

1. What immediate advice is given?
2. What predictions are made?
3. What immediate application is apparent?
4. Is there a dispensational effect to be considered?
5. Are there "inorganic element(s)" that will indicate fulfillment?

While these are not particularly difficult, they are points that enable the student to come to a conclusion by study, not by jumping on an intuitive hunch.

1. *What immediate advice is given?* Students are often so anxious

to get to the predictive part of the prophecy—the lure of the future is enormous—that they miss the advice in the prophecy which was to guide the party hearing it at that time.

A clear illustration is seen in Isaiah 7 when the prophet tells Ahaz that the plot that is hatched against him will not come to pass. In having the historical background in mind, the student knows Ahaz is looking for help from the king of Assyria[6] and is compromising the worship of the Lord to get that help. The practical advice is not spoken but powerfully suggested. God will not let this plan that is put against Ahaz to be successful. The practical advice given is to serve God and give up this compromising alliance.

When the prophet tells Ahaz to ask for a sign and the king refuses to do so, the immediate advice is to recognize him as an unbeliever. Following that the prediction of the virgin birth is given. The practical advice would have saved Ahaz a lot of grief but by ignoring it he increased the difficulty the nation faced. As indicated earlier, the prophet speaks to the present and only speaks to the future to indicate the sovereign will and strength of the Lord.

2. *What predictions are made?* This subject will be seen in greater detail when the study takes up a representative prophecy. It is important and, since the predictions are sometimes made in figurative language, it is vital to know what they are. They may be identified by a verb in the future tense or by a simple declaration that God will do this or that. Very often the prediction—that may at first seem simple and individual—is actually complex and involves several parts. This complexity often gives greater credibility to the whole message since it is obvious that they are beyond the possibility of a good guess or a coincidence.

3. *What immediate application is given?* Often in a prophecy the truth that is being taught will be given an immediate application. In Isaiah 7, when Ahaz refused to ask for a sign, the prophet replied, not to Ahaz, but to the whole ruling class of Judah (identified as the house of David). The Lord will give a sign, not necessarily to Ahaz—since he is unwilling to ask for one—but to all the kings that will follow him, all the rulers that will sit on the throne of Judah.

This prophecy will obviously have a long history, but the immediate application is that God will give a sign and those who are wise will be aware of it and be ready for whatever the Lord does.

4. *Is there a dispensational aspect to be considered?* Whether one is a dispensationalist or not is not the point of this query. All Bible scholars recognize that some commands and instruction belong to one period and not to all. That is why we are not sacrificing lambs today or building altars for burnt offerings. It is possible that a prophecy may be intended for a king or a people at one time and, being fulfilled, have no directive ministry to anyone else. The building of the Jerusalem temple serves as an example. The plans came from the Lord but the Lord did not tell us to build similar temples throughout the world. The prophetic work centered on the ministry of Solomon and many of the prophecies are for that age.

As noted before, the goal of the student is to learn from everything but to distinguish particular actions in accord with the time references given in the Word.

5. *Are there inorganic elements that will indicate fulfillment?* An inorganic element is a piece of information in the prophecy that has no special meaning to the ultimate prophetic fulfillment but is an immediate piece of evidence to convince the recipients of the prophecy that the prediction will indeed come to pass. An example may be seen in the prophecies that are given in 1 Kings 13 when a prophet foretells the doom of the northern kingdom and the downfall of its false priests. In doing this the prophet gives the name of the Judean king who will come into this territory (it is Josiah—a king who will not rule for nearly 250 years) and desecrate this altar built by Jeroboam.

To the specific prophecy he adds a sign in verse 13 about the altar being rent and the ashes poured forth. This happens almost immediately in verse 5, although there is no indication earlier that it will not be contemporaneous with Josiah. It is an inorganic element—not a feature of the main prophecy—but a definitive piece of information that, when it occurs, signifies that God has spoken and the whole prophecy will be fulfilled. These aspects of the prophetic witness serve to show the credibility that is to be given to the message that has been given.

Level Three: MESSIANIC PROPHECIES

Level Three for all the prophetic types is very similar and does not need a long or complicated discussion.

1. Details in the Hebrew

2. Evidence of fulfillment or lack of such

3. Relation to similar prophecies

1. *Details in the Hebrew:* The prophetic literature is sometimes written in prose and at other times in poetic fashion. An understanding of Hebrew[7] is enormously helpful although not indispensable. It would be valuable to have enough understanding to comprehend the notes in Bible commentaries or study Bibles. Almost any of the "self-study" courses in Hebrew would be adequate to this end.

2. *Evidence of fulfillment or lack of such:* Helpful information on this line may be found in any of the major study Bibles. In the case of a lack of fulfillment, the student must consider whether the prophecy is literal or to be taken in a figurative sense. At times this matter is assisted by historical research.

If there is evidence the prophecy has been fulfilled, it becomes necessary for the student to note each aspect of the prophecy, whether directive or predictive, and determine what the prophecy meant when given, and what evidence it gives today for the enactment of the will of God.

3. *Relation to similar prophecies:* This is an interesting factor since the prophets often speak of similar events or situations. Compare Isaiah 2:1-9 with Micah 4:1-8 and note that these two prophets were contemporary, although Isaiah's ministry seems more general while that of Micah more directed at the leaders of the nation.

Comparison of similar prophecies will often yield a synthesis of ideas that give greater detail to the nature of the message.

AN ILLUSTRATIVE STUDY

Putting these concepts to work: Micah 5:2-7

This is a favorite Messianic prophecy. The intention in this exercise is to deal with the first part of it and only to scan the second. Verse 1, in the Hebrew Bible, is assigned to chapter 4 in another prophetic discourse. Verse 2 begins with the adversative "but" and that is why our study is beginning at that point in the English Bible (KJV). Verse 1 ends with a pronouncement on the "judge" of Israel while verse 2 moves to address Bethlehem (a speech figure!) and talk about the future events of that community.

It is not so complicated as it may seem; the chapter divisions were made by men, and there are other places where the breaks are not in the better interest of our understanding. The prophecy student will note many things of interest in the study of the passage, being careful to survey the historic background and the other basic materials needed in the study of a passage.

2 But thou, Bethlehem Ephrata, *though* thou be little among the thousands of Judah, *yet* out of thee shall he come forth unto me *that is* to be ruler in Israel: whose goings forth *have been* from of old, from everlasting.

"Bethlehem Ephrata." It is assumed the student will investigate the term "Ephrata"—a combined speech figure composed of an apostrophe and a personification.

The italicized words indicate an ellipsis, and the phrase *"thou be little among the thousands"* may indicate hyperbole. The contrast is set with the elliptical *"yet."* Bethlehem is so small but the ruler of Israel will come from there. As well, this ruler is one whose activities do not start in Bethlehem; they have an everlasting character. In other words, the comings and goings of the ruler have been from everlasting days. This is a pointer to the Messianic character.[8]

In this verse are a few predictions along with the general statement. It is predicted that 1) Bethlehem will continue to be a recognized site until the ruler comes; 2) it will continue as a Hebrew

community; 3) the eventual ruler will come from there and he will
be 4) a servant of God to rule His people. These items may seem
small but they are pointedly important in the history of Israel and the
coming of the Messiah.

The essential fulfillment is seen in the New Testament in the
record of the Lord's birth and the place where the wise men of Israel
believed it to be. But while the ruler would come from there, he did
not come as a ruler but as a servant to minister to His people.
Therefore verse 3 introduces what is almost a contrary thought.

> 3 Therefore will he give them up, until the time *that* she which travaileth
> hath brought forth: then the remnant of his brethren shall return unto the
> children of Israel.

The prediction is that the ruler will not rule immediately but give
up the people until—and there in the text a condition of time is
entered. The pronoun *"she"* requires identification and may be tied
into 4:7, 10 and seen as the nation Israel. The nation is personalized
in the concept of "travail"—laboring to produce—and the ruler will
give them up until that action is accomplished. But when that is
accomplished there will be a reunion of all the members of the family, the brethren returning to the children of Israel.

The prophet does not tell us when these things will be, but it is
significant that the ruler has proceeded according to plan even
though he does not take up his rule until the suffering of the nation
is complete and there is a reunion of all those people who are to be
under his rule. Please remember this is not a commentary on the
prophecy, just an illustration of what one needs to know to study it.

> 4 And he shall stand and feed in the strength of the Lord, in the majesty
> of the name of the Lord his God; and they shall abide: for now shall he
> be great unto the ends of the earth.

The pronoun *"he"* certainly has the *"ruler"* as the antecedent.
The term *"stand and feed"* is a metonymy describing how the ruler
will be strengthened. The pronoun *"they"* seems to describe those in
the reunion of verse 3 and they are depicted as being set or established, with the ruler being great throughout the world.

The student will have augmented the list of specific predictions given after verse 3 with the concepts that the ruler will not take the rule but will wait till the travailing process is over. He then will see a reunion of all that are His. He will manifest the glory of God and the people who are His will be established while He is made great over the entire earth.

5 And this *man* shall be the peace, when the Assyrian shall come into our land; and when he shall tread in our palaces, then shall we raise against him seven shepherds and eight principal men.

"Man" indicates the ellipsis, but in this verse one is brought to see the historical setting. The land is faced with an Assyrian invasion and it appears that it will be a devastating affair. But in the providence of God the nation will have its deliverance when there is raised within it adequate leadership.

Note the numerical collocation *"seven...and eight."* There will be no end to the leadership God will provide and, although the foe seems to be overwhelming, there will be a deliverance. The peace will be in knowing what God will do and what will be done by this *"man"* and the leadership provided by the Deity. *"Assyrian"* in the historical context makes sense literally but the term may indicate any aggressor who so seeks to dominate the people of the Lord.

6 And they shall waste the land of Assyria with the sword, and the land of Nimrod in the entrances thereof: thus shall he deliver *us* from the Assyrian, when he cometh into our land, and when he treadeth within our borders.

The leadership God will provide will be adequate for the task. Note that *"us"* is elliptical. Another pronoun might be supplied, but the first person pronoun is used to agree with *"our."*

The student will inquire about the *"land of Nimrod"* and again will need to see the historical background for this passage.

7 And the remnant of Jacob shall be in the midst of many people as a dew from the Lord, as the showers upon the grass, that tarrieth not for man, nor waiteth for the sons of men.

The prophet speaks of a great day when "Jacob" will be a blessing to all mankind—not because men want to make him that, but
because the Lord has done it.

The student will note the different designations for the people of
God and will be able not only to put together a list of Messianic predictions but also a list of things predicted for Israel. Verse 7 features
some well-drawn similes and builds on the "remnant of Jacob." This
phraseology needs considerable study beyond this prophecy.

Now it is not fair to terminate our study of the portion at this
point. But that is the case for the present study. Note that the prophecy of the coming ruler is the grounds for peace on the part of his
people, no matter what comes. See that no enemy is able to deter
permanently the work of God, that even God's people in their rebellion are not able to end His gracious intention. Notice that God will
provide what is needed for any time of difficulty and will continue
His program of blessing. To see these things clearly, we must take
into account the historical background, details of the language, an
analysis of what is predicted, and the realization that it is given as an
encouragement to all the people of God, both then and now.

NATIONAL PROPHECIES—REGARDING ISRAEL

Prophecies of the Messiah are often closely interwoven with those
of the nation of Israel. That is logical, of course, for the Messiah will
be of Israel and will accomplish the blessing of Israel and establish
its role in the world at large. The prophecies for Israel are found
throughout the Old Testament and cover everything from the initial
promise to Abraham to the words of Paul in Romans 9-11.

There is, in the Israelite economy, a spiritual people and an ethnic
people. There are times when it is hard to make a satisfactory distinction[9] between the two, but the student must keep this always
before him. It is more of a problem in the New Testament than in the
Old, but the potential for confusion should be always close to the
scholar's mind.

In this work, the concern is for the study of prophecies given to
Israel as a nation. The sphere of the work does not allow any deeper
thinking than that. Our interest then moves to these national prophecies and follows the three-level procedure.

1 Level One: NATIONAL PROPHECIES

The general principle still applies that the student will be given to a prayerful reading of the Word of God and gaining a grip on the historical background of any passage when it is isolated for study. In *Level One,* in order that the study may be more productive, the student will need to comprehend these things:

1. How Israel became God's people
2. What God expected of them
3. How God delivered them and made them a special people
4. How God revealed His will to the nation

These may seem very basic or even self-apparent, but it is on these aspects that God speaks to the nation through the prophets in all the generations that follow.

1. *How Israel became God's people:* A good place for the student to begin this study is Deuteronomy 7 and related passages. From this point, move to the call of Abraham and the promises made to him by the Lord (following his obedience in Genesis 12). The history of the patriarchs will show how God protected this word of promise. While there were many other people in the created society, God chose this band for Himself. Following the deliverance from Egypt, it will be seen how God gave the people a land and an image and for this reason, if for none other, God had the concept that He was their God and they were His people.

2. *What God expected of them:* There are many starting points for this information, but probably Exodus 19 is one of the most important. Leviticus 19 will add to the picture that God expected them to be a holy people who would declare to the world a holy God. He did not expect them to be perfect in the law, otherwise He would not have prescribed a sin offering and a Day of Atonement. He *did* expect them to be sensitive to His leading and direction.

These ideas are expressed here in an *ad hominem* fashion, for the Lord knew about them and knew of the national weaknesses long before we became aware of it. The expectation is that they would turn to Him and He would have the Creator-honor of which He was completely worthy. The covenantal codes in Deuteronomy will be a vital part of the student's study at this point. When we have an idea of the expectation of the Lord, then we are ready to proceed and hear what the prophets will say as they are instructed by the Holy Spirit.

3. *How God delivered them and made them a special people:* Following the deliverance from Egypt—by blood and power—the Lord showed great deliverance to Israel both in the wilderness and in the taking of Canaan. His grace shadowed their every move. Now when the student reads a prophecy about the nation, he can feel the heart of God beating for His people. A survey knowledge of the kingdom of David and Solomon and the divided kingdoms that followed is a necessary part of this picture. To see Israel delivered from Sennacherib is a fascinating account and, as much as it encourages us, their tendency to idolatry and spiritual adultery depresses us.

4. *How God revealed His will to the nation:* Israel, at times, acted as if it had no knowledge of what God wanted (Micah 6 shows us a picture of that). But God was perfectly clear in His will and intention as well as in His desire. He gave the essential foundation documents in the Law and He augmented this through the prophets.

Therefore when a prophecy is studied, it is, in reality, an insight into the will of God. The Lord used circumstances to go with the words, but there was no lack of knowledge. Instead at times it was a lack of compliance by a people who seemed to forget their Lord too easily—although that fault, it appears from our own day, was not limited to Israel by any means.

Level Two: NATIONAL PROPHECIES

In *Level Two* the background materials grow in importance. While the major part of these are available in the Bible itself, it is useful to use the bibliographic materials as well. The most helpful of these is the Bible Dictionary and a work surveying the Old Testament. Note the points that are of particular interest:

1. Research the covenantal promises of Deuteronomy

2. Study the book of Judges in particular to see how God responded to Israel in times of blessing and judgment
3. Summarize the historic setting of the prophecy
4. Study Solomon's temple prayer and, in the light of his requests and commitment, put the prophecy into proper perspective

1. *Research the covenantal promises:* The strongest expression of these are in Deuteronomy (especially Deut. 27-30). Since many of the prophecies are concerned with Israel's behavior under varying circumstances, the promises of blessing and judgment are fundamental[10] to any utterance of the prophet. The prophet speaks from the foundation of the will of God as expressed to the nation. Much of the message is not new but is rooted in previous revelation.

2. *Study the book of Judges to see how God responded to situations regarding blessing and judgment:* This is a suggestion to the student, not an assignment, but this book (one of the former prophets) gives the clearest picture of the consequences of apostasy and the blessing of God when His people call on Him. Not every national prophecy will be committed to these items but many of them will be in this area. To see how the Lord has reacted is a good clue to anticipate how He will react. It is to be remembered that the directive aspects of the prophecy are as important as the predictive elements.

3. *Summarize the historic settings of the prophecy:* This is one of those factors that appears constantly, yet is easily and often overlooked. The audience is part of this information and the development of Israel's history is another. The character of the leadership of the time is important as is their response in regard to the national interest. Help in this area is usually available in a commentary or a survey book. The student should not hesitate to make use of these valuable tools.

4. *Study Solomon's temple prayer:* The text is found in 1 Kings 8 and 2 Chronicles 6. It is a dedicatory prayer but, among other things, it goes into a discussion with the Lord that follows the line: "If we do this, will You do that?" It is almost like a contract indicating what

Solomon anticipates God will do in certain circumstances. In the
study of a national prophecy (that comes after the time of Solomon,
of course) it is interesting to see how the requests of the king at this
dedicatory moment are answered by the Lord, not by quotations or
specific statements but in the way things are accomplished.

Level Three: NATIONAL PROPHECIES

In *Level Three* the attention is turned to these points:

1. An understanding of biblical Hebrew
2. The nature of, and problem with, spiritual adultery
3. The language question
4. Fulfillment aspects

1. *An understanding of biblical Hebrew:* Should it be troubling
that this is mentioned in every Level Three, it is only done so to
emphasize the potential importance of this discipline. Not everyone
can have the opportunity for such work but, if it should occur, even
a smattering would prove useful if employed in the study of the text.

2. *The nature of, and problem with, spiritual adultery:* There is a
wealth of material on this subject in the book of Ezekiel, and it is
possible to understand it in the light of the command to *"have no
other gods before"* the Lord. Of all the offenses that may be committed against the Lord, none seems more severe than this one. It
challenges the very roots of the relationship between God and His
people. The allegory on this line is drawn clearly in Hosea but the
inferences are legion in the Old Testament. God will not share His
glory with another, and whether the other is a pagan temple or a worshipful idea, the Lord will have His people for Himself alone.

3. *The language question:* This item has probably caused as many
sleepless nights as any other in the nature of these studies. The student will need to determine if the prophecy is given to the nation as
an ethnic body or to a spiritual Israel, an invisible body. Whether the
language is figurative or literal must be decided. The student will
recall that literal language does use speech figures, instead of using

words consistently as real representatives of concrete objects. The guideline recommended in this work is that the language should be understood as literal unless 1) the context suggests otherwise; 2) there is a direct statement that indicates otherwise; or 3) if the literal interpretation suggests an absurdity or contradiction that would be harmful to the integrity of the Word of God. It is a serious matter and all of us should retain a degree of humility before pronouncing our thinking as correct and that of everyone else as being in error.

4. *Fulfillment aspects:* The student must determine if there are evidences of fulfillment of this particular prophecy within the Bible or in the scope of historical reference. A study Bible will help in this regard, and there are several books on fulfilled predictions that may help as well. If fulfillment has been accomplished, then the prophecy is studied as an indicator of the way in which the Lord works. If it has not been fulfilled, then the student looks for those pieces of information that will help in seeing fulfillment when it does come or in identifying it historically when it did come. Fulfillment of predictive prophecy is always exciting and one of the indications of the truthfulness of the prophet and the dependability of God.

AN ILLUSTRATIVE STUDY

Putting these concepts to work: Jeremiah 25

Jeremiah 25 is helpful for illustrating the treatment of a national prophecy. The passage is selected and read prayerfully and then we look to the items that will assist in the study. Jeremiah is identified, the time of his work is noted, the circumstances of his life, and the relationships with the authorities are all put in order. These are basic materials needed for any passage, of course, but it is always good to remind ourselves of the primary things that must be done. The full text of Jeremiah will not be printed but significant portions will be reproduced from the King James translation of the Bible.

1 The word that came to Jeremiah concerning all the people of Judah in the fourth year of Jehoiakim the son of Josiah king of Judah, that *was* the first year of Nebuchadnezzar king of Babylon.

With the help of a Bible Survey book or a commentary, the student is able to date these events within a year or so of the exact time. Note how careful Jeremiah is with his specifications of data. That the message is given to *"ail the people of Judah"* does not preclude people of the northern kingdom but Israel had been in captivity for a long time and most of the Israelites who had escaped the exile were living within the confines of the territory of Judah.

Jehoiakim is the second son of Josiah to rule and the student will be sure to read of his reign and that of his predecessor. The mention of Josiah stirs memories of a man of God who struggled for revival in Judah, and the note on Nebuchadnezzar helps to place the whole scene in a proper Near Eastern context.

> 2 The which Jeremiah the prophet spake unto all the people of Judah, and to the inhabitants of Jerusalem, saying,

"Unto all" indicates the message was for everyone, not that Jeremiah spoke to each one. It is interesting that he makes a specific note for the inhabitants of Jerusalem and and so makes certain that no one can feel outside the declarations to come.

> 3 From the thirteenth year of Josiah the son of Amon king of Judah, even unto this day, this is the three and twentieth year the Word of the Lord hath come unto me, and I have spoken unto you rising early and speaking, but ye have not hearkened.

The dates are instructive and the expression *"rising early and speaking"* is a figure to show how committed he was to the service of God. It is a sad note that they had not, as a nation, hearkened.

Verse 4 repeats the concepts of verse 5 including the speech figure and the charge, *"you have not hearkened nor inclined your ear to hear."* *"Ear"* is a speech figure (*synechdoche*) and means that the whole intelligence factor had been kept from listening to God.

In verse 5 the initial pronoun *"they"* has for its antecedents the *"prophets"* of the previous verse and their message—by now a historic theme—follows:

Turn ye again now every one from his evil way, and from the evil of your doings, and dwell in the land that the Lord hath given unto you and to your fathers forever and ever.

6 And go not after other gods to serve them, and to worship them, and provoke me not to anger with the works of your hands: and I will do you no hurt.

That was the message consistently given by the prophets over many years. The matter of spiritual adultery is not mentioned by name, but implied in the text. The message is clearly literal and addressed to Israel as a whole.

7 Yet ye have not hearkened unto me, saith the Lord: that ye might provoke me to anger with the works of your hands to your own hurt.

"That" introduces a result clause: God will do them no hurt but they have defied Him and and have done so to their own hurt. In this prophecy, the directive part is to give up the things that irritate the Lord and accept His blessing.

In verse 8, Jeremiah speaks for the Lord, following in the train of the prophets who have gone before him and, since the people have not listened to the words of God,...

9 Behold, I will send and take all the families of the north, saith the Lord, and Nebuchadnezzar the king of Babylon, my servant, and will bring them against this land, and against the inhabitants thereof, and against all these nations round about, and will utterly destroy them, and make them an astonishment, and an hissing, and perpetual desolations.

"Families" is surely a metonymy for the armed forces coming from the northerly direction and they, with Nebuchadnezzar, will accomplish a great destruction not only over Judah but the lands round about. Note the metaphor in showing how God will treat these nations that fall before His judgment: *"an astonishment,"* etc.

And no one will be happy. Note the speech figures describing the loss of joy in the day of God's anger in verse 10.

11 And this whole land shall be a desolation, and an astonishment, and these nations shall serve the king of Babylon seventy years.

The prophecy will continue, and one may read of its fulfillment in Jeremiah and of the conclusion of the years in Daniel. In the following verses, the Lord will express His displeasure with Babylon and the neighboring territories—moving forward in prophecy to a day when all the nations will face the wrath of God (v. 33).

In this portion of the study, the interest is in the national prophecy. This chapter will be taken up again when prophesies for the nations are discussed. At this point, however, it is possible to see the exact nature of the predictive and directive prophecies given by Jeremiah and the literal way in which this judgment will be enacted.

THE KINGDOM PROPHECIES

By definition, the kingdom prophecies are those utterances that speak of an age when the kingdom of God will be a physical reality on the earth. The Lord Jesus will rule and the great promises of the Abrahamic Covenant will be completed. Some of the prophecies of the Israelitish kingdom typify this time as well; that is why David is seen as a type of the Lord in a reigning capacity.

There are many other interpretations of these prophecies, however, and we need to be aware that Bible students over the ages have not been unanimous in their understanding of these things.

With regard to the kingdom of God identified as the Millennial Kingdom, the three most common views are these.

1. The *Premillennial* view believes that the Lord will return and establish a literal kingdom on the earth.

2. The *Amillennial* view believes that the Lord has established the kingdom and it is a spiritual one, centered in the Church and that He, in time, will return when all the program is completed.

3. The *Postmillennial* view teaches that the Church, through the spreading of the gospel, will bring the world to Christ and a kingdom of peace will grow out of it at the conclusion of which Christ will come again.

There are variations to all of these views[11] and all are ably presented and defended by various Bible scholars. If one wonders how students can look at the same texts and come up with such different ideas, the answer is mostly in the understanding of language.

Premillennialists tend to understand language literally (about the kingdom) while the Amillennialists see it in an allegorical sense and the Postmillennialists take a view that is essentially literal but emphasizes an internal working rather than an external working. It is a complicated matter and the student is not expected to unravel it or to solve it, but to understand what is said and to evaluate and determine the course one thinks is most faithful to the biblical method and message.

At that point one teaches what one believes, but does so in an aura of understanding and fraternal love. Students in all camps of thinking will discover excesses among their own teachers and those teaching otherwise. So humility should be a prime feature even though we should not be hesitant to explain the facts of the matter as we personally understands them.

Questions will also arise about the dispensational appointments in these prophetic studies and such are not the objects of our work at this time. Suffice it to say that those who love the Scripture and the Lord often use terminology that creates more "heat than light." In the discussion of biblical issues every student should be concerned with *"speaking the truth in love"* and displaying that the person who loves God also loves his brother. With these caveats in mind, the study of the kingdom prophecies may proceed.

Level One: KINGDOM PROPHECIES

Remembering that prophecy is both foretelling and forth-telling, the student will find these points instructive when beginning the study:

1. The historic circumstances in which the prophecy is given
2. The nature of the prophecy
3. Identification of speech figures and character of language

1. *The historic circumstances in which the prophecy is given:* This

is determined through reading the Bible itself and consulting a commentary or a survey work. The circumstances lying outside the biblical material can only be gleaned in one of these latter works and there may be considerable research involved. But no word originates without an historical context and understanding that context often helps in marking the meaning of the passage or the intent of the prophet. This point is true for all prophecy studies, of course, but it seems to be especially needed for the kingdom prophecies as they often arise in response to some national challenge or as a means of encouraging fidelity to the Lord.

2. *The nature of the prophecy:* Similarly discerned from the reading of the prophecy, the point is to determine whether the prophecy is intended as a corrective for some problem, a rebuke for some particular party, a matter of encouraging information, or a grounds for some definitive doctrinal teaching. More aspects may be realized by the student but the thrust is: "Why is the prophet giving this prediction at this time?" That requires some insight into the total prophetic program and may require a little inventiveness as well! However, when one has thought through this matter, it is not only a help to understanding what the prophet hoped to discover in his time but also helps in relating a present application to present needs.

3. *Speech figures and character of language:* Since the prophecies are often given in poetic fashion and are also often marked with imagery and highly descriptive language, the student needs to be aware of the speech figures that occur and what they mean.

By considering character of language one is determining if it is literal, figurative, etc. The literal concept has been mentioned frequently enough in this work that it need not be repeated now. But if the character of the language seems to lean to allegorization, there is no need to be fearful of it or to try to twist it into something else.

The prophets spoke as the Holy Spirit moved them and the task of the student today is to understand what they said and not to seek to make the message what the modern student might want it to say. Many speech figures are seen in the Hebrew text that may not be visible in the English text as they are not easily translatable. The student who does not have some facility with Hebrew will need to rely on the English text and identify the figures that are apparent and make sure they are understood correctly. As a matter of fact, the student with some Hebrew facility has exactly the same problem, although that student will find more speech figures and language devices to consider.

Level Two: KINGDOM PROPHECIES

Level Two will find the student working more intensely with the text of of the passage and discerning these things:

1. The relationship with this passage and similar prophecies
2. The predictions and directives that are given
3. The immediate use of the prophecy

1. *The relationship with this passage and similar prophecies:* A topical Bible (or a chain-referenced Bible) is a great help in this since it can hardly be expected that the student would read the entire Bible and mark these passages for one's own study. That might be ideal but does not seem practical. At the same time, any helpful book might not list everything so the student must be aware that there may be pertinent material not readily laid out for one's perusal.

In comparing similar passages the student will need to see 1) if there is a common history; 2) if there is a common intention; 3) if the same item is treated to the same degree or end; 4) if both passages use the same character of language; and 5) if the advice or directives given are consistent with one another. It is helpful to have several copies of the text so that they may be studied in parallel form and these copies may be made by photo-copying or any one of several modern means. Of course passages may be viewed side-by-side in any Bible software program or printed off the computer to make hard copies for comparison.

2. *The predictions and directives of the passage:* It is always possible that one of these might not occur in the passage at all, but it seems less than likely. Listing the predictions in one column and the directives in another seems to be a good approach. The advice in this work is to keep the listings in the order of exact expressions of the

text, first of all, and then in deductions or inductions made from the
text. But one must exercise some care in noticing the prediction
because it is not uncommon for them to be underlying in the text and
not seen immediately. No, the student should not manufacture something artificial, but should look with keen perception so as not to
miss what is there.

3. *What is the immediate use or response regarding the prophecy?*
From the text itself one reads to see how the hearers reacted or how
the prophet took advantage of the message he had given to urge
some further action. There are times when this is very apparent and
other times when it is not! The student looks hard at the prophecy to
make a determination. If none can be seen, do not manufacture a
sequence. But if some immediate use or response is visible, the student is given direction in applying the prophecy in a present setting.

Level Three: KINGDOM PROPHECIES

Only two items need mention in *Level Three* and the student
might be able to guess them at this time.

1. An understanding of biblical Hebrew
2. Application of the prophecy throughout the Bible

Of both of these items enough has been said that it need not be
repeated. Both items offer the student the assurance of accuracy in
the analysis made. The second helps us keep in step with the unity
of Scripture and shows how the Word of God has consistency within itself.

AN ILLUSTRATIVE STUDY

Putting these concepts to work: Micah 4:1-5

There is no lacking of kingdom prophecies and many of them
involved Messianic prophecies as well. For this illustrative work the
prophecy of Micah 4:1-5 is considered. The total prophecy is considerably larger, but this segment relates specifically to the kingdom

and is serviceable for the purposes of this work. The text is printed
from the King James Version.

> 1 But in the last days it shall come to pass, that the mountain of the
> house of the Lord shall be established in the top of the mountains, and
> it shall be exalted above the hills, and people shall flow into it.

"In the last days" equals the concept of the "days afterward." In
the prophecy these last days follow the destruction of Jerusalem
(3:12) and the ruin of the Judean economy. Historically the prophecy is given in the days of Hezekiah (Jer. 26:18) and likely following
the ruinous reign of Ahaz, since the prophet was given a corrective
message to strengthen the reform ministry of Hezekiah. The mountain is Mount Zion, of course, and the *"top"* of the mountains is a
metonymy to indicate the place of exaltation. The *"hills"* over which
it is exalted may be a metonymy for other religious systems or simply refer to the topography. That the people will *"flow"* into it is a
metaphor: they will move as a stream in a continuing undulation.

> 2 And many nations shall come and say, Come, and let us go up to the
> mountain of the Lord, and to the house of the God of Jacob: and he will
> teach us of His ways, and we will walk in His paths; for the law shall go
> forth from Zion, and the word of the Lord from Jerusalem.

"Many nations" indicates conversion of the Gentiles with their
recognition of the supremacy of the God of Jacob. Proof of their sin-
cerity is in the fact that they will accept His teaching and walk in His
ways. Zion will be the center point of justice and Jerusalem will be
a focal point for the teaching of the Word of God. The predictions
are easily seen.

With regard to the language, verse 1 may not be physical but refer
to the station Zion has—although it could certainly be physical.

Verse 2 seems to be literal in the prediction of a Gentile conversion and a yieldedness to the law. Needless to say, there are other
interpretations, but this appears to be the most satisfactory.

In the last two clauses Zion and Jerusalem should be thought of
as one (type of speech figure: *hendiadys*) and the terms "law" and
"word of the Lord" seen similarly. The truth of God will come forth
from His place of occupation.

3 And he shall judge among many people, and rebuke strong nations afar off; and they shall beat their swords into plowshares, and their spears into pruning hooks: nation shall not lift up a sword against nation, neither shall they learn war any more.

The *"he"* must refer to the Lord; *"swords and plowshares"* combine figures of metonymy and synecdoche, the terms indicating instruments of war but representing the whole arsenal with two instruments. The prediction is of an age of peace. Those not at peace will suffer the rebuke of the Lord. National entities are designated, not individual citizens, although it might be assumed that what would be true of nations would also be true of citizenry.

4 But they shall sit every man under his vine and under his fig tree, and none shall make them afraid; for the mouth of the Lord hath spoken this.

The picture is one of great peace. The speech figures are plain. The statements could be interpreted figuratively, but the literal sense is easier and more available. The authority of this is the *"mouth of the Lord,"* mouth representing the speech figure *anthropapatheia* which indicates the attribution of human passions (or parts) to God.

5 For all people will walk every one in the name of his god, and we will walk in the name of the Lord, our God for ever and ever.

It is not that the people will have different gods, for all nations will come to the knowledge of the Lord. *"Every one"* represents the nations beyond Israel who will walk in the name of God, but Israel (Judah in particular) will walk in the name of *"our God"* as Micah reflects how different things will be in this age. And they will do it for ever—the speech figure suggests unbroken fellowship with the Lord.

The preference in this work is to take this prophecy literally, and believe that it shows a time when the world will trust the Lord, and peace and safety will be the rule. Prosperity will be the common way of life, and external fear and danger will be controlled. That is what is called the "Kingdom Age." To the people of Micah's time it was both a promise of blessing and a challenge to get back to spiritual basics. The only comfortable life would be one lived in and with the knowledge of the Lord. If that is the way it is to be in the Kingdom, that is the way it should be now! Obedience and worship should mark the life of the children of God. In a sense, we learn for today from what we will be tomorrow. But the fact that we should learn it today does not in any way suggest that it will not exist in reality and in perfection in this promised Kingdom age.

SITUATION PROPHECIES

There will be a natural overlapping of our materials and many prophetic messages may involve two or more prophetic concepts. But there is sufficient individuality in them all to make these separate categories without becoming redundant.

Situation prophecies are those in which the prophet speaks to a particular situation and may prescribe a solution to an immediate problem or predict for a future setting. General principles may be gleaned from these, but usually the particular word is directed just to that given situation. It does teach in an illustrative way and, when coupled with the overall teaching of the Scripture, becomes a useful directive for many occasions when the problems are similar.

There are many of these settings in the Bible. The tools for working with them will be described and an illustrative passage follows.

1 Level One: SITUATION PROPHECIES

For most types of prophecy there are points in common in the preparation for study and/or teaching. The following are important basic steps:

1. The historical background
2. The problem or situation calling for the prophecy
3. The personnel involved
4. Speech figures and wording

1. *The historical background:* It is important to determine when this particular event took place and who was involved in the action. This is part of the basic study for almost everything because the set-

ting for the matter often indicates what needs done and what one should be doing. The student should be certain of proper names, locations, and events connected to the prophecy. The Bible Dictionary is a great friend at this point, and the commentaries also usually have good background material. Much of the historical data is learned from the text itself, but there are many things that are outside of the text. For these we need special help from others who have made the research a project.

2. *The problem or situation calling for the prophecy:* In many ways this is part of the historical background, but it is a more immediate item and so a separate heading is given to it. It is not such a broad subject as the historical data and does not require a detailed answer. Knowledge of this aspect is key to seeing how the prophet handles matters and what his advice means.

3. *The personnel involved:* Situations do not happen in a vacuum, and the nature of the persons involved is instructive as to how things have come to pass. A biographical study is in order for all those involved; and the greater their involvement, the greater the need of the study. Among the prophets of the Bible are a few outstanding names and if one has done a biographical study on Elijah, for example, it would be adequate for every Elijah encounter—with the understanding that a new situation might add something to the biography. The student does not have to repeat a study where one has been done (it is not good to manufacture work). But there are many aspects to personality. In dealing with biblical characters, it is good to see different facets emphasized by various sources.

Sarah, for example, has a rather negative cameo in the Old Testament, but in the New Testament she is only mentioned for good! A study on her personality and life would be incomplete without the New Testament references and the study of a biography might well go beyond the immediate text of a setting or what the student already knows. The lesson is to have a thorough understanding of the personnel.

4. *Understand speech figures and wording:* The advice of this work is that one should not wear oneself out looking for speech fig-

ures, but wherever there is something perplexing, duplicative, or not easily explained, a speech figure may be involved. The figures given in APPENDIX 1 are adequate to have the student begin, but the appendix material must not be viewed as terminal. Commentaries that are essentially grammatical will often offer help on these occasions and when the student has identified a figure once, it should be locked in the thinking process, for it will certainly be seen again.

A practical rule is that one does not press the language to a doctrinal conclusion unless all the wording is understood and agrees with the pattern of Scripture.

2 Level Two: SITUATION PROPHECIES

Only two items impose themselves in the study for *Level Two*.

1. Study the broader context of the prophecy
2. Determine the character of the language: is it literal or something else?

1. *Study the broader context of the prophecy:* In agreement with the student's concern for the historical background is the need for comprehension of the broader context. If the prophecy concerns a king in any of the Hebrew kingdoms, the student will want to see the events that led up to the kingship and the results that grew from it. The broader context will often demonstrate a reason for an occurrence that will make the point of the prophecy more clear. If one wonders how broad the context is, the answer is simply that whatever is connected to the prophecy by implication or assignment, that is the broader context. The total amount of material may vary from chapters to books! But it is all worthwhile.

2. *Determine the character of the language:* As much as possible identify the character as literal, allegorical (figurative) and so forth. Remember that the presence of speech figures does not make language aliteral, for speech figures are part of all language. But if the language suggests an understanding that does not seem comprehensible in a literal form, look for a figurative meaning. Ecclesiastes 12:1-7 is a good place to see where a literal verse (v. 1) is followed

by a series of figures that obviously constitute an allegory. When
one has made this determination, it aids in seeing the total purpose
of the passage, whether it is predictive or directive.

Level Three: SITUATION PROPHECIES

We meet again these common tools to help our understanding in
Level Three. One might even guess some of them:

1. Appreciation for the Hebrew
2. Knowledge of fulfillment
3. Special problems of fulfillment, text, or meaning

1. *Appreciation for the Hebrew:* In APPENDIX 3 some examples
are given to indicate the value of biblical Hebrew. They may be
impressive or they may not be. But without reiterating what has been
said regularly, if one has the opportunity for this study, it is well
worthwhile.

2. *Knowledge of fulfillment:* Discovered through perusing materials in one's study Bible or a commentary, it is vital to see if the matter has been fulfilled in the Old or New Testament. Sometimes a prediction is given to show how something *could* happen, even though
the prediction might not be fulfilled on that spot. The Amos citation
in Acts 15 is a good example of this. James tells us that all the words
of the prophets (and it is plural) agree with what is happening, and
Amos is cited as a clear example indicating what will take place
some day. The conversion of the Gentiles at that time pointed to the
ultimate fulfillment that would come, as in Micah 4.

3. *Special problems regarding fulfillment, the text, or meaning:*
There are some Old Testament prophecies that are not yet fulfilled
in the predictive aspect. There are others that apparently have been
fulfilled, but we do not have the clear fulfillment statements. These
are admitted problems and the student must be aware of potential
solutions, and not be definitive until all things are clear. Text problems pose a difficulty for one not having the service of Hebrew and
in such cases the student will need to rely on the commentators and

study Bibles. Such problems are not faith destructive! They are challenging, but not damaging to the truths of the gospel and the grace
of God.

AN ILLUSTRATIVE STUDY

Putting these concepts to work: 2 Kings 3

For a *Situation Prophecy* the selection goes to 2 Kings 3. The
passage will not be cited at length, but aspects of it are noted to present a situation in which the prophet spoke predictively while giving
some sound advice directively, even if in an indirect way.

3:1-3 Reading the passage the student will see the need to return
to 1:1 and follow the events preceding this chapter. There are plenty of names for study and a historical situation for which some
archaeological work is helpful. Since the prophet of record is Elisha,
the material in chapters 1-2 will be important to see how he came to
his position, and how God demonstrated His authority through him.

3:4-8 Note carefully the action of Mesha. Study the character of
Jehoram and think about his relationship with Jehoshaphat. What is
the problem with Jehoshaphat's confession: "I will go up. I *am* as
thou *art, my people as thy people* and my horses as thy horses"? And
when Jehoshaphat asks how they should go, the advice is to go the
way of Edom—hardly the way for quick success. The student will by
now have checked it out on a map.

3:9-10 So Jehoshaphat and Jehoram move out and the king of
Edom joins them. They take a circuitous route for seven days and
exhaust their water supply. Now there is no water available and the
king of Israel laments that God has gathered them here to fall under
the hand of Moab (note the *synechdoche*), whom they have come to
punish, but who is secure in its own territory and has its water. See
the situation?

3:11-12 So in the face of tragedy, Jehoshaphat asks if there is a
prophet of the Lord nearby from whom they may obtain advice. One

of the king of Israel's servants tells them that there is a prophet nearby—Elisha. Note the speech figures used to describe him and the
implications of this. Jehoshaphat knows Elisha and that the Word of
the Lord is with him. So the three kings go to see the prophet.

3:13-15 Elisha immediately rebukes the king of Israel and tells
him he should see some of his own prophets. The king of Israel
protests that the situation is that the Lord (!) has called these three
kings together to be destroyed by Moab. Elisha, seeing Jehoshaphat,
tells them that he would not even look at them (a speech figure) if it
were not for Jehoshaphat's presence. He has a minstrel called to play
for him (music is a quieting influence in prophetic work) and, as the
music is played, the Lord speaks to Elisha.

3:16-20 Elisha directs them to make the valley where they are full
of ditches. They are told they will not see wind or hear rain but there
will be plenty of water for all, and to this prediction he adds that they
will defeat the king of Moab. See how the directive and predictive
elements harmonize and address one another. The kings are advised
on how they will treat Moab after the victory. In the night there is a
flood of water out of Edom—without wind or rain, and the ditches
are indeed filled with water.

3:21-25 The Moabites had no knowledge of the water, and early
in the morning they were fully armed and mounted in defensive
positions against the expected thrust. But when the rising sunshine
reflected off the surface of water in these ditches, it looked red and
the Moabites assumed it was blood. They rushed forward for the taking of the spoil. But this was no ordinary military attack; it was a
disorganized band gone to plunder, and when they came to the camp
of Israel, the armies of the kings were awaiting them. On this occasion they inflicted a great defeat on Moab.

3:26-27 The king of Moab decided to make a giant thrust at the
king of Edom and was frustrated by it. It appears that the Edomite
king was filled with triumphal joy and offered his eldest son as a
sacrifice to his pagan god—although it is not really clear whether he
did this or the king of Moab did this. But the affair was so repre-

hensible that the allies fell apart with disgust, especially for Israel. The text merely tells us they returned to their own lands.

The prophet Elisha is the hero of the account. He predicted how the relief would come and what the military result would be. To accommodate the prediction, he gave the advice that led to its fulfillment. He showed respect to Jehoshaphat, but clearly indicated his displeasure with the compromising situation. The situation was that three kings were close to being destroyed—through their own folly. But the Word of God was adequate: they were spared and the foe overcome. The predictions came to pass as the prophet said, and the directives worked in the manner he had prescribed.

PERSONAL PROPHECIES

A personal prophecy is one intended for a particular party in a specific sense. It may overlap with some of the other prophecies, but the idea is that here is an individual to whom God has something to say directly. Since it is personal, it may serve as an object lesson or illustration for later generations, but the point of it is to show the power of God and His Word, leaving a lesson for the generations that follow. It differs from the situation prophecy in that it does not necessarily show immediate development but may be a characterization for one's entire life. In approaching such a prophecy, the following stages guide our thinking.

Level One: PERSONAL PROPHECIES

Since these prophecies relate chiefly to individuals, the following items are important:

1. Know the historical circumstances
2. Know the person involved (and the prophet)
3. Know the events triggering the prophecy

1. *Know the historical circumstances:* Details of the history behind the encounter are very important. Most of these must be gleaned from the Bible itself, although a Bible dictionary will prove

a great help. One must be careful to see as many of the details as possible, for very often some item that might seem unimportant will become the foundation for what is said. In the nature of the circumstances the predictive and directive elements are better seen as well.

2. *Know the person involved, as well as the prophet:* We cannot know too much about the person who is the subject of the prophecy. A study of the character, of the interaction with God and the prophets of God is valuable. The work in which the party has been involved and the particular actions for which the person is accountable are important. Where aspects of the individual personality are available, they should not be overlooked. The biblical text is the major source of information, but commentaries will help and biographical studies will also be of good assistance.

3. *Know the event(s) triggering the prophecy:* Although this is somewhat part of the background as well, it is a matter that needs special attention. Out of the entire life of an individual or a group, it comes to pass that at one time a particular prophecy is given. So the immediate event will make the purpose of the prophecy and its teaching value more apparent. It is almost as if the Lord says, "That's enough—here is My statement." The attitudes of people before God become an instructive tool and these events are useful to that end.

Level Two: PERSONAL PROPHECIES

The most important point in *Level Two* is to determine what is given in the prophecy by way of direction and by prediction as well. It is not as simple as it sounds, and there are some conditional aspects with regard to the current matter. One of these is the prospect of repentance.

Many prophecies are conditioned on the basis of the right response from the party in view. Nineveh, in the days of Jonah, is a good example of this development. There seems to be a hint in most personal prophecies that *if* a proper step is taken, better results may follow. This is not always true, but it is fair to think that it is usually implied.

3 Level Three: PERSONAL PROPHECIES

In *Level Three* we find the following items useful:

1. Understanding of biblical Hebrew
2. Reality of fulfillment
3. Teaching for the present establishment

1. *Understanding of biblical Hebrew:* Since these are personal prophecies, a lot of the material is addressed for the benefit or direction of a given person. This is something like a personal discussion with the Lord and is often conducted in the first person. Many of the intended thrusts in a dialog are screened in translation and overlooked. While this may not affect any major doctrine, it does take away something of the intimacy or directness of the prophecy. A smattering of Hebrew is a big help in this instance and many of the study Bibles (particularly the Concordant Bibles) will touch on this.

2. *Reality of fulfillment:* This is not always tracked out in the Bible, but when it is, the importance cannot be over-estimated. Study Bibles and those with enclosed references will usually point the way in this study, but the student must pursue it for himself. The reality of fulfillment grips us in powerful ways as it demonstrates the power, wisdom, and capacity of the Lord for achieving His purposes. Since many persons in the Bible are not given a very full biography, there will be cases where the fulfillment is not shown. In such cases, we rely on the fact that, where fulfillment is shown, it offers credit to places where it is not shown.

3. *The teaching for the present establishment:* Although these prophecies are given to individuals, there remain lessons for all who read about them in later years. The truth of Romans 15:4 is certified in these lessons: *"For whatsoever things were written aforetime were written for our learning, that we through patience and comfort of the scriptures might have hope."* While they are not directed *to* us, they can be applicable *for* us. The wisdom and justice of God, as well as His intended will, are generally seen in very clear form, and from that important lessons may be gleaned.

A very big part of the work of the student is to develop these
lessons into practical reality for the present ministry or work. Some
help will be found in commentaries, but the prayerful reading and
thinking of the student is of prime importance.

AN ILLUSTRATIVE STUDY

Putting these concepts to work: Jeremiah 22:24-30

There is no shortage of these in the Scripture, but the one chosen
for this study is from Jeremiah 22:24-30, and out text is again printed from the King James Version.

24 As I live, saith the Lord, though Coniah, the son of Jehoiakim, king
of Judah, were the signet upon my right hand, yet would I pluck thee
from thence.

In the background, the student will review the life of Jeremiah and
the kings of Judah for whom he served. Coniah is also known as
Jehoiachin or Jeconiah—variants of his name. His career must be
studied and the particular nature of his rebellion must be understood.
What a statement Jeremiah makes as he brings the message of the
Lord! Coniah obviously has no standing with God at all. The date
and occasion are part of the historical background, as well as is the
spiritual condition of Judah (especially the inhabitants of
Jerusalem). Some sad facts will appear when one sees the reforms
of Josiah and the waywardness of his sons. We will be reminded that
moments of great blessing are not far removed from moments of
great failure, if the Lord is ignored.

25 And I will give thee into the hand of those of those who seek thy life,
and into the hand *of those* whose face thou fearest, even into the hand
of Nebuchadrezzar, king of Babylon, and into the hand of the
Chaldeans.

Note the speech figure with *"hand"* used three times in this verse.
The spelling of the name of the king of Babylon has an "r" in the
place of the liquid "n" and probably reflects an ethnic hearing of the

term. The prediction is plain: Coniah will be taken prisoner by the enemy and fall a victim to Nebuchadnezzar and the Chaldeans.

26 And I will cast thee out, and thy mother who bore thee, into another country where ye were not born; and there shall ye die.

There is apparently nothing Coniah can do about it. The sentence is exact and specific with regard to his family and his deportation. As noted earlier, the student will understand the severity of this judgment better when the total historical background is in view, and the unstable character of this king is seen. His rule is very short and its end is hastened by his perfidious behavior.

27 But to the land to which they desire to return, there shall they not return.

In that God promises a return to the land, it is noteworthy that the king and his family are not going to be participants.

28 *Is* this man Coniah a despised broken idol? *Is he* a vessel in which is no pleasure? Why are they cast out, he and his seed, and are cast into a land which they know not?

Note the ellipsis forms (italics)—words supplied to make the text more readable. And the interrogations are in the speech figure family of *erotasis,* which is identified in APPENDIX 1. These are not rhetorical and require an answer, even if it is self-evident.

29 O, earth, earth, earth hear the word of the Lord...

Apostrophe and *personification* are the speech figures prominently displayed here.

30 Thus saith the Lord, Write this man childless, a man that shall not prosper in his days: for no man of his seed shall prosper, sitting upon the throne of David, and ruling any more in Jerusalem.

This is a very important prediction for it states that no descendent of Coniah's will sit on the throne of the house of David and prosper. The prediction is not that there will be no children at all, but that none will successfully follow him to the throne of David.

In Matthew 1, we learn that Jesus is a descendent in the Judean family but he is not of the seed of Coniah—the Virgin Birth replaces that. And in Luke 3, we learn that Jesus is a descendent of David through his mother. He rightly claims the throne of Judah. The curse on Coniah is not His, but the blessing of David's is His.

In this case the study of fulfillment is critical, and we marvel at how the Holy Spirit has given us the truth while stating the full facts of situations and personal histories faithfully.

What does one learn from Coniah? Nothing in the sense that this is our commission or judgment, but a great deal in the sense of the control of the Lord and the importance of living in His will.

INTERNATIONAL PROPHECIES

The Bible touches on many subjects and many lands. It is chiefly a record of the redemptive program of God and the revelation of His will and Word. The nation of Israel takes up a great deal of space and, in general, the Word is not directly concerned so much with the other nations. Yet all the major prophets and some of the minor prophets have portions that deal with nations outside Israel, and there are frequent references on this line in other parts of the text. Jeremiah 45–52 has a great concentration in this area, as does Ezekiel 25–32 and Isaiah 13–23.

Among other reasons, there is the fact that God is just. While the Gentile nations are not the covenanted people, God looks for truth throughout all mankind and speaks against evil and idolatry wherever it is found. God speaks with the authority of a Creator and Owner of all the territories of the earth.

The attention paid to the nations around Israel may have been for the purpose of showing His people that He was not "picking" on them, but was concerned for righteousness among all peoples. It also served as an equalizer since most of the nations discussed had at one time or another attempted to oppress the people of God.

Whatever the case, the Lord had messages for these peoples also, and the prophets delivered them without reluctance (Jonah excepted). Consideration of them in this work is somewhat limited, but the study goes through the three levels with the hope that the student will be conversant with the work of God, regardless of the personnel or ethnicity.

Level One: INTERNATIONAL PROPHECIES

At the foundation of the study of these prophecies, the following materials are most basic:

1. Knowledge of the nations mentioned
2. Understanding of the relationships of Israel with these lands
3. General knowledge of the social/political/economic conditions

1. *Knowledge of the nations mentioned:* Beginning with the table of nations in Genesis 10 and continuing through the whole of the Old Testament, there is a continued reference to nations proximate to Israel, and sometimes far away as well. One cannot master the history of all these nations, but it is good to be informed about those that were Israel's neighbors. Although the work was written long ago and is not easy reading, the history of Herodotus is a worthwhile secondary source for the Bible scholar. This is true as well of the other ancient histories written before this modern age and its re-evaluation of historical material.

However, a Bible dictionary or encyclopaedia is a good source and probably much more convenient. When the student looks up a land or a people group, he or she should have a pencil and notebook ready to note significant items. If one does this well once, it is a con-tribution to a lifetime of study.

Information gleaned this way will help in understanding the geo-graphical arrangement of the Near East as well as gaining knowl-edge about the cultures reflected in the lives of the different nations. Many of these nations have disappeared in the passage of time and the student will be especially interested in those that continue to this day. Many of the prophecies will have been fulfilled, but the student will be interested in those that seem not to have been fulfilled.

2. *An understanding of the relationships of Israel and these lands:*

Why, for example, is there a continuing conflict with Edom and
Moab? Why were the Philistines such a persistent foe and what happened to them historically? How could the king of Tyre take such an
interest in Israel to mount a friendship first with David and then with
Solomon? Note how the prophets warn Israel about depending on
Egypt and question that relationship. Why would the king of Assyria
take such an interest in Israel when it was only a tiny state and his
vast empire did not really need it at all?

Notice how easily Israel (at times) assimilated the pagan religions
and practices. Ezekiel 9 offers a good introduction to this subject.
One might ask what was wrong with the Lord that His own people
were so ready to give up on Him. Many of the prophecies given to
these nations are a direct reproach to their attitudes towards Israel
and the nature of their religious practices. Obadiah offers a nice
study on this line, but the subject is not limited to one book or one
passage—it is the heart of most of the prophecies against the nations
around Israel.

3. *General knowledge of the social/political/economic conditions
of the lands:* This sort of information is taken from the commentaries and the Old Testament survey books. Some information is
found in the Bible. For example, Amos offers a brief insight when he
discusses the economics in Israel.

The worship practices should be observed in one's study and the
evils that were done in the name of Marduk and company will open
the eyes of the student to the horror of pagan worship.

Many of the wars (such as that discussed earlier in 2 Kings 3)
grew out of economic stress, and the shuffling of politics was very
often influenced by this. Students at times are reluctant to pursue
these things because they do not seem to be "Bible study." The fact
is that they are at the very heart and foundation of Bible study, for
the study of the Bible is the study of mankind and his relationship
with God and God's people.

Level Two: INTERNATIONAL PROPHECIES

Level Two in the study of these prophecies will concern itself with
the following:

1. The nature of the predictions and directives
2. The authority of the prophets
3. The response of the nations, when available

1. *The nature of the predictions and directive:* At this level the student needs to observe exactly what is prophesied, both in the directive and predictive matters. What does God want these countries to know, and what does He want them to do? Such thoughts will occupy a good bit of reading in the text and in related works. When reading the predictions for the Gentile nations in the major prophets, one must ask what right these persons had to speak so forthrightly to people who neither knew the true God nor showed a propensity towards knowing Him.

2. *The authority of the prophets:* The "right" they had to speak to the nations comes from the fact that the Lord is the Creator of all people, Master of all places and the only one worthy of worship by mankind.

Some of the greatness of His authority is witnessed in the Jonah account. A prophet with no Assyrian credentials suddenly emerged and gave a foreboding message that went to the heart of the nation. When one has a commission to speak for God there should be no awkwardness in exercising the matter.

3. *The response of the nations* (when available): One quickly sees that the response of the nations was, on the whole, one of ridicule or defiance. The study of this aspect, however, is important because it gives a clue to every successive generation about how people will react to the truth. It is not always a negative reaction, but when it is, that is what one may expect of a civilization that is opposed to the Lord. Readers of the prophecies will take great care to see how the prophecies were received, and we may then be more faithful with our own duties in giving out the Word of God.

Level Three: INTERNATIONAL PROPHECIES

The material will sound familiar, but that does not mean it is unimportant or can be taken for granted:

1. An understanding of biblical Hebrew
2. Knowledge of fulfillment or lack thereof: historical fulfillment

1. *An understanding of biblical Hebrew:* Much more emphasis on this point is not necessary but the student does not want to forget the priority that this discipline will have if one has the opportunity to become acquainted with it.

2. *Knowledge of fulfillment or lack thereof: historical fulfillment:* In many cases when one has read the prophecy, it will be determined that information about the subject is outside the Bible and in historical data. History is not needed to determine the truthfulness of the Bible, but it is very informative and often gives corroboration to what is known to be true since God has said it!

When one reads the prophecies for Tyre, for example, and then follows up the predictions with a study of Alexander's conquest of that interesting place, it is quickly seen how the prophecies, made years earlier, are fulfilled, although it is doubtful that Alexander realized the nature of his work.

The fact of the matter is that God frequently used parties to accomplish His work when they did not know He was using them— and would have rebelled if they had known it (Isaiah 10 shows an example of this in the treatment of Assyria). Study Bibles will contain some of this information; encyclopaedias will give more. Commentaries that are oriented to the devotional nature of the text will likely have more information than the technical commentaries that deal more with text questions and problems. This is a rewarding study, and is better undertaken when the other matters are in hand.

AN ILLUSTRATIVE STUDY

Putting these concepts to work: Jonah

For this purpose, the book of Jonah is selected, partly because it is well known and partly because it offers a short, succinct prophesy for a Gentile nation. The text will be displayed when needed, but most of the narrative may be summarized and the student will be able to follow it easily in his own Bible.

Jonah was commissioned to go to Nineveh and cry against the city because its wickedness had come before God. The cultural and historical background will be very helpful to the student at this point, as will familiarity with the role that Assyria played in the Old Testament. The more positive side is seen in Isaiah 10 and the more negative side is seen in the prophecy of Nahum.

That Jonah did not want to go there is obvious: he took ship for Tarshish, a place not specifically known except that it was in the west and he was supposed to go to the east.

At sea, his adventure came to grief and, in the belly of the great fish, he prayed with fervency. When he was cast out on the shore in a rather unceremonious manner, the Lord again told him to go to Nineveh and this time he went. Undoubtedly his earlier decision was swayed by ethnic pride; this is clearly seen in the fourth chapter

But he went and entering the great city (it was a very large and populous place. The archaeology finds of Nineveh[12] are well known today). There he cried out and said, *"Yet forty days and Nineveh shall be overthrown."* The prediction is given in literal fashion and has a condition of time attached, although there is no word about repentance or of God's making any sort of alteration of the decree.

However, no doubt to the great surprise of the prophet, the people and even the king believed. This is especially telling because those who have studied the history will know that Nineveh was in a very strong position at this time.

Calling for national repentance and a change of ways, the king of Nineveh touched the Lord so that the Lord did not do what He has proposed to do.

Nineveh, incidentally, would later be overthrown very completely, but not in 40 days. The concept of forgiveness is implicit in prophecies of judgment and, in this case, there was a change in the program of God as far as time was concerned. Nineveh would soon go back to its old ways and suffer the destruction Jonah had predicted but for the moment it was spared.

And was Jonah pleased? The student must see Jonah's reaction and try to understand what was in the mind of the prophet, but for this international prophecy we have all the information needed.

IN CONCLUSION

There are other ways of grouping prophetic literature, but for this work no more will be considered. The study of the books in entirety can follow the same general treatment as the smaller portions considered for illustrative purposes. Taking a book in its entirety is, however, a much larger task and requires a good deal more work. Generally one should follow the logical divisions in a book and treat the sections individually while at the same time relating them to the dominant theme of that book. Most importantly, the student should see the Word of God as the great field of information and thereby seeks to understand it more fully and apply it more appropriately.

IV
STUDYING OBJECTS OR SUBJECTS

It seems likely that there could be no end to this sort of study but we will confine our treatment to a few particular items. They are placed together for the simplicity of our study, but will be treated individually in the pattern that has been used throughout this work. All of these matters might be treated in greater detail but this presentation is intended to summarize things one should know in proceeding with the study. It must be assumed that everything previously discussed retains the relevance given to it, and all this serves as background material for this section. The items to be discussed are as follows:

- a person
- an event
- an object
- an institution
- a word
- a text
- a theme
- a teaching

Some of these things overlap but each has its own place and will be treated accordingly.

THE STUDY OF A PERSON: DEFINING THE STUDY

The study of people is both challenging and rewarding, one of the

more interesting areas of consideration. Biography is always challenging and instructive and there is room for a lot of it in Bible study.
The Scripture is full of the accounts of the lives and activities of
many persons—and it neither lionizes nor canonizes unnecessarily.
It is refreshingly frank in its appraisals; the honesty of the evaluations is another of those items that increase our confidence in the
Word of God.

Therefore when we look at a person we are especially interested
in the performance of that party in the will of God, and in the factors that "made" or "defeated" that life in the process. The eventual
goal is to learn life lessons that will be applicable in any age. This is
not always apparent but a guarded study of the person in the context
of his/her time will always enable us to come to some very useful
applications.

In the process it is certain that some theological areas will be
enforced as well, and the way in which the Lord accomplishes His
work through these fleshly instruments will also be clear. As we
work through the levels of information, the student will also recall
the basic four points of Bible study sketched originally on pages 21-
22 and reemphasized from time to time: *thankfulness* to the Lord for
His provision of this truth for us; *humility* to see ourselves as learners; *industry,* a willingness to work; and *teachability*.

Level One: THE STUDY OF A PERSON

In *Level One* the interest is in the following as being very basic
for the study of a person:

1. The name of a person   — WHO
2. Family and heritage   — WHERE (look BACK GND)
3. The position of the subject — WHAT (STATUS)
4. Life circumstances   — WHEN HAPPEN → WHAT
5. Achievements: good or bad — HOW   ARE THEY

1. *The name of the person studied:* Was it Shakespeare who
queried, "What's in a name?"[1] Although our literary grasp may be
weak at the moment, one cannot help but being impressed at the
name given to a person. Some names, apparently, were simply pulled

out of a hat, some were named with great commitment and dedication, and some were directly given by the Lord. Whatever the case,
the name identifies the individual. It is important in that regard and
may be significant in other ways as well.

There are many books on the meanings of names in the Bible
(note our BIBLIOGRAPHY) and these are generally reliable. The student should know the name, know how to pronounce it, and be wary
of other persons with the same name—an occurrence that is not
uncommon in both Testaments.

Some caution must be used in treating the meaning of the name
as a means of defining character, although there are passages where
such usage is perfectly plain, as in 1 Samuel 25:25 where Abigail
notes that her husband, Nabal (the root meaning is fool or folly) is
really a fool and folly is always with him. His name adequately
defines his character! One wonders why a mother would choose
such a name for a child; the suspicion is that she just picked it out
of a hat, so to speak, or was insulting his father. And whether Nabal
grew into the name or was a victim of circumstances, we cannot say,
but the name defined the man. This is not always the case but must
be kept in mind as a potential clue about the person studied.

When name changes are directed by the Lord, it is always significant. The names of Abraham, Sarah, Israel, etc., are good examples.
Likewise when persons in the Scripture reassign a name, there is
considerable importance. An example may be seen in Jeremiah 20:3
when Jeremiah renames Pashur (the name seems to indicate one
having a godly portion in heritage) and calls him "Magor-missabib,"
with the meaning that fear is all about him. Jeremiah is saying by the
name change that Pashur has no godly heritage but is simply a cow-
ard and is scared to death, thus explaining why he rebels at the
prophetic truth.

A further interesting example is in the New Testament when the
Lord revises Peter's name. While it is not so definitive, the change
in the name of the Apostle from Saul to Paul offers an interesting
study as well.

The student should not treat the name as a theological finality but
as a point in better understanding the person in the biblical accounts.
The etymology may be very helpful or it may not be. Context and
history will be more decisive in this study. But knowing the name

will help you understand why few mothers today name a daughter Jezebel or a son Nabal.

2. *Family and heritage:* These are much more important in ancient times than they are today. All of Israel was concerned with genealogy and the birth orders of families. The student can often discover this because the text will say "son of" and while "son" may not mean immediate descent, it does prescribe a family direction.

It is interesting to go to Genesis 49 and study the predictions of Jacob for his sons and see how the history of the family is marked in the names. The subject was very important for the priesthood and for the prophetic promises of kingship. In the study of family history one will often discover aspects or conditions that prevail in the individual under consideration. The student should not force this issue, however, and if there is nothing in the text to suggest it, one should not try to demand it.

But notice how the instability of Reuben, identified by his father in Genesis 49:4, is characteristic of his family as seen in Judges 5:15. It does not mean that every Reubenite will have this flaw, but it is a factor to be considered in the genetic structure of that family.

In this regard, it is interesting to see how the person being studied has interacted with other family members. When we find extreme cases such as Jehoram—who killed all his brothers in order that there would be no rivalry for the kingship—it is immediately seen that his rule will be marked by various forms of violence and deceit. The account is found in 2 Chronicles 21. His name has the etymological significance that "Jehovah is exalted" but such was not the case with his reign. He was out of character with his father's family but in character with the Baalite family of his mother. The student is reminded that genealogy alone does not determine the character or performance of an individual.

3. *The position of the person studied:* This is usually quickly resolved in the case of kings and priests, but in other officials and servants it is not always so easily discerned. What was the position of Isaiah in the kingships when he served? Was he simply a prophet, or a secretary in the court of the kings as well? When the position is not defined, the scholar may make "educational guesses" so long as

one remembers this, and does not assume the guess is a fact.

The position held by Nehemiah, for example, is extremely important with regard to his service and missions to Judea. These positions are not always clearly defined in the Bible, but many are known to us through history and archaeology. Reference texts in both these fields are readily available and some are listed in the BIBLIOGRAPHY. Knowing the position will help in understanding how that person performs and what factors God has employed in using this servant.

4. *The life circumstances* (both usual and unusual, as the case may be): These factors are not so readily discernible, depending on how much is told in the biblical narratives and the wider or narrower range of the life of the person. Some circumstances are matters of birth—including such things as inheritance, responsibility, and genetic factors such as Ehud's being born left-handed.

Some circumstances are set by the parents, as with Samson who was consecrated a Nazarene from birth, and Samuel who was promised as a servant of God before conception. Likewise Jeremiah was destined for the prophetic ministry before he was born. There are many other examples of such things.

A situation like that held by Joseph as a boy was a result of family affairs, but it was a conditioning influence for the rest of his life.

While he did not know it, the career of Josiah was prophetically stated long before he was born and he carried out the prophesied part of it flawlessly. To see the relevance of these circumstances, the student must be a diligent reader of the Bible and concern himself with every mention of the life of the person studied.

Usual circumstances relate to the expectation of duty in an office or a function. In this category are the friends, the foes, the peers, etc., of the individual. With that must be an understanding of the challenges faced and the pressures that influence the designated life. Character studies in the Bible are helpful in this line and some commentaries will be illuminating as well. But essentially it is the student working through one's Bible that makes the difference in excellence and mediocrity in the study of biblical persons.

5. *The achievements—successes or failures of the person:* The

biblical text will supply a lot of these, but it takes careful reading to be sure of the assessment of the biblical writer. The student will need to realize what was expected and what has been accomplished. When it cannot be determined what is expected, the student summarizes what the individual did and compares it with the general revelation of the will of God. Many matters are never concluded in the Scripture and the student will see how his subject attempted to do something and then you will need to speculate on the outcome.

It must be remembered that failure and success are cyclic matters, and where failure is repeated, it is not likely to be reversed. In the accomplishments of others and the understanding of how they accomplished their achievement, the student gains an inkling of how one's life should be spent in the testimony of the Lord.

Ultimately this is why we study the lives of people. The intention is not to try to live their lives, but to learn from their experiences and service something that will enable our present witness to be more firm, as well as learning what things are harmful and how they may be avoided. It is somewhat akin to Longfellow's *Psalm of Life* when he wrote:

> "Lives of great men all remind us
> We can make our lives sublime
> And departing, leave behind us,
> Footprints on the sands of time."

We do well, therefore, to pay good attention to the lives of the people in the Bible. Between examples and didactic statements, we have a great field of guidance for everyday living.[2]

Level Two: THE STUDY OF A PERSON

In the study of a person, most of our work is in Level One. It is basic and fundamental to the project and, on the whole, fairly easily observed. *Level Two* involves two important matters not so easily observed and not always applicable, but the nature of these points confines them to a separate heading. The features are:

1. Evaluation of the person in the Bible
2. Biblical application of the person in the Bible

Undoubtedly the greatest chapter in the Bible in both of these areas is Hebrews 11 and the summaries that are contained therein. But there are similar references throughout the Bible, and the student must be sharply watchful for these.

1. *Evaluation of the persons in the Bible:* When coming to this aspect of the study, the Book of Jeremiah contains many evaluations of persons of his time, and earlier persons as well—including his analysis of Baruch in chapter 45. Daniel 9 presents an insight into the work of Jeremiah and how it was regarded in Daniel's day. Needless to say, the books of Kings and Chronicles contain many of these comments as the works of kings and others are seen in biblical perspective.

The evaluation of the Bible will often be corrective of some of our ideas. Lot is a good example; he gets much criticism in Old Testament studies, but in the New Testament he is known as "righteous." Similarly Sarah, although not receiving many compliments in the Old Testament, is given the virtual status of a heroine in the New Testament.

All of the Bible is our field of study and, while we are concerned with the Old Testament and the Old Testament characters, the New Testament frequently has the last word on these.

2. *Biblical applications of persons in the Bible:* There is, perhaps, less of this, but a good study may be had in Malachi 2 where the life of Levi is used to apply the desire of God for the priesthood to the people of Malachi's time. It is evident that the priesthood of Malachi's day had fallen out of the desired service of God, and the prophet applies the truth of their father's commission to their duties.

A concordance is a good tool for pursuing this study as it enables one to note all the occurrences of the name of the person and then to see how it is used Bible-wise. Remember that the same name may be used for different people, and that means the student must always have the right person in view. But with that reminder, this approach should be fairly simple. An interesting study will be found in Jeremiah and the use of the Rechabites,[3] the children of Rechab. The student will be interested to see how the life of this godly father is applied in the situation of Jeremiah's day.

It is worth mentioning again that the student should not force an application where the Bible does not make one apparent. There is a fine line between what we miss in the Bible and what we put into it, and both aspects are incorrect. The honest student does not want to neglect truth nor to invent it.

Level Three: THE STUDY OF A PERSON

In *Level Three* the concentration moves to very practical things in the study of the Bible. The lessons that are learned, are the most desired things but it is a mistake to try to rush to them without taking the preliminary materials into account. Here we will treat two matters:

1. Essential, practical lessons for today
2. Typological significance

The first of these items is relational: relating the past to the present. The second is theological: seeing the work of God in a prefiguring sense.

1. *Essential, practical lessons for today:* Taking a detailed look at any person—and remembering that truth is uniform in all ages—the student will look to see what aspects in the life of the subject are practical points to apply in every age. These will often relate to obedience, faithfulness, use of particular gifts and skills, etc.

On the negative side, they will demonstrate the causes of failure or disillusionment and disappointment. The context of situations from earlier times will differ from the present age, but the conditions governing human behavior will have great similarity. While the student cannot assume a duplication of exact conditions, it may be expected that there is a general continuity of conditions that will help in this analysis.

As in other matters, caution must be exercised and all the relative data considered. It is too easy to jump from a general point to a specific application. General applications are more easily established, however, and there is nothing to be feared in that. One might study the character of King Saul and agree with Samuel that *"to obey is better than sacrifice"* (1 Sam. 15:22). The specifics of Saul's situation are not likely to be repeated, but the general point of doing what one wants to do regardless of what God has said, that is a general application that will bear on our lives many times. The person learns that obedience is the primary point in pleasing God, and disobedience has no excuse or standing. The character of this obedience will be determined by the message the Lord has given. In that sense it does not make much difference whether one is fighting with the Amalekites or driving on a modern highway. The lesson lies in the simple truth that to obey is better than sacrifice.

2. *Typological significance:* Typology is a particular study that will come to our attention in a later segment. Essentially a type is the use of one object (subject) to predict the coming of another. A type is not just a matter of two items resembling one another, but a portrayal of truth in which the first object not only teaches something about the second but, as noted, predicts its coming.

In the case of a person, a good deal of particular study is due, and reference in the Bible itself is most helpful. Regarding the references of Psalm 110 and Hebrews 5, there can be little doubt that Melchizedek (Gen. 14) is a type of Christ—a type of Christ in his mediatorial role and in the worship sequence.

Typological significance, however, does not indicate a totality of identification, but identification at a given point. David is seen as a type of Christ in the establishment of kingship but not in David's administration of that kingdom, in which he made serious mistakes.

This item is placed in Level Three because, while it is very important, it is also very difficult, and a victim of subjectivity in some cases. It is a part of the unity of Scripture, but such considerations must be careful, precise, and have some biblical warrant. It must be understood as well that not all Bible teachers agree on this treatment, and the student is forced to respect the view of others while establishing his/her own identity in thinking about this subject.

In summary, the study of persons in the Scripture is most rewarding and likely the most attractive. The Bible student is urged to engage in it frequently for the benefit of guidance regarding things that please and displease the Lord, and the factors that further or hinder His program. When the bulk of the preparatory materials are at

hand, or in view, the student is well prepared for an adventure with
the life of the chosen subject.

STUDYING AN EVENT

Defining the study: By an event we mean a particular occurrence
in historic perspective. In other words, something that actually happened and is recorded in Scripture for our learning. Most of these
matters will be found in the historical books, although some are also
noted in the other literature of the Old Testament. The prominence
of events in Israel's history is seen in the continual reference to foundational events (Creation, deliverance from Egypt, etc.), timely
events such as the wars and movements of the kings, and even the
conquest of Canaan. Any reading of the Historical Psalms will show
a continuing reference to these things (the psalm is not the event but
the events become illustrative materials for the psalm). It would
appear that the study of events is second only to that of persons for
number, interest and profit.

Level One: THE STUDY OF AN EVENT

In *Level One* the concern is with the basic materials one needs for
this study, and most of these are learned directly from the Bible with
the help of a study Bible or a particular work about the event considered. Four items are very important:

1. The event: what it was, or what happened
2. The location: where did it occur?
3, The time: when did the event occur?
4. The participants — W H O

1. *The event: what it was or what happened?* This might seem
self-apparent but actually it is deeper than that. Take, for example,
the crossing of the Red Sea, one of the events of the Exodus from
Egypt. On the surface it is merely an escape from the pursuing army
but in further analysis this event 1) demonstrated the mighty power
of God; 2) worked with the other parts of the Exodus to fulfill the
promises made to Abraham in Genesis 15; 3) allowed Israel to see

the punitive powers of God; showed the presence of God in a meaningful relationship with His people (the cloud and the fire); 5) established the reality of the call and ministry of Moses and Aaron. No
doubt several other fine points could be added to the list.

What happened was the crossing of the sea but this gave a foundation for Israel's history that is one of the most quoted or cited
events in the Old Testament—only creation is given more citations.
We know it was not a small event, but hardly realize what a great
role it would play in the development of the nation. This is true with
almost every event— there is a great more to it than may be seen on
the surface. One does not have to "imagine" the import of the matter, but simply study to see in a full sense what really happened.

2. *Where did it occur?* The importance of this may vary from
event to event. The location of the item in any study is a factor in
explaining or understanding what happened and why it happened as
it did. There are many times when we cannot locate the exact spot—
history has not always been fully noted.

The Red Sea crossing, incidentally, is one of those events, since
the Hebrew term is not "Red Sea" but "Sea of Weeds." However,
earlier translators simply felt it had to be the "Red Sea" and so translated it that way. No one knows exactly where the crossing occurred
except to say that it was at a body of water which one could not wade
through without divine help.

Knowing where the event occurred will often help one see the significance of it, and also explain the complications that may have
been involved in the story.

3. *When did the event occur?* This will refer to 1) the year; 2) the
time of year; 3) relationships to special events in Israel's history
such as the sacred holidays; 4) the time of day; and 5) the dispensational arrangement. It will also include any other such temporal matters as the time of the life of the individual involved, or the place on
a program time-wise that was assigned to the event.

Most commentaries make notice of this and some study Bibles
assign such times. With regard to all dates there is usually a "plus or
minus" factor since the dates of the ancient times are not always
quickly identified and the sychronisms that would help in this mat-

ter are not available much of the time. Very often in the Bible a time will be assigned (not by date but by historical reference or human experience, for example: *"In the year that king Uzziah died"*) and the student will be satisfied with that. Knowing when the event occurred may or may not prove significant, but, if available, it is information the student needs for further analysis.

4. *Who were the parties involved?* Once again it would seem obvious that one would need to know this, but the obvious things are often overlooked. The parties give meaning to the event and whatever is learned from the event will be passed on to others.

The student should be aware of individuals as well as groups. These may be identified with a Bible dictionary or commentary. Do not be content with simply reading the name but investigate, discovering as much as possible about the persons involved.

Historical studies of the people or people groups involved will often provide illumination as to what happened. An example of this may be seen in the identification of the parties in the Edomite warfare discussed in 2 Kings 3.

The event in which Israel and Joshua accepted the Gibeonites (Josh. 9) provides an example of the consequences when failure to correctly identify the visitors caused Israel considerable anguish in days to come. Many of these things are apparent in the narratives but the whole event must be scanned for this information.

Level Two: THE STUDY OF AN EVENT

While it may not be possible to cut off each line of study at a precise point, *Level Two* moves into three areas concerning the event.

1. The actual outcome of the event
2. The historical significance
3. Biblical applications

These three items are largely derived from the Bible itself and the historic texts that may apply.

1. *The actual outcome of the event:* Many biblical events have a

future or prophetic cast, and the student will need to realize how this event has been worked out, not only at the time of occurrence, but in future reference as well—if any of this information is provided. This section regards what really happened in this instance and what part it played in the program of God's dealing with His people.

2. *The historical significance of the event:* At this point the idea is to see how the event influenced, altered, or perhaps directed the history of the nation or the people involved. Some very small events have great effects historically, for example, such a small thing as a Hebrew slave maiden telling how an Assyrian general may have help for his leprosy (2 Ki. 5). It is necessary to understand that all events have historical consequences and the Bible student should learn what they are, or were, and be ready to judge their relative importance in connection with the study.

3. *Biblical applications:* In this case it is necessary that the student determine how much of this there is—by direct statement or inference. If there is none, one should not attempt to manufacture it. If there is, then it will be important in understanding the event. A good bit of the material given broad reference in Romans 15:4 is in this category, and strong examples may be seen in 1 Corinthians 10:11 with the expression, *"All these things happened unto them for examples..."* The idea here is that the events are didactic—teaching events—and from them the present age of believers should learn a great deal about pleasing and displeasing the Lord.

Level Three: THE STUDY OF AN EVENT

Level Three calls on the student to do some comparative and literary study, and incorporates three aspects on these lines:

1. Observations for living
2. Theological implications
3. Typological significance

1. *Observations for living:* Since the great point of the Scripture is to make us wise in the ways and will of the Lord, this is probably

an obvious exercise. But the observations for living must be developed from the text and the actual message of the text. The student must be certain that all such observations are consistent with the total biblical revelation, not contradictory to some known truth. This is not such an easy area as it may appear since the wording of the observation must be applicable to our day, and the message of it in accord with other doctrines of the Word of God. The student should list as many observations as possible and study the list in the light of these cautions.

2. *Theological implications:* "Theology" defines the concept of the study of God and His will. In this part of the study, the student determines how the event reflects on the character of God and His dealing with mankind. Whatever it shows in this area, as the student sees it, must agree with the total revelation of God, His ways, and His will, as was stated in our former discussion. One cannot read 2 Kings 2:23-25, for example, where Elisha dealt with the mocking children—as bears came out of the woods and wreaked havoc on them—and conclude that God does not love children! All theological lessons must be kept in the total theological community.

3. *Typological significance:* This challenge asks whether the event prefigures some later event and offers guidance with regard to it. The typology of the flood and the prediction of some great day of testing with the comments in 1 Peter 4:21 offer an interesting study on this line. The predictive element is key in this sort of study, not the mere resemblance of issues or facts.

The study of events involves all parts of the Old Testament, and many of the large events include numerous smaller events that fulfill the total meaning of a passage. There are two tendencies among Bible scholars that should be avoided. One is the temptation to take very large amounts of Scripture for a study and thereby overlook many things; the second is to concentrate on *minutiae* and overlook the large picture. In this regard, the student needs to see the total text and treat it as a unit—not overlooking the details, but not allowing them to obscure the whole picture either. It is not an easy task, but one that is necessary for accuracy in Bible study and application.

THE STUDY OF AN OBJECT

By an object we mean a physical item of any proportion. This is not a major part of the work of the Bible student, but is often helpful. In a later study the matter of institutions will be discussed and we will find many objects within an institution or an event worthy of added study. Perhaps what must be stressed is that there is very little in the Bible that is purely incidental. Especially in the Old Testament, every item that is mentioned is deserving of scrutiny.

Level One: THE STUDY OF AN OBJECT

In *Level One* attention is placed on three lines of thought. These do not take long, detailed treatments, but may be quickly surveyed.

1. What is it?
2. What is its normal, usual usage?
3. Is there any unusual usage suggested in the passage? Any divergent or abnormal feature? — HOW —> USED

1. *What is it?* As a rule this is easily answered but an understanding of the object is at times more difficult. In Exodus 4:2, for example, the Lord asked Moses what he had in his hand. Moses replied, *"A rod"* (KJV). And it is true that is what it was, but in reality the object was not just a rod, but a token of divine power. There were many sticks and staves in the desert, but this was no ordinary staff when used in the work of God.

2. *What is its normal usage?* The answer is defined by culture, historical knowledge, and other factors. If the object is something with which the student is not familiar, a Bible dictionary will be the best source of quick help. With this basic understanding, the student is prepared to observe usage that is not usual, discussed in Point 3.

3. *Is there any unusual usage of the object or any abnormal feature seen in the passage?* This is determined, of course, by knowing the normal usage. In the book of Zechariah, the prophet will see things that he can identify physically (1:8, for example[4]) but which

he does not understand. He will ask the Lord what these things *mean,* and the Lord will tell him what the objects represent or teach. The horses mentioned are of various colors and will represent the omniscience of God in an unusual way.

It must be noted that an object may have a different significance in different passages, but the uniqueness of them in such an account as that of Zechariah suggests immediately that they are special features. In this case, the text is explained by the Lord, but in other cases the determination of an unusual aspect of the object will be left to the Bible interpreter who should proceed with caution—but not fear!

Level Two: THE STUDY OF AN OBJECT

Two items merit our attention in *Level Two*:

1. How is the object featured in the account?
2. Observe other biblical usages of the same object with a different meaning in other accounts

1. *How is the object featured in the account?* Essentially this is a matter of a close study of the account. The rod in the hand of Moses and under the authority of God will be a sign of God's power and an indication of His intended deliverance for His people. The rod was a physical help to Moses, of course, and a divining help in the providence of God as when Moses was instructed to strike the rock with it (Ex. 17:6). At another point (Num. 12), it will be the means of establishing the Mosaic/Aaronic authority over the nation, although in this case it is Aaron's rod. From a physical point of view, the rod was not necessary in any of these cases. God could have simply spoken or told His servants to speak, but the symbol became an indicator of the reality of God's providence.

2. *Observe other biblical usages of the same object with a different meaning in another account:* The rod of Psalm 23, however, is not so much a physical rod at all, but a spiritual force in the hand of God to help His people as they work through life. But the term for rod in the Psalm is not the same Hebrew word as in Exodus 4.

Therefore the Bible student must be careful in this regard. There are at least five Hebrew words translated as "rod" in different places in the Old Testament. A concordance is a huge help in this matter, and will prevent this sort of mistake. The observation must be of the same original word that is given different usage in another passage. Any data in this category will cause the student to be careful about a random assigning of meaning to the term used.

Level Three: THE STUDY OF AN OBJECT

Level Three concentrates on the understanding and application of the object now that the basic items are in place. Two lines of thought are usual:

1. What is the basic lesson God is teaching with the object?
2. What spiritual principles are enforced by this setting?

As a rule, students tend to rush to these conclusive points, but the thought in the study is this: when the basic materials are covered, then the major application is more certain—better established both theologically and practically.

1. *What is the basic lesson God is teaching with the object?* A student will need to put it in his/her own words. Staying close to the text in describing what is taught by the object should not be difficult; although the student must remember that others might word it in a different fashion. With Moses, the rod was an object to teach the man who was to be the leader of the people that he could depend on the power of God, whether challenging Pharaoh or meeting the danger of having no water in the desert.

2. *What principles are enforced by this study?* As in the foregoing paragraph, the student must think it through! The principles of obedience, trust, and dependence on God—these are all seen in the Mosaic rod object. One may think of other concepts of serving God that are enriched by this object. But whatever principle the student may find illuminated by it, the finding is based on solid study and a knowledge of all the details possible.

AN ILLUSTRATIVE STUDY

Putting these concepts to work:
Person, Event, and Object illustrated in Jeremiah 19

Jeremiah 19 presents an opportunity to study these three items together. This will not be detailed, but a suggestive analysis and, as in many other things, the student will be on his own after that. At this point the student should read the chapter carefully and prayerfully, keeping in mind the basic concepts sketched earlier (pp. 21-22) and reviewing mentally, at least, the concepts in the study of an historical account.

Following our levels in the studies, the student will know the man Jeremiah, where he comes from, what his genetic connections are, the general circumstances of the nation in his time, what God has told him to do, and what the general reactions have been to his message. He will understand the prophet's commission in this passage and have a grip on the significance of his name. He will know how Jeremiah's own family regards him and what standing he has among other prophets. The student will also know who the "elders" of the people are, and the chief persons in the country. He will know why the elders are willing to go on this adventure with Jeremiah, and will see how it affects them in the following chapters.

Of the event, the student—through applying the keys to studying events—will know what it is, where it takes place, what is significant about the name and its change, why the event is outside Jerusalem, and what is the intended purpose of the gathering.

In the case of the object, the studies will have the student know why an earthen jar is used and what is significant in its ceramic description. The symbolism of the bottle (jar) will be clear in the mind of the student and, when it is broken, one will know why it was broken and what the point is that the prophet is making. The outworking of the event will be seen in chapter 20 and following, but the immediate reaction may likely be guessed.

The forcefulness of the action, the passage, and the message cannot be over-estimated. But this is only one of the many cases in the literature of the Bible where a thorough study of all the details leads one to yield to the expressed will of God or to be ready for dire consequences. There are many other practical lessons and some theological insights, as well, with regard to the consistency and program of the Lord, and the maintenance of some of the prophecies which were given when Solomon prayed for the temple and, much earlier, when Moses instructed Israel in the blessings and cursings of Jehovah.

THE STUDY OF AN INSTITUTION

Defining the study: The study of an institution is made somewhat more complicated than other individual subjects due to the difficulty in definition. Generally we understand what one is until we come to the point where we actually put the definition in writing. In very technical terms, an institution is a societally recognizable entity that is perpetuated as a feature of its culture and is established as a law, a practice, a custom, or a societal order. In light of that, some institutions are the home, marriage, the ten commandments, the temple, and the gathering of believers in church order. It is not an endless subject but does have an enormous potential listing.

An institution is something that may be recognized historically (as it did exist in a culture) or practically (as it continues to exist). Hence the "home" or "family" is an institution that has been a part of society from the beginning and continues that way today. The temple, on the other hand, was an institution that lost its practical ideal after the destruction of Jerusalem by Titus. In this latter case the institution may continue as an ideal or a visionary project and still have meaning, but the actual use or identification of it has been limited by the effects of history. For further definitions of "institution," *Webster's Dictionary* is recommended as well as the *Oxford Dictionary of the English Language.*

But all the identifiable institutions may be studied in the same way following the three-level approach. For some there will be great masses of material, while for others the material may be sparse. The student must remember to avoid making the institution more formal and precise than it is, while avoiding the common error of not identifying it at all. The overall study is important to us, for in it we are looking at how things have been handled in the past with a view to application in the present.

Level One: THE STUDY OF AN INSTITUTION

As the most basic level, *Level One* is occupied with five items, and in this order:

1. Identification: what is the institution?
2. Why was it created, organized, or established?
3. How was it implemented?
4. What role did (does) it have in its culture?
5. Are there dispensational limitations imposed upon it?

To a large extent, these are observation points as one reads about the institution in the Scriptures and enforces that study by the use of the Bible dictionary, commentary, or study Bible. Some parts of the answers will be theoretical and will depend on the grasp maintained by the student on biblical imagery.

1. *Identification: what is the institution?* In keeping with the previous discussion about defining the idea of an institution, the student will find that a number of things qualify for this designation. The study of such will be topical by necessity, but identifying the particular area of study is by no means automatic.

The family is an institution, and within it are the institutions of marriage relationships, child training, support for life needs, etc. All of these may be treated either singly or lumped together, but the student needs to identify the area in which the study is particularly pointed. It may be best for the student to identify the more basic institutional forms and then build a total picture from them.

In our study, this matter should not be so complicated as it may seem, but an identification that is too large will make a very lengthy study and often leave one with an incomplete picture of the very item being researched. If the institution, for example, is the tabernacle, the student will have several institutions to study in completing the tabernacle study, including such items as the Levitical Order, the sacrifices of the Lord, the religious celebrations, and the priesthood, as well as the services performed in the tabernacle and usage given to it in the history of Israel. Carefully defining the institution simply limits the boundaries of research and study.[5]

2. *Why was it created, organized, or established?* What was the need for this institution? That is the question. Was it given for the better ordering of society, for religious affirmation purposes, for designating specific performance areas for individuals, for aiding in the fulfillment of the prophecies of the Lord? These determinations need careful thinking by the student, and, while in most cases the reason for the institution is fairly clear, there will be times when the student will simply have to speculate on the matter. In knowing why it came into being, however, the student has a very useful tool for thinking through what is expected of the institution. And with this he has a measurement tool for evaluating the institution and thereby seeing its relative importance or service.

3. *How was it implemented?* This is largely a matter of history, and the Bible is the chief source for the earlier institutions. Later ones, such as the synagogue, will have information in the culture levels of histories and tradition. The nature of implementation is often a clue as to what the people actually thought of the institution. When Moses was given the instruction for the tabernacle, it was the liberality of the people that quickly provided all that was necessary in the way of material. There was an enthusiasm that made the whole project more meaningful.

Similarly when Joash renewed the life of the temple, the giving[6] was such that the people had to be told to stop. The initial implementation did not always auger for continued zeal, but it indicated the importance that was initially recognized, and made a recovery point for times that might come later. After the actual creation of the institution, the role that it had in the life of the people becomes an important part in the study. How much attention was given to it? Answering this question prepares the student for the following consideration.

4. *What was the role of the institution in its culture?* Once again, this is largely defined within the Bible for the older institutions, while the later ones may have historical referencing that will prove helpful. This question is also conditioned by the nature of the institution—whether it was governmental (as with a law that was instituted and enforced by law), or purely societal, such as the home

whose role in society depends largely on the acceptance and pro-
mulgation by the populace

If the law of God as given in Deuteronomy 6, for example, had
been followed with care and fidelity, the whole standard of national
life would have been increasingly enriched. But when His law was
overlooked or ignored, that institution had mostly a condemnatory
influence on the culture. Bible dictionaries are a help in such matters, and commentaries are also often useful, although they may tend
to extend the matter beyond the institution of that time and bring it
into the present situation in a way that its service to a previous culture may be overlooked.

5. *Are there dispensational limitations imposed on the institution?*
Basically the answer is that there may be, and the matter must be
studied carefully. Earlier in this work, the matter of dispensations
was discussed and, while some Bible scholars do not appreciate that
term, it must be seen that some items and institutions are limited to
a particular age or economy. There is no physical tabernacle today
and, in fact, the institution *per se* ceased to exist long before the
Lord's time. But the institution of law as a means of ordering society covers all ages. Particular laws within the broad sphere may have
limited use or a "timed" usage. This question is best answered in a
biblical sense by seeing how the total revelation (Old and New
Testaments) deals with the matter. Suffice it to say that we do not
dispense with an institution because we do not "like" it or appreciate its contribution, but, in the passing of the ages, some practices
are phased out. While they may give us valuable lessons, with even
present day applications, it is recognized that they belong to a particular age, and must be studied in that context.

Level Two: THE STUDY OF AN INSTITUTION

In *Level Two* our concern moves to more biblical information
about the institution and treats these three items:

1. What care was given the institution?
2. What aspects of life harmed or aided the institution?
3. How is the institution viewed in the New Testament?

1. *What care was given the institution?* This is determined some-what by the sort of institution addressed. If it were a law, the question would indicate how it was observed or honored. Had the institution been an establishment, such as the temple, the question would ask how it was cared for, and supervised, over the years of history.

If the institution is something like the home or family, then the question is how society has honored the institution as time has gone forward. Consequently the material in the Bible is needed to show the particular way in which the institution was honored, or, as the case may be, dishonored. Some data may be gathered from a Bible Encyclopaedia where the institution is discussed in detail or a study Bible with annotations on the subject. This is, however, another of those subjects for which there is no substitute for a simple reading and re-reading the texts of Scripture.

2. *What aspects of life harmed or aided the institution?* While thinking of this matter, the student must reflect on the institution and how it was handled by society. The factors that aid an institution are matters such as obedience, devotion, commitment to the Lord and His purposes. The things that harm: neglect, indifference, defiance, and self-will at the expense of truth. You may add to both categories, but the studies of the past and how these attitudes have "made" or "broken" the intentions of the Lord are fascinating lessons, especially today as we still wrestle with the concepts of obedience or defiance.

A study of the Sabbath law in the Old Testament and the stress laid upon it—in Jeremiah, in particular—will help the student see how the attitudes of the people towards the institutions God gave resulted in the blessing or condemnation of the Lord. What was ruinous in the past is most likely to be harmful in the present.

3. *How is the institution viewed in the New Testament?* This ties in directly with the question of a dispensational disposition in the case of any institution, since the truth is that Scripture has self-agreement, and the totality of Scripture is what makes or breaks a teaching.

Many Old Testament institutions are discussed in the New Testament, the tabernacle in Hebrews 10 being a very good exam-

ple. Material of this sort is available to the student through a study
Bible or through one's own reading. A study Bible will often have
the references pulled together. While the student should not assume
all references are cited, it is most likely that the major identifiable
portions are there, and from them the student may reach to others.

Level Three: THE STUDY OF AN INSTITUTION

Level Three carries the focus of the study into three areas in
which the perception of the student is critical—in other words, a
more minute examination of the institution and the texts that discuss
it. Three items are suggested:

1. Are there symbolic elements in the institution and, if so, what
   do they symbolize?
2. What is the role of the institution in Israel's history?
3. What typology is involved in the subject studied?

1. *Are there symbolic elements in the institution and, if so, what
do they symbolize?* This item will be more important when the institution is better defined as an establishment or as a thing, rather than
a societal principle. A symbol is the use of one entity to portray
another, and the Scripture abounds with symbols.

Numbers are often seen symbolically, colors are often given symbolic meanings, objects of every sort are given assignment in this
line. But it is an area where a very keen sense of imagination may
lead one into absurdities, so the student must use caution. Speech
figures as discussed earlier in this work will offer some help and the
study of objects previously noted is also applicable. Studies in the
tabernacle, the temple, the feasts of the Lord, etc., are especially
subject to strong symbolic studies and, at times, to lengthy allegorical interpretations. While the student must be careful in the handling
of such material, he cannot afford, for example, to miss the tabernacle symbolism in Hebrews 9 or that of the brass serpent in John 3.

2. *What is the institution's role in Israel's history?* Having defined
the institution, the student must know something of the history of
God's people and how this subject was a part of it. The kingship

institution, for example, shaped the kingdom on a political line which would prefigure the rule of the Lord in a coming age. The role of this institution is critical in the spiritual and societal development of the nation and while many other items are not so sweeping in dimension or influence, all played a part and the student should see that part. The prophetic institution is a key element in the spiritual life of Israel with both positive and negative thrusts. Until the student has a grip on this aspect, one will not be able to properly understand or estimate the service of the institution.

3. *What typology is involved in the subject studied?* Types and symbols are very close in usage except that the type always has a predictive element. Not all Bible scholars agree on this, and our work in this booklet cannot determine rightness or wrongness in all the views. That there is a *bona fide* typology in the Bible should be plain to all, but the degree to which it extends is not so plain. Bible commentaries and study Bibles should be a help to the student in this area, although one must remember that the ideas of scholars do not have the solid force of the Bible itself.

As a very general principle, the student may follow the concept of 1 Corinthians 10:11 that there are objective lessons in the great majority of things noted in the Old Testament as they are applied to us. We also have the example of Hebrews 9:9 with the idea that the aspects of the tabernacle as discussed were "figures" for us to foretell what God would do in days to come.

The study of the institutions is a rewarding study and offers the student a great deal of help in dealing with the institutions of today, and forming the policies of the present. Much of the material is illustrative, but illustrative in the sense of pointing to real life as we live it day by day.

THE STUDY OF A WORD

Defining the study: The study of a word might seem to be a very simplistic thing about which no special notice is needed. But the student has, no doubt, heard preachers and teachers often refer to a word and pronounce upon what it *really* means.

On the other hand, Bible readers are often challenged as they read

another Bible translation and discover that the text has a different
reading from what they have been accustomed because of a word
change. The study of a word can become the occasion for a whole
book and is certainly a needed part of every Bible student's equip-
ment. Presentations in this work are necessarily brief, general—and
cautious—for the old expression, "what's in a word," is more meaningful than one might think. The progress of the study will continue
with the three-level format.

First there are some cautionary notes. Several times the use of the
original language has been mentioned and there is probably no one
area in which this sort of knowledge is more needed than in the
study of a word. That is because the word(s) we study are translated
words, and, while we are very thankful for the translators and their
works, we must recognize that the important word is not the translated word but the word behind it—the source word, so to speak.

The concordances, dictionaries, and some study Bibles will show
the student the original language word, but there is much more for
the student to do than simply recognize the basic form. Much of this
is very hard to gain without some familiarity with the basic language. A student does not have to be a master of the subject, but
should know enough about it to realize basic distinctions and to proceed cautiously with the pronouncement of what this or that word
really means!

Etymology, in itself, is not a sufficient guide in these matters,
although it can be very helpful. But what is most helpful is some
acquaintance with the language behind the text and a reasonable
comprehension of *semantics*—the science of language.

This is not intended to discourage the student from word study but
rather to encourage a more thorough familiarity with the language
picture. The end result will be a more assured presentation of the
text, and the ideas that come to the attention of the student in the
process of study.

Hebrew is the essential language of the Old Testament and there
is a bit of Aramaic (a Hebrew cognate or *vice versa*) thrown into the
bargain. Hebrew is a much more simple language in syntax and
grammar than Greek or Latin, but has a number of features that
become meaningful with study.

Its vocabulary is much smaller than that of English, and this results in a given Hebrew word having the potential for more than one meaning or translation into English. How the translator will handle it depends on how he sees the word in context, and in the technicalities of use that occur in Hebrew.

Similar to Greek, but less determined, is the situation with sentences containing a condition. Both languages can show more of the certainty or uncertainty of the condition and consequence than may be shown in plain English.

In both of the ancient languages, the use of verb tenses is more sharply defined than it is in present-day English as these matters are hardly studied at all any more. Gender, declension, mode, etc., are all more significant in the older languages and much less definitive in English.

As noted earlier, there are many helps available in these areas today. The multitude of translations offers the student a comparative understanding of a term. The interlinear Bible publications may be helpful, and the study Bibles that concentrate on this sort of material are useful. It must also be remembered that grammar is often not so rigid as the grammarians make it seem, since they have to make their determinations on inductive rather than deductive approaches.

A number of useful works are mentioned in the BIBLIOGRAPHY of this work, but the best of these generally require at least a recognition of the letters of the ancient alphabets.

Perhaps this is a good place to insert a favorite subject: the knowledge of the English language. Unfortunately many of our present age know less about English than can be otherwise imagined. A review course would be helpful so that the student knows in his own language the basic ideas about participles, infinitives, gerunds, complimentary clauses, particular tense usage, etc. It may sound humorous now, but in the process of teaching ancient languages, this writer has often found it necessary to stop and give lessons in English—or at least suggest them in a hearty way.

Level One: THE STUDY OF A WORD

Level One is the most basic level and, while often the simplest for which the student must gather material, in this case it requires considerable exercise as it treats the following items. The basic idea, however, is that of locating or isolating the word to be studied and the section proceeds along this order:

1. Identify (name) the word (English or in your Bible)
2. Identify the word from which it is translated
3. See if this root word is translated otherwise; remember the particular translation in your text shows the mind of the translator
4. See if any other root words are given this same translation
5. List or mentally observe all the occasions in which the word is translated as you have it in your text and note how the root word may be translated otherwise in other texts

This is a lot to do and requires a good bit of work with a concordance and a dictionary, but it is effort well spent in gaining assured knowledge of the word one wants to discuss. When all this has been done, the student now has isolated the Word, knows what it is, and what the potential may be for varying translations and interpretation.

1. *Identify the word:* This is an apparent point, but in doing this the student identifies it as to its part of speech (noun, verb, adjective, adverb, preposition, etc.) and how it is used (subject, object, modifier, etc.) as well as how it is classified with regard to tense, number, voice, etc., when these things are applicable. In other words, the student knows the word in his Bible in all of its parts, and this prepares him for a further step.

2. *Identify the word from which it is translated:* For the study at this point, the term "root word" will suffice. The root word is the word in the original language from which the word in your text is translated. This material may be found in a comprehensive concordance that views the particular translation one is using. There are such concordances today for all of the major translations and the student will need to be familiar with how this book is put together and how it may be used—materials that are normally found in the introduction of the work.

3. *See if this root word is translated otherwise and remember that*

particular translation shows the mind of the translator: It is not uncommon for a word in the original to be translated as much as five or seven different ways, with all of the translated words having the same general idea but not the precise flavor of one another.

If the Hebrew word the student is studying is translated only occasionally with the English word in the student's text, but a majority of times is translated with another English word, the student must proceed slowly before making any conclusions on its use. The mere counting of usages does not prove the case one way or another, but it does mean that the student needs to think through the context, etc., and view the possibility of other ideas.

4. *See if any other root words are given this translation:* The concordance is a great help in this case as well. If another word is translated this same way, it may give some insight into the broader usage of the language. There are times, however, when the student looks for all of these things and finds neither help nor contradiction.

5. *List or mentally observe all the occasions in which the word is translated as you have it in your text, and note how the root word may be translated otherwise in other texts:* The tabulation of all occurrences in this fashion gives the scholar what is known academically as the *usus loquendi*, meaning that the word is studied in the light of the texts in which it occurs. If the student makes a careful note of this, the material will serve for a long time. Mental observations often do not last! The diversity of translation possibilities is also apparent and warns the student about over-emphasis on a given form.

At this point the student has isolated or located the word and has an exact concept as to how and where it is used. He is also aware of variants in translation and the possibility of other root words being translated this way.

2 Level Two: THE STUDY OF A WORD

With the basic information at hand, the student continues to survey the word itself and to watch for the following data:

1. Is the word simple or compound?
2. Study the fuller meaning of the translation through consulting a major dictionary (*The Oxford Dictionary of the English Language* is undoubtedly the best)
3. What special impetus does the word have in the passage being studied?
4. Are there overtures or nuances in the passage that suggest the word may not be used in the usual style…touches of sarcasm, for example? These steps are intended to aid the student in identifying the word syntactically or semantically.

1. *Is the word simple or compound?* This is more a question on New Testament words than the words of the Old Testament since Hebrew does not have as much of this feature as does Greek. Yet words or terms like the "valley of death" are apparently compound and the fuller meaning for them is taken from the compounding items. The simple word is just the word as a basic entity, while the compound joins two words together to give one expression. This is quickly observed, but an interesting and important point.

2. *Study the fuller meaning of a word in a comprehensive dictionary:* The great majority of English words have multiple shades of meaning. The shades do not contradict one another but show the diversity of this language. An example might be seen in the word "show." As a verb it means to display something, but there are several ways in which that display might be made, including one that is simply verbal. As a noun it may indicate anything from a simple sign to a Broadway production. To know the diversity of definition in a word is important for the complete understanding of the term. One is often surprised to discover that a word has shades of meaning not known in common parlance but known to lexicographers, and thus may be used in translation to indicate a fine point of meaning.

3. *What special impetus does the word have in the passage being studied?* This is largely determined in the mind of the student, although consulting commentaries may assist in forming an opinion. Even such simple words as the articles may have a great impact on the text, the emphasis of "the" being critical at times. It is also pos-

sible to reverse this concept and ask what would be lost in the text if this term were not used. It is good to note that this is a matter for the student to think through, and not a matter for presentation in most cases. A student draws the conclusions that are needed or implied, and uses them as a foundation for the teaching.

4. *Are there overtures or nuances of meaning that may indicate a word is not being used in the regular form or style?* The most common feature in this line is that of sarcasm or a sardonic expression in which the speaker uses a term that is not intended to be understood in the normal, literal fashion. Features such as this may also be part of rhetorical questions, and the word that is being studied may have a more figurative intention in the passage at hand. There is considerably less of this in Hebrew than in Greek, but the occurrence is always a potential item, especially when people are talking or discoursing with one another.

With this material in hand, the student has identified the word in its context and is prepared for the final stages of the study.

Level Three: THE STUDY OF A WORD

What remains for the student in *Level Three* is to put the information to work and promote the study. Two items are suggested for guidelines:

1. What is the "teaching" of the word in this study?
2. What cautions may be needed for understanding the word?

1. *What is the teaching of the word in this study?* This is the place to which the student has been aspiring. It remains for him/her to put it into the speech that best declares the importance of the term. A wise student will generally not attempt to make a finalized dogmatic statement that settles all issues, but will offer an assessment of meaning that is genuinely helpful.

2. *What cautions may be needed for understanding the word?* The student will note the variety of usages that may be involved in the term, but will not do this in a pedantic manner with such technical-

ities as to make the research unavailable or unimportant to the hearers or readers. Advice will be given to the effect that one text or one
word is not the substance of the total teaching, but must be put with
other materials that relate to the subject. We remember that no doctrine (teaching) is fully studied until all relevant material has been
investigated. These are necessary cautions in word study but should
not limit the study or the student's desire to promote this activity.

THE STUDY OF A WORD: Some Procedural Advice

Looking over the subject at large, the present writer is hesitant to
prescribe any necessary format for the study, but with the levels of
study in mind, the following is the procedure usually followed in this
work. It is not a mandated idea, but a notation on how some scholars (or would-be scholars) approach the study.

1. The word to be studied is chosen
2. A concordance is consulted to determine the root word and
   where the word studied is found in Scripture
3. The concordance is used to see if other root words are translated this way.
4. A chart is prepared, showing the root word and the occurrences
   of the translation word. It may look like this:

The word identified (English)_____ The root word _____

References	How used	Semantics	Added notes
(chapter/book)	(noun, verb, etc)	(literal/figurative)	meaning

If the word is very common, it might prove too exhausting to list
all references. The page should be wider than this for extended
notes. There are several ways to arrange the chart, but the idea is to
get the material at one's fingertips.

A second chart will take up root words given the same translation—the concordance will show this—and another chart will show
passages in which this root word is translated otherwise. This is simply basic data, and the steps in each level will allow the necessary
inductions for the meaning and use of the term.

WORD→EVIL

A good word for this sort of study is the word "evil." The student
will recall the words of Job 2:10 when Job surmises that we cannot
expect only good from the hand of God, but also evil. The study of
this word will enable the student to understand the various ideas
expressed in the word "evil." One will discover that much of "evil"
is just the everyday consequences of life! Not many sermons or lec-
tures will be given on "evil," but many biblical texts are simplified
when we understand this word. While the student is at it, a broaden-
ing of the study to include "sin," "iniquity," "transgression," etc., is
also helpful. The fuller meaning of these terms is often overlooked.

As noted earlier, there are many helps for this sort of study today,
some by computer and some by books. The BIBLIOGRAPHY will note
some of these, but the student who has the opportunity to do some
work with the original languages will find great advancement and
ease in the use of these resources.

THE STUDY OF A TEXT

Defining the study: Obviously, *the* text is the complete written
Bible. *A* text is any individual part of that which we may choose for
a particular study. In theory, it should be a completed sentence with
subject and predicate, but in practice it may be any group of words
conceived of as a basic thought by the Bible student or preacher.

Ideally the text would be the biblical portion which is being presented in a message form, whether spoken or read. Its length will
depend on the intention of the person using it, and the purpose for
which it is employed. It is important that no text be wrestled from
the context in which it is found for any particular reason. The old
adage is that "a text without a context is a pretext" and while that
may be overly severe, it is a good point for a beginning consideration. Messages may be given on the line of several disciplines:
expository, textual, biographical, topical, etc. But whatever form is
employed, a text is needed and therefore to study a text in a meaningful and proper way is necessary preparation.

1 Level One: THE STUDY OF A TEXT

In this very basic consideration the following items are addressed:

1. The grammatical identification of the text
2. The place of the text in its context
3. The subject of the text
4. The particular action of the text
5. To whom the text is addressed

1. *The grammatical identification of the text:* This is largely a matter of determining the sentence or clausal structure of the passage considered. Is it an independent clause (subject, predicate, etc.) or is it a dependent clause needing the total sentence structure to fulfill its meaning? It may be in the latter category but the student wishes to use it by itself—and that is certainly permissible so long as the student knows it is not the complete thought.

One might, for example, read in 2 Corinthians 6:1 the statement that we are *"workers together"* (implication—with God) and make that a focal point of a message. But it needs to be seen that it is not the complete thought of the sentence, but rather a clause introducing an item for exhortation. This does not mean it cannot be used for the student's point. It *does* mean that the student must be aware of the incomplete nature of a clause that is not a final thought in itself.

2. *Consideration of the place of the text in its context:* Item 1 leads directly to this point. The student must see that the text is part of a total picture of truth. It may be desired to treat this one aspect, and that is often done, but it needs to be studied in the light of the total passage to prevent undue emphasis on one point that might obscure other points. What is to be determined is how this text completes or affects the rest of the Scripture about it. This is not a major study, but a very important preliminary step, especially in the Old Testament where it is easy to spiritualize a given point.

A message was called to my attention with respect to Isaiah 40:31 and the text, *"they shall run and not be weary"* as an exhortation that a servant of God should not become fatigued in the process of life. Most of the rest of the verse and passage was overlooked, and no explanation was given to the critical thought about those who *"rest in the Lord."* The whole picture of truth needs to be visualized when a text is studied.

3. *The subject of the text:* This is mostly a matter of seeing the

idea discussed in the text. The idea might be a person, a teaching, some action, etc. The point is to know what the text is discussing. This is sometimes not specifically stated, but must be read from the context and the general understanding of the teaching.

(4.) *The particular action of the text:* This exercise answers the question: What happens in the text, or what is supposed to happen? The proclamations in Daniel 2, where we are told that all were to fall down and worship the image which Nebuchadnezzar had erected, tell what *should have happened*; the passages that talk of the worshipful obedience of Daniel's friends tell us what *did happen* as a result of their loyalty to the Lord.

(5.) *To whom the text is addressed:* We understand that all of the Bible is written *for* us—for our learning and instruction—but not all is written *to* us (in the sense that it is directive). Therefore it is necessary to determine the party addressed. It is sometimes a person, sometimes a group, at other times the world at large, and even, occasionally, a person who is not yet on the scene but who will come some day. In keeping with our other guidelines for Bible study, this is important in order that we do not attempt to take a duty or privilege, particularly assigned to another, and make it our own area of privilege or responsibility.

Level Two: THE STUDY OF A TEXT

This level of study takes on a greater dimension of Bible familiarity, and may well call for your attention to a concordance or a text Bible. At this level our study is geared to:

1. Possible parallel texts
2. Parallel texts and contexts
3. Further citations of this text in the Bible

1. *Possible parallel texts:* A parallel text is a text that says essentially the same thing, but in a different location in Scripture. The wording may not be identical but the idea is essentially the same. Note, for example, Psalms 40:13, 40:1 and 71:12. The similarity of

citations is more common in the wisdom/worship literature but is
found throughout the Bible, including passages in the New
Testament as well. If ministry is given on a text where there are parallels, it is possible that these may shed more light on the idea
expressed and make the exposition more meaningful.

2. *Parallel texts and contexts:* In following the previous note, one
will need to determine if the contexts regarding the citation are similar or diverse. (They will not be identical in historical position, of
course, but may be in very similar circumstances.) The student will
note carefully that, if the context differs, it will be necessary to see
if the text is used in a different manner. See the repetition of the text
in Psalm 57, verse 5 and 11, and determine if the use in context indicates any difference in application. And while in Psalm 57, compare
verse 7 with Psalm 108:3 and see how this text is used to give a different flavor to the idea.

In both of these, a concordance or text Bible is a big help. Older
tools like the *Thompson Chain Reference Bible* are also helpful.
One's reading of Scripture will call some of this material to mind,
but it takes a lot of reading to get a complete feel on the subject.

3. *Note where the text may be cited in other biblical passages:* The
thought in this sequence is a direct citation of the text such as may
be found when the New Testament quotes the Old or where a writer
in the Old Testament quotes from another Old Testament writer.
Compare Isaiah 2:1-4 and Micah 5:1-5 and note as well the use of
Habakkuk 2:4 in the New Testament. The wider use of a text may
give one a much better idea of the fullness of its meaning.

Level Three: THE STUDY OF A TEXT

Level Three treats one technical matter and two practical items
that need to be considered in any study.

1. Textual problems
2. Interpretation of the text
3. The use of the text

1. *Textual problems:* A textual problem is a situation that develops

when a biblical text has different readings in the basic manuscripts. It is technical enough that, unless one has some facility in the original languages, it can be very provoking. The student who has no such familiarity may become aware of textual problems by reading various translations or by the use of a study Bible. To ignore them completely is not wise, but for a full discussion a great deal of study and background help is necessary.

The vast majority of biblical texts have no such problems, but if the student becomes aware of a problem in this field, the best thing to do is to recognize the difficulty and not make the questioned area of the text the major part of the presentation. One may consult other scholars and more detailed works, but it is not an easy field without considerable training. Since less that $1/10$ of one percent of all texts are affected (a good estimate), it must be one of those shadowy realities of which one must beware, without becoming preoccupied.

A very small example may be seen in Isaiah 6:3 where the standard Hebrew Masoretic text reads *"Holy, holy, holy"* while the Dead Sea Scroll text (by far the oldest text on this passage) reads just *"Holy, holy."* There is a critical mark (*paseq*) in the Masoretic text indicating that the editors of that text were aware of a different reading but did not favor it. So if one were to argue for the Trinity on the basis of the three "holies," it would be a specious argument at best. Watch for these critical affairs and do not jump to conclusions. The area is one needing considerable expertise for full determination.

2. *Interpretation of the text:* It is important that the student interpret the text in harmony with the unity of the Bible. If one reads Psalm 138:8 and concludes that there is a fatalistic thrust in the world and one can live life with no consideration of conduct or procedure, he has interpreted the text incorrectly. The thought that the Lord will complete that which concerns me does not relieve me of my responsibility or involvement in His worship and testimony. The teaching is not to make us indolent, but to reassure us of the well-placed trust we have in such a God of power and grace. Bible verses may not be set against one another for contradictory purposes since the Bible is one book and does not disagree with itself.

3. *How will the text be used?* This becomes a matter of individual

preferment, and the student must seek to understand whether the text is best used to advance a doctrine, teach a life lesson, or illustrate a given point of thinking. These three suggestions do not exhaust the possibility of usage, but are areas in which the student may think in terms of application and teaching.

The proper study of the text (or a text) is necessary for the correct presentations of biblical truth. It is the study *of* the Bible, not just *about* the Bible, that is most instructive for the life and ministry of the Christian. One must avoid the tendency to simply "grab a text and run with it," and instead be a patient attender to the Word which God has given.

THE STUDY OF A THEME

Defining the study: A theme is a recurrent idea in Scripture—an arrangement of materials under a common subject. The theme of a book is the major concept it treats, while a subject theme is the tracing of an idea or ideal throughout the Bible.

In the case of the first item, it will be said that the "theme of Zechariah is the importance of building the house of God," while in the second case it may be said that the subject of the "brevity of life" is a theme seen throughout the Bible to challenge people to live in the light of eternity and the fact of meeting God some day.

The use of themes enables us to concentrate on given specific teachings drawn out from the whole body of Scripture. And while all must be seen in the light of context, the thematic statements really constitute a context in themselves.

Theme study requires a great deal of Bible reading and careful study in the Word of God as a whole, although, as with many other things today, there is plenty of help available on the subject. No added help, however, is adequate to replace one's own study of the Bible. In this examination of themes, the three levels of study continue to guide us from the simplest to the most complex matters.

Level One: THE STUDY OF A THEME

In *Level One* three items are discussed:

1. Determining the theme
2. Determining the understanding
3. Placing the theme in common, understandable words

These suggestions may seem overly simple, but they are basic and without them the import of the theme may not be presented clearly.

1. *Determining the theme:* There may be many themes in a book of the Bible, and, while the student does not need to isolate all of them, it is important to identify in particular the theme that will be discussed. In the larger books of the Old Testament there will always be a major theme and many sub-themes. In the poetical books (especially Psalms and Proverbs) there will be a multiplicity of themes, all of which are developed more or less in an individual manner and expressed under rather general themes such as "worship," "praise," "daily dependence," etc.

The student will become aware of these themes as one reads—and rereads—the books! It is then important to isolate the particular theme to be discussed. Whatever other material the student wishes to include will be developed in support or demonstration of the theme. If the student finds multiple themes in a passage, it is not necessary to present them all at one time. Prudence would suggest that one might be sorted from the others and used for instructional purposes.[7] The specific nature of the theme should be stated succinctly and clearly.

2. *Determining the understanding:* It is one thing to state a theme, and another to explain what it means; both are necessary. Psalm 39 has several thematic propositions but the dominant one, in my judgment, is the "brevity of life." This concept is seen frequently in the Psalter and takes a major role in Ecclesiastes. It does not mean that life is short in the sense that it does not last long enough, but that our activities and programs must be gauged in light of the fact that we do not have an unlimited amount of time with which to work. The idea is not to sit and sulk about age or the passing of years, but to take the time that is available and give it to do the will of God.

That life is brief is to be a stimulus towards holiness, not necessarily an argument for doing things more rapidly. It is possible to

LIFE & TIME

state the theme but not to understand it. This is seen when folks say, "Life is short, so live it up!" In this concept of the brevity of life we do not find an impetus for involvement in thousands of things just for the sake of involvement, but rather that its brevity might make us more aware of the Lord and His intentions for us. To be certain of a proper understanding, the student will need to survey the theme in its use throughout Scripture and thereby have a fuller grasp as to its complete meaning.

3. *Placing the theme in common and understandable words:* Very little need be said about this, but it is vital in the matter of presentation. Bible students have a tendency to express things in theological terms that often are foreign to the hearer. Clarity of expression is a goal to be sought and, as a rule, if one will express the theme in language that little children would understand, most adults will be able to understand it also.

Level Two: THE STUDY OF A THEME

Level Two also discusses three aspects in theme study:

1. See how the theme is initially developed
2. Determine if the theme is limited in time
3. Discover how the theme is used in comparative passages

1. *See how the theme is initially developed:* Psalm 39 gives a good opportunity for this observation—and the student must recall or re-examine the data on the study of the Psalms. While there are several themes in this psalm, the one I have mentioned earlier is the one that dominates my thinking; it is the matter of the brevity of life.

It is first announced in verse 4 (English Bible), following the writer's disappointment in his own inability to fulfill high aspirations. He simply writes, "Let me know how few days I really have and how frail I am." This is expanded in verses 5-6 as he notes that the Lord has authored these things so that, in verse 7, he has hope only in the Lord.

His subsequent prayer will be developed in the light of the fact that life is brief but he would like to live it for God as he goes. Why can he not attain the standard he desires in verse 1? Life is too short and we are too weak. If we know the nature of our being and the brevity of our life span, we are better able to undertake those things that are possible for us in the will of God.

2. *Determine if the theme is limited in time:* In this matter the student endeavors to see if there is any dispensational limitation on the theme, or if the subject is universally true at all times (not all Bible scholars agree on this distinction). The theme of the Babylonian Captivity enunciated in Jeremiah, *et al*, was a theme limited to an historical situation in Israel's history. But the theme that obedience honors God, and that He will deal with the rebellious and sinners is a theme that has eternal understanding. In the case of the theme that has some time limit it is possible to use applications from it and tie these to other situations. Those themes that have eternal understanding are obligatory in every age. Some discernment is needed on the part of the student: while one must not neglect any aspect of truth, we must be certain that the truth aspect is equally applicable in all settings before attempting to make it a mandatory obligation. Not everyone has an Abraham experience.

3. *Discover how the theme is used in comparative passages:* Note how often the "shepherd theme" as given in Psalm 23 is found in the scripture of both the Old and New Testaments. There is enough material on this subject to cover several presentation opportunities!

In proper contexts, there are some heavy words about poor shepherds and applications of good shepherdship. Not all themes have so many comparative passages, of course, but there is virtually no theme that is an independent thought of its own making. Topical or study Bibles help us see this, and, while the student will hardly be able to present the total teaching of any theme, he will be able to give an accurate and adequate treatment to the overall subject.

Level Three: THE STUDY OF A THEME

Level Three returns to a practical aspect of the study of a theme and does not have the intricate or technical material of the study of a text. Two items seem necessary under this notation:

1. What is the intended accomplishment of the theme?
2. How will the theme be applied in present living?

1. *What is the intended accomplishment of the theme?* This must be determined by a careful study of the context and the theme itself. In the case of Psalm 39 the intended accomplishment is to cast the hearer on the Lord for whatever strength or achievement one wishes to make. In some cases the desired end may be stated (as in the fourth commandment), but in many cases it remains to the student to summarize this point and make it explicit by clear and understandable language. That it must be thought through carefully before any conclusion is stated would seem to be obvious.

2. *How will the theme be applied in present living?* This, too, is a decision for the student. As with the study of a text, it may be used to illustrate a doctrine, indicate some correct or incorrect practice, or enforce some aspect of the will of God for our lives. But nothing in the Bible may be deemed extraneous. It all has meaning for us—even in the parts not written directly to us. The truths of 2 Timothy 3:16-17 will guide us in this matter, and we will find how the totality of Scripture enables us to be the completed persons God desires.

Theme study is fascinating work with wide ramifications for expanding our knowledge of the will and witness of the Lord. It cannot be done in a hurry and, in fact, is a lifetime challenge.

THE STUDY OF A TEACHING

Defining the study: A "teaching" or a doctrine is a statement establishing some point of truth from the Scripture. Doctrine is usually thought of as implying some more formal statement while a teaching is seen as a broader application. In reality the distinction is hardly needed and the terms may be used interchangeably. The Bible is the Christian's source of teaching and from it come the points of faith that direct our fellowships and lives. Therefore the correct appropriation of any teaching is necessary for the health of the Christian community and its witness to the world.

Analyzing the teachings of the Old Testament is an important part of the Bible student's work, and we approach again at three levels.

Level One: THE STUDY OF A TEACHING

1. State the teaching clearly, showing the biblical data on which it is based
2. Determine why the teaching is necessary and what it will accomplish

These two points are foundational to the approach to any doctrine or teaching. Relevance in the teaching is the major issue and study on the lines of these points will help to determine that relevance.

1. *State the teaching clearly, showing the biblical data on which it is based:* What is said now will be relevant to all Bible study but has special significance to the student of the Old Testament. This is due to the fact that so much of the Old Testament is historical and illustrative of biblical truth. It teaches directly as well, but some of the teaching is directed to the establishment of the worship of Israel (as with the tabernacle, for example) and the particular relationships God had with Israel as a covenanted people (items such as the Babylonian Captivity and the like).

It is possible to take a point in some such area and make it a didactic issue, as some teachers did with Isaiah 39. When Hezekiah is rebuked for receiving an embassage from Babylon, the passage was interpreted to mean that our country should not have ambassadors from non-Christian countries. Persons convinced of such things present their ideas with considerable force, but to make this sort of political alignment—a teaching of the Bible based on an account in the history of Israel—is to overlook much of what God has said with regard to governments, and to introduce a contradictory teaching that only serves to confuse.

Working in biblical teachings requires a thorough commitment to what God has said and to *all* He has said. The Old Testament student, therefore, needs to state the teaching (the doctrine) clearly, and show how it is based in the Bible and how it relates to other instructional materials in Scripture. It is a vital issue requiring time, patience, and perseverance.

2. *Determine why the teaching is necessary and what it will*

accomplish: In a real sense, all biblical teachings are necessary for an understanding of the total concepts of the will of God for His people. But some teachings are not appropriate (or required) at a given time—although times will come when they are. For example, when one is questioning concerning salvation, it is probably not the best time to be discussing the date of the Exodus. But in the course of life some teachings become immediately more necessary and need more stress at that time.

I suppose the big point in this case is the sensitivity of the teacher to the Word of God and to the audience with whom he is communicating. The question that meets us is simply this: what does one hope to achieve or accomplish with this teaching? The student should be careful in this regard, and more pointed that just to say, "better Bible knowledge." While we will not diminish the importance of that, it must be noted that it is too general to vindicate or enforce every teaching at the same time.

Level Two: THE STUDY OF A TEACHING

In *Level Two* we meet some practical points that keep the teaching meaningful and foundationally sound:

1. Correctly view the "dispensational" cast of the teaching
2. Determine how the teaching has been used in the Christian community
3. See how our understanding agrees or disagrees with others.

There is a certain amount of personal reflection in these items, but the student must face that as a part of one's total viewpoint.

1. Correctly view the "dispensational" cast of the teaching: There are many schools of biblical interpretation, and this present work is not an attempt to identify or deny various understandings. By "dispensational" it is not intended that we can have a stereotyped characterization of one element or group of Bible students. Instead we want to recognize the fact that some things are relevant in one age that may not be relevant in another. "Storehouse tithing" is a teaching that is heard today, with the concept taken from Malachi—that all giving should be through the "storehouse." But the storehouse was the temple/tabernacle and a part of Israel's worship system in the physical realm. It is difficult to make the devotional realities of those institutions to be the realities of today. The principles and ideals are surely true but the actual observance belongs to another time—which is why we do not have a burnt altar sacrifice in the church of today.

This is not an attempt to get interpretive uniformity, but to warn that it is possible to go to all sorts of extremes in such areas. Wise students will keep the entire Bible in perspective, but will concentrate on the didactic concepts for the age in which they are working.

2. *Determine how the teaching has been used in the Christian community:* Some understanding of historical theology is needed at this point, and there are some helpful works[8] available on the history of doctrines. Biblical commentaries may assist in this area as well and the student is seeking to discover the impact of this teaching in the history of the Christian community.

Very often Bible students will come to a point of truth or instruction and feel certain it has never been taught before. While we cannot say this will not happen, it is safe to say that it does not happen very often! Research in the work of others will usually show that the Spirit of God has enabled others to comprehend the message as well.

Some teachings have always raised more questions than answers, and some have been divisive to the people of God. It is not that these things should not be discussed, but that they should be presented with an understanding of what their service has been, and an appropriate respect is made accordingly. The age of the earth is such a question in Old Testament study and, while we have varying appreciation of the concepts scholars develop about this subject, we should understand that the debate is more likely to prove divisive than edifying. No suggestion is intended that we should not study these things, but we should keep them in proper perspective.

3. *See how our understanding agrees or disagrees with others:* This point does not tell us whether the teaching is appropriate or accurate, but it does shield us from novelty, and may make us aware of some failing which is fatal to our logic but which we may not

have seen "on our own." To some Bible students it is almost humbling to think they should be concerned with what others have thought, but this is a necessary humility.

All of us are limited in various aspects of out total viewpoint of truth, and we should be honest about that, being considerate of the gifting of the Spirit of God to others. One does not "give up" on the teaching if one is certain it is a biblical concept, but it is good to be broad enough to see what others think, and how they have applied this truth in their time.

Level Three: THE STUDY OF A TEACHING

Some of the material in *Level Three* may appear repetitious and, in fact, may be so. But in the study of a teaching, the student is attempting to present the fact or directive as to what the Bible has to say. The results of the study should produce a concrete picture of truth, and not be a vague discussion of opinions. So it is that these three considerations are important as the closing steps in the study of a teaching:

1. Be certain the teaching is held uniformly in the Bible
2. Be careful that the teaching is neither a novelty nor a frivolous opinion
3. Prepare to share the teaching with others and determine ways to know they have learned from it

All of these items have an intense personal side and, in some ways, this is the hardest part of Bible study for our comprehension. There are not many concrete ideals of standards that may be given for our insight, except the Bible itself. But that is surely more than just adequate so we are able to look realistically at these matters.

1. *Be certain that the teaching is held uniformly in the Bible:* Any given teaching may have great emphasis in one part of the Bible and be barely mentioned in another part. Our suggestion is not that the teaching is found on every page, but that wherever it is found it is agreed on with regard to content and intention. The Bible does not contradict itself, and it is important that the student, understanding

this, does not seem to make it contradict itself. Many theological debates would never have existed, or would cease to exist, if the uniform measure of God's revelation were allowed to stand on the simple ways in which they are presented in the Scripture. This is especially needed for Old Testament study since we tend to use the illustrative material in a directive way rather than in a defining or demonstrating way.

2. *Be careful that the teaching is neither a novelty nor a frivolous opinion:* No Bible student will even admit that such is the case, but if it is an idea that no one has ever thought of before, proceed very cautiously. The Bible student must not allow imagination to be the documenter of truth. It is helpful to present material in fresh and varied ways, but one must be certain the medium of presentation does not dwarf nor obscure the teaching.

3. *Prepare to share the teaching with others and determine ways to discover that it has been comprehended:* Easier said than done, that is certain, but it needs to be attempted.

Find some way whereby the hearer expresses the reality of what has been taught. Questions and answers, opportunities for critique, life action, etc., are all possibilities, but if the student of Scripture just mouths the words and does not plumb the mind of the hearer for application and understanding, something very important may well be lost.

In drawing this segment to a close, it must be noted that nothing is needed more today than the teachings from the Bible as they affect our lives. Truth is always being challenged in very deceptive ways, and the best way to deal with this is to present it again and again with greater vigor and better documentation.

THE STUDY OF PHENOMENA

Defining the term and the study: The term *phenomena* (*phenomenon* is the singular) defines remarkable or singular events not patterned by recurrence or accountable on a life-cycle basis. For our consideration there are five classes to be discussed:

1. Miracles
2. Signs
3. Wonders
4. Dreams
5. Visions

There is considerable overlapping among these, but the usages will allow individual treatment. Some occurrences may fulfill the definition of all five items at the same time, but there are others that belong distinctively to one class.

THE STUDY OF MIRACLES

By definition, a miracle is an event or an eventuality transcending the normal or expected course of events, and not governed by predictability of recurrence or the ordinary processes of life (you may find alternative definitions in a dictionary or thesaurus).

In the New Testament, three words are used to indicate a miracle (work, sign, wonder) while in the Old Testament two basic terms are employed (sign, wonder) both of which may indicate other phenomena. The word "miracle" is not widely used as a translation term in the Old Testament, but events of miraculous stature are common.

Miracles, therefore, are identified on the basis of what happened more than on the use of a particular word. In other words, there are many miracles[9] evident in the Old Testament, but not all are identified by a particular term.

Miracles may occur as the event itself, in the timing of it, or in the perception of what has happened. It is sometimes difficult to distinguish these factors, but they are significant in the study of the miraculous. One must remember that Satan has some miraculous power also, and a miracle in itself does not necessarily mean the Lord has done it. To determine the validity of a miracle for spiritual purposes, the student must return to the authenticating test for a true prophet, and in that data will also be found a basis of the evaluation of a miracle.

Miracles serve a variety of purposes. At times they are used to authenticate a message from the Lord or to identify His servant. At times they are directly given for emotional and/or physical release.

Sometimes they occur to meet the challenge of national disasters. They are not done for a simple novelty value, however, not to satisfy the curious or to stimulate the idle wishes of a crowd.

Miracles of healing and miracles showing control of nature are the most common, but when the Lord decides to work, none of us should attempt to interfere and hinder it.

May we pray for a miracle? Surely it is not wrong to ask such a thing if the honor of the Lord and the furtherance of His testimony are the key issues. For personal convenience? That is probably not a good basis for asking a miracle of the Lord, but we may ask: only the Lord knows what will be granted or accomplished.

While there is no absolute rule on the frequency of miracles, they do seem to come in clusters, particularly at the beginning of a new age or economy. When Israel was called from Egypt, there was a great quantity of miracles, both in their departure and in their time in the wilderness of Sinai. Likewise in the days of Elijah and the threat of Baalite worship among the people of God, there was an intensity of miraculous events.

This is true in the New Testament as well, with the proliferation of miracles in the ministry of Christ and in the days of the early Church. In such settings, the miracles definitely serve an authentication factor. This in no way rules out miracles at any time since they are part of the work of God, but it is of interest to see how they are used to confirm the faith of God's own in such times of trial.

In the study of the miracles we will proceed on the same order as in the other materials, with a suggestion of areas of inquiry to help in developing levels of understanding.

Level One: THE STUDY OF MIRACLES

In *Level One* we are concerned with some very basic things that are mostly a matter of study in the biblical text. Four items are considered:

1. What is the occasion for the miracle?
2. Who are the persons involved?
3. What is the actual proceeding? What is the miracle?
4. What is the positive evidence that a miracle has occurred?

Parts of these discussion points are self-evident, but it is important to see them all as grounds for understanding what has happened
and what the miracle means. For this consideration of miracles we
will use the text in 2 Kings 6 for a demonstrative passage on all five
of these points. The nature of the problem is cited in verse 8, and the
narrative continues from that point.

1. *What is the occasion?* The occasion giving rise to the miracle
will always tell a lot about what the Lord's tactics are, and to what
end He is working.

The Syrian king is at war with the king of Israel and laying all
sorts of devious schemes to trap him. One of the Lord's prophets is
able to tell the king of Israel what is happening, and where to go and
where not to go. The king of Syria is constantly frustrated in his
plans and, in a move of aggravation, attempts to find the person in
his camp who is a secret spy for Israel. He is answered by his own
advisors that there is no spy among them. Instead Elisha, a servant
of Jehovah, knows everything the king of Syria is planning to do,
and is able to inform the king of Israel, thereby foiling the Syrian
plans. In a fury, the Syrian asks where he can find Elisha, and is told
that he is presently in the city of Dothan.

Acting quickly, that very night, the Syrian king sends a force,
moving swiftly to surround Dothan, capture Elisha, and end this
information leak against him. By the next morning the city is completely surrounded—it is not very large anyway—and Elisha and
those with him face inevitable capture and certain death.

2. *Who are the persons involved?* It is noteworthy that neither of
the named principals was there. The king of Israel remains in his
capitol; he is not involved. The king of Syria remains, with his army,
at the place of encampment. The Syrian warlord is represented by
horses and chariots and a great host of men identified in verse 23 as
the *"bands of Syria."* In all likelihood this was the equivalent of a
guerrilla band in our day, a hired force to achieve the goals of the
king without jeopardizing his personal corps.

The prophet Elisha is central—he is the wanted person and apparently is defenseless. Next to him is an unnamed servant but a youth,
perhaps a prophetic novitiate.

3. *What is the actual proceeding? What is the miracle?* In the totality of the action, there are actually three major miracles with some parts of a sustaining action.

Elisha's servant is helped by the first. He is fearful, and Elisha prays that God will open his eyes When we say something like this, we are usually asking that someone will be better able to understand a situation. But in this case, the Lord wanted this young man to actually *see* the armament of God. With Elisha's urgent request to God having been given, the young assistant suddenly sees that the mountains about Dothan are filled with chariots of fire and horses around Elisha. The Lord is not going to have a big battle but the assistant "sees" and he certainly will understand. It was a miracle in that God allowed him to see.

This is followed by a second miracle when the Syrian host comes to take Elisha. Suddenly, in verse 18, in response to the prayer of Elisha, the host is struck with blindness. This is no normal thing. It is totally unexpected, but God has worked a miracle for a teaching purpose. Elisha will challenge the host to follow him and he will take them to the person they want—they have little choice, I think. But when they follow him, he leads them into Samaria, right into the middle of the forces of the king of Israel.

Then the third miracle takes place in that Elisha has their eyes opened and they can see—but what a frightening sight! The king of Israel asks if he should kill them; Elisha says he should not. Feed them, he responds, and send them to their master. He does this, and then the offending host is allowed to leave. In the text (v. 23) we are told that these bands never came back to fight Israel again. This guerrilla force has seen something that they did not want to see again, and God had provided deliverance for Elisha, and for Israel in a chain of "small" miracles.

4. *What is the positive evidence that a miracle has occurred?* We often hear of miracles in healing and such things, but then find the intended victim dies of the same problem in which it was claimed the healing had taken place. The evidence that a miracle was performed in this occasion is twofold: 1) that Elisha was delivered and would continue to serve God in Israel; and 2) that the Syrian "bands" came back no more. The Syrian army was another thing; it

will come again—but the people who had "magically" escaped certain death would not take that chance a second time. The study of a miracle such as this fills one with an appreciation for the power, wisdom, and timing of God.

Level Two: THE STUDY OF MIRACLES

Level Two in the study of a miracle involves three aspects that are closely tied to the occasion and circumstances:

1. How is the miracle categorized? (healing, nature, combat, etc.)
2. What theological emphasis does the miracle show?
3. What are the wider results of the miracle's enactment?

Most of the information needed for Level Two is discerned directly from a Bible. Commentary and character study books are helpful as well. The benefit of these works is that they often point us to something that we would have otherwise overlooked.

1. *How is the miracle categorized?* Generally this is not hard to determine. The miracles in 2 Kings 6 can be seen as "combat" and, in a sense, as "healing." This information helps us see the contexts in which the Lord does great work. The student should have many notebooks for Bible study and somewhere a listing of this type of information should be kept. There are some special books written for this sort of study (Lockyer's *All the Miracles of the Bible*, for example). It becomes apparent that the miracles are not predictable, and the circumstances are not the only consideration.

2. *What theological emphasis does the miracle show?* It is rare that a miracle only stresses one point, but since they are given for teaching purposes as well as for goal attainments, it would be remarkable if they did not have a theological emphasis. In the passage of 2 Kings 6, it is possible to see how God's omniscience and omnipotence are stressed. Very visible also is the fact of the care of God for His servants and, in this case, it is not only Elisha but also the young man who needed these lessons for his personal growth. God's plan or sovereign delights are frequently highlighted in mira-

cles—such as those performed in Egypt to enable the deliverance of Israel. It is important to remember that the miracle is not performed for stage value or for a mere showing of the unknown: it has a positive purpose, and tied to that is the honor of the Lord.

3. *What are the wider results of the enacted miracle?* At times these are readily apparent in the text; sometimes they must be assumed. In the case of an assumption, one must be governed by practicality and common sense or judgment.

Considering the passage in 2 Kings 6, think of what the effect of the miracle was on the youthful attendant. It would be fair to say that he never forgot it, and very likely never doubted the power of God again. Very likely it gave him an increased appreciation for his master as well. We know that the king of Syria lost a supporting group of marauders, but since he was not personally involved it is probable that he learned nothing from the situation (see 6:24!).

The New Testament helps us to understand that not many persons are won by miracles, but many of the Lord's people are encouraged and strengthened by them. That is no small benefit.

Level Three: THE STUDY OF MIRACLES

In *Level Three* our concentration is on some of the practical aspects of the miracle study. We are concerned with these items:

1. How is the miracle seen in the Bible?
2. What does it teach for life today?
3. To what extent do we seek to explain a miracle?

1. *How is the miracle seen in the Bible?* Some miracles are seen in the Bible in a special sense, like that of crossing the Red Sea. The fact of God's deliverance by this means is one of the great themes in the worship psalms, and a part of Israel's history that cannot be forgotten. Those we have seen in 2 Kings 6 have no mention in other parts of the Bible, although there is a general reference to the work of God in such ways in Hebrews 11.

If the miracle becomes basic for some other biblical foundation material, then the student will be able to see it in a clearer light and emphasize the purpose and work accomplished. If it is not further noted in the Bible, it does not lose anything of its character or factual recording, but it means that the study is very much confined to the discussion of the miracle by itself in its time.

2. *What does it teach for life today?* One of the major problems in Bible study and Bible teaching is the failure to relate the truths seen to the present life. Every biblical account must be seen in its own context and its own theological-sociological perspective. But this becomes rudely academic if the teaching setting is not seen as being relevant to the study and to the hearer's society. It is one of the reasons why many Christians do not get excited or serious about the study of the Bible.

If, on the other hand, total attention is given to present relevance, the theological aspects may be sacrificed and the student loses the enrichment that should be his. It is something of a delicate balance, but one that should be sought without injury to all parts of the teaching. It is a very legitimate question to ask: what should I learn today from this miracle that will enrich my witness, my worship, and my personal enjoyment of the fellowship of the Lord and His people?

3. *To what extent do we seek to explain a miracle?* While this is an important question, my quick answer is that we do not attempt to explain it at all. The circumstances, situation, persons, events, etc., may all be seen in the light of what has happened, but pragmatic attempts to show how God does things will create more problems than answers. A miracle must be accepted; it cannot be diagrammed or explained in its workings. When something is predictable or programmed, it is not properly a miracle but the end result of a careful program. With God there is a careful program, of course, but we do not know what it is and cannot manipulate it.

I have read several books explaining the long day in Joshua 10, the crossing of the Red Sea and the Jordan, and even the miracles of resuscitation of the dead. When these books are put to careful scrutiny, they do not stand up nor do they explain the happenings. We simply receive the miracle and live in the good of it.

Miracles are impressive when they are handled well in the study of the Word of God, and in both Testaments there is adequate room

for research and study as to the ways of God and the execution of
His ways.

As noted earlier, these miracles, often abundant at the beginning
of a new era, certify the reality of the claims of the servants of God,
and are authenticated by their agreement with God's Word by the
various tests of truth given in Scripture. The miracles in Israel's history are used consistently in the Psalms to point out the reality of the
care of God, and His selection of Israel as His "peculiar" people.

THE STUDY OF SIGNS

By definition, a "sign" is a specific act or demonstration that ver-
ifies a messenger or a message from God. It may be a miraculous
affair as well, but its purpose is to allow the observer to know that
God is real in the situation and His Word is vital. While the miraculous may be present, it is not required, and some natural or predictable occurrence may be used as a sign in a commonplace way.

What the sign does mostly is to establish credibility. We have
many tests for this today (but still have trouble doing it well),
although in the ancient world it was more difficult, not having the
technological advances that help us now. Anyone could claim almost
anything and there was no "truth serum" available. Facing that problem, in the providence of God, specific signs were often used for the
certification process. An excellent situation is seen in 1 Kings 13.

There an unknown prophet confronts Jeroboam I, the wicked king
who led the revolt following the death of Solomon. He is remembered as the one who *"made Israel to sin"* in 1 Kings 22:52. In the
account of 1 Kings 13, the prophet speaks of things to come (v. 2) as
he faces Jeroboam's idolatrous altar. Having given the prophecies,
the prophet gives a "sign" to indicate the validity of his word—the
sign is the statement that the altar will be ruined.

When Jeroboam acts vengefully and orders the prophet seized, he
is smitten by God and the altar, previously intact and functioning, is
immediately broken, the ashes spilling out from it, as the prophet
had said. This is the sign indicating that the prophet had spoken the
truth in his prediction, and one would not have to wait three hundred
years to see it fulfilled. Any observer would know that God had spoken. The sign demonstrated to all that God had revealed a point of

truth. It did not say when it would be seen to be fulfilled, but it would occur. Ultimately the lesson meant that the godly should have nothing to do with the pagan altar set up by the king. By its very nature it is obvious that the sign may be any entity suited for the purpose at the time, and there are enough of them given in the Old Testament to justify our study.

The major Hebrew word translated as "sign" indicates something with a signaling characteristic. There are a few other Hebrew words of occasional use, but all indicate a token or demonstration of power from a higher source.[10]

Level One: THE STUDY OF SIGNS

It is not our intention to make every aspect of the Old Testament seem like a major course of research. But the fact remains that the more thorough our studies, the more useful the results. *Level One* touches on three basic points:

1. The situation in which the sign is given
2. The giver of the sign
3. What is the sign?

1. *The situation in which the sign is given:* Consider the situation regarding Moses in Exodus 4. He has been given the commission by God to return and lead the people of the Lord out of Egypt. He thinks they will not be ready to follow him, and asks what he can do to gain their belief. The Lord gives him two signs for immediate use (v. 8 uses the term): his rod and his hand. He will throw his rod down and it will become a serpent, becoming a rod again when he properly retrieves it. If that is not enough to make them think he has had an encounter with God, he will put his hand into his bosom and it will emerge in a leprous condition. Then he can put it back again and it will come out clean. These demonstrations will show his people that he has an authority and power that they can trust and thereby commit themselves to his leadership.

Other signs will be given to persuade the Egyptians to cooperate, but these are power signs to authenticate Moses as the servant of God. The first shows him a master of nature and the second shows him a master over life. Oppressed in Egypt as they were, the Israelites needed a leader who could show overcoming powers in such cases; the signs are to that effect. Anyone could remember the sign and be gripped by it. To know the situation in which the sign is given will, therefore, often explain why a particular sign is used. It will also make it plain why a sign is necessary. As with miracles, signs are not given to amuse or indulge people, but to provide a visible representation that something remarkable has happened.

2. *The giver of the sign:* In this category we mean the person or institution giving the sign. Obviously God is the One who really gives it or assigns it to His servant. Seeing the giver of the sign in the situation will help us understand why it is needed, and how it is received. Note the signs that God established in Genesis 1:14.

3. *What is the sign?* It may be argued that sometimes the sign is an object and at other times an action. If the object and the action are more or less simultaneous, I think the distinction is not necessary. The sign given to Ahaz in Isaiah 14 is clearly that of an object-action united: the virgin birth. It seems most likely that differentiation on this particular matter is not very important so long as the student can identify the sign and see how it is given.

2 Level Two: THE STUDY OF SIGNS

Three points of study constitute the bulk of the work of *Level Two*:

1. Why is the sign needed?
2. Is it intended for immediate or future use?
3. Is the sign something easily recognized or it is obscure?

1. *Why is the sign needed?* As a general rule, signs are needed where intellectual assent is not given outwardly. It is the doubting nature of the individuals concerned that make a sign important; this is stressed in the New Testament as well as the Old. Insight is given into the nature of the problem and the reactions of the involved parties when the sign is in view. There may be times when emotional or

intellectual assent is given, but there is a question as to when and how something will be accomplished. The sign is intended to endorse that.

In Isaiah 14, the doubting king of Judah is told to ask for a sign, but he will not. He has already rejected the advice of God, so a sign is given to all the people of God so that even those with the greatest of doubts will be able to identify God's work when He acts. The sign is needed for confidence of heart and for the consideration of those who are not sure of the times and seasons.

2. *Is the sign intended for immediate or future use?* This may be determined by the context or by some related Scripture. Most common is the fact that the sign is not given with a sharp time sequence; instead there is a statement of fact that this or that will happen.

In the case of Isaiah 14, the sign is described but the fulfillment of its message is in the distant future. This differs from 1 Kings 13, where the prophecy is in the distant future but the sign is immediate.

If the sign is immediate, it is calling for some quick action; if it is for a future event, it is pointing to an awareness that should mark the lives of the people of God. In either case, the sign is to be studied with an eye to what God expects of His people in the light of what He is doing.

3. *Is the sign something easily recognized, or is it obscure?* The object serving as a sign may be easily recognizable, but the actual meaning of the sign may be obscure.

An example may be seen in Isaiah's children, who are noted as being signs (in Isaiah 8:18) and are given symbolic names. Anyone could look at the child and say, "It is a child," but what the child-sign meant prophetically is another matter.

The first child is a sign that there will be a remnant of God's people left, despite a desolation. The second child is a sign that the devastation is coming soon and the righteous must be prepared for it.

In the view of the people, the significance of the children may have been missed, but in the totality of Scripture it is plain that God was giving signs for the direction of His people.

No matter how recognizable the sign, careful scrutiny is needed for its study and meaning.

3 Level Three: THE STUDY OF SIGNS

In *Level Three* our concentration is on materials developed in the text. There are only two aspects. A commentary or a study Bible is the better help in this case. Of great advantage also is a notebook kept by the student of items that correspond in the Scripture, items that are noticed in one's regular study or reading and then incorporated into a notebook. This should be organized on the lines of book study or subject study. The two items greeting us at this level are:

1. Do other Bible passages note this sign?
2. How is the sign fulfilled or its purposes accomplished in the Bible?

1. Do other passages note this sign? Genesis 9:12-13 tells us of a sign (*token* in the KJV) the Lord gave to Noah[11] as part of His covenant with him. The sign would indicate that God would not again destroy the world as He had with the flood. You will find this sign in at least two other places in the Bible, and he will want to search out what it signifies in those places. It may be giving the same message God gave to Noah, but in a different context.

If any sign is used in multiple occurrences, it is a good indication that it has a special meaning for times other than the one in which it originated.

2. How is the sign fulfilled or its purposes accomplished in the Bible? The study in 1 Kings 13 gives a good study example of this point. The sign is given that the altar will be destroyed—but no time is set on this. When the king attempts to take the prophet prisoner, he is immediately afflicted and the altar destroyed. The sign is immediately fulfilled and certifies the prediction.

In Isaiah 14, the sign is not fulfilled until about 700 years later and the New Testament writers tell us that it was fulfilled in the coming of the Lord Jesus. Completion of what is indicated by the sign is another demonstration of the power and faithfulness of God.

In concluding the study of signs, the student will see the use of true and false signs in Jeremiah 28. Note the prediction and sign of Hananiah; then note the prediction and sign of Jeremiah. Observe

the fatal sign that Jeremiah gives concerning Hananiah, and how the
truthfulness of his prophetic stature was demonstrated in contradiction to that of the false prophets. Several similar cases will be found
in the Old Testament. Giving a sign is easy, but seeing it used mean-
ingfully is something that comes from the hand of God.

THE STUDY OF WONDERS

By definition, a wonder is an act of power and amazement intended to draw full attention to some point of truth or a special message
from God. A wonder may be a miracle or it may be a common thing
that takes on an uncharacteristic posture, surprising the viewer. The
great wonders in the Old Testament are the acts of God that force
attention to Him. His servants are given, at times, the capacity to
perform wonders for the same purpose. Such is the record of Moses
and Aaron in Exodus 11:10.

Wonders, as in the case of signs and miracles, may be counter-
feited. The student will recall the magicians in Egypt with some limited powers in this line. The prophetic tests of Deuteronomy 13 and
18 need to be used to determine the validity of a wonder as much as
they may be used to see the truthfulness of a prophet[12] or his prophecy. Neither the miracle nor the wonder is self-sustaining, but must
gain validity through the instruction of the Word. If the phenomenal
occurrence does not measure up to the biblical standard, it is to be
discarded and given no influence with the people of God.

The main Hebrew term translated as "wonder" suggests amazement and there are a few other terms translated similarly that have
various shades of meaning, including "wonderful" in the sense of
being extremely pleasant or attractive.

Level One: THE STUDY OF WONDERS

The most basic items for the study of a "wonder" are these:

1. What is the wonder?
2. What makes it remarkable in its time?
3. What is the situation that calls for it?

1. *What is the wonder?* The term "wonder" is used to describe the

particular item that causes amazement. (It is not used in the sense of the Christian song, "The Wonder of it All.") To define the word as used is simply to tell what it is or was. The wonders of God shown to Pharaoh were, among other things, the plagues. The student will discover that the wonders of God include many things from the acts of creation to the specific assignment of a particular deed. It is important to note that it is not the use of the word "wonder" but the startling presentation that draws one's attention to the divine initiative. When the terms are used by the biblical author, one may quickly identify the wonder; but when the term is not used, it is the effect on the subjects that makes the character of the wonder apparent, and makes it important to have an exact identification.

2. *What makes it remarkable in its time?* The object or event is shown in such a way as to surprise or alarm the subject. The little cloud of 1 Kings 18:44 became a wonder to the prophet Elijah as the rainless sky was suddenly threatened with a great rain. Ordinarily there is nothing about a cloud to send one on a rapid journey, but at this time and under this unusual set of circumstances, it was a wonder—remarkable in the context of the time. Asking why the wonder is noteworthy at the time often gives a clue to the nature and need of the situation.

3. *What is the situation calling for the wonder?* Why is a wonder needed at this time? That is the question. It is almost always true that there is some difficulty, some decision, some needed action, that could not be initiated without some sort of shock. And a wonder, on the whole, is a sort of peaceful shock in many cases. We are accustomed to things happening at a very slow and determined pace; the wonder speeds things up a bit. It promotes action that otherwise might have been delayed. The sudden judgment of the man gathering sticks on the Sabbath probably made many others think twice before defying God.

Level Two: THE STUDY OF WONDERS

Three items are involved in *Level Two* and these are mostly discerned in the study of the biblical text:

1. Who are the persons involved?
2. What reaction does the wonder produce?
3. Is the wonder a normal occurrence used in a striking way, or is it an amazement otherwise unknown?

1. *Who are the persons involved?* Generally speaking there are two main parties: the one calling for the wonder or stating it, and the group to whom it is shown. Discerning this, one may better see whether the wonder is to strengthen the giver, to challenge the hearer, or to have a common meaning to both. The whole picture is given for us, of course, but it is important to see it in the context as stated.

2. *What reaction does the wonder produce?* The reaction is not always what the student might expect or desire. When the wonders were shown in Egypt, the hearts of the Egyptians were hardened (particularly that of Pharaoh); and while the Israelites should have been filled with confidence, we learn that, during their march to Canaan, these wonders were not the teaching lessons that they should have been. They do, however, work together to provide lessons and instruction for all generations thereafter.

3. *Is the wonder a normal occurrence used in a striking way, or is it an amazement otherwise unknown?* This is determined simply by a study of the text, and it will help us in understanding that the ways of God are not always our ways. Whether the wonder is normal or paranormal will not make it more important in the total development of the work of God with His people. But it will teach us that God may use perfectly normal events—or something radically new—in achieving His purposes. This means we must learn to trust God, not the circumstances.

Level Three: THE STUDY OF WONDERS

We address two aspects of this study in *Level Three*:

1. What other biblical passages mention this wonder?
2. What is the particular teaching purpose in the wonder?

1. *What other biblical passages mention this wonder?* A concordance or a reference Bible is the best help in this matter, and one will often be surprised at the frequent mention of some of the wonders of God. Creation is a great subject and, in the history of Israel, a dominant wonder is the crossing of the Red Sea, as well as the things done in Egypt. The importance of such particular acts of God becomes obvious when the breadth of reference is seen. Often the student is gripped with the realization that God works for the ages more than just for the moment.

2. *What is the particular teaching purpose in the wonder?* This cannot be answered on a page of discussion, but must be discerned in the text itself. Wonders, as with signs and miracles, are not given for amusement or personal intrigue, but to enforce some message or lesson from God. Any two students looking at the wonder may discern two or three lessons apiece—and they may all be somewhat different in statement. It is important that any teaching the student discerns is compatible with the whole of Scripture, of course, but beyond that there is no list of official lessons that will be equally understood by all.

IN CONCLUSION

In drawing this part of our discussion to a close, the point is made that God has many means of making us aware of His greatness and purpose. We cannot insist that He use one means to the exclusion of the others, nor can we demand that He employ any one for our benefit. The challenge is to learn to observe Him in His Word and His work, and be thankful that by grace we can know the Creator of the universe as our Father and our God.

In general, almost everything God does is a wonder to us (Job 9:10) but the particular wonders hold a fascination for us. A good example may be seen in 2 Kings 7, when the camp of the Syrians was abandoned as the Lord made them fear there was to be a surprise attack by their mortal enemies. The Syrian siege of Samaria had caused great stress and a huge famine. The wonder, so far as Israel was concerned, was that suddenly the siege was over and the

Syrians gone! This act was reported by the lepers who had gone out
early in the morning in hopes of getting something from the Syrians.
When they reported the camp abandoned, the people of Samaria ran
to the abandoned camp and seized the spoil and forsaken food. The
famine was over without their having fired a shot, so to speak!

We are filled with amazement at the work of God, and it continues to challenge us to believe His Word and trust Him in all sorts of
settings today.

THE STUDY OF DREAMS

By definition a dream is a visual presentation occurring during a
period of sleep. The term "dream" is used in modern parlance to
describe an ideal or a hope or even an ambitious enterprise. It is not
used that way in the Old Testament. Dreams have fascinated us for
centuries, and the attempts at interpreting dreams–discovering what
they portend or mean–have been many. Some dreams may seem perfectly logical, while others may be totally absurd. But dreams, in the
Bible, are phenomenal in that they are not predictable or logically
recurrent. The biblical dreams in the Old Testament offer a very
interesting study in a well-defined area. We will proceed with our
three-level methodology.

Level One: THE STUDY OF DREAMS

In this basic study of dreams, we are concerned with two major
items:

1. The historic setting of the dream
2. The source of the dream: Is it from God?

1. *The historic setting of the dream:* This material includes the
nature of the biblical context, the developments surrounding the participants, the stage of life of the dreamer, and even the consequence,
to some extent, that will follow. One will think of Joseph's dreams,
the dreams of the baker and butler in the Egyptian prison, etc., and
how these dreams were the virtual answers to some of the issues of
life and personal development in the principal characters.

That the dream is often immediately attached to the historic context is no accident, and the understanding of that historic context is often the key to the meaning of the dream. Remember that we are involved in the study of biblical dreams, not one that the student may have had on a recent night!

2. *The source of the dream: Is it from God?* Observing the text, one will often see the notation that God is speaking through the text.

Jacob's dream in Genesis 28 offers an interesting study at this point. Initially it would seem that the fact of the dream was merely a result of fatigue in his journey. But in the content of the dream it becomes plain that the Lord is speaking to him, and reasserting his right to the covenant. One would necessarily conclude that the dream was from God.

But could not God have told him or shown him these things in a more normal manner? Such questions cannot be answered now. The fact is that God spoke through the dream and Jacob understood it that way and responded that way.

Whether the dream is from God or not will depend on 1) direct statement or 2) obvious application. In either case, the dream is directive, and the consequences that develop following it are the proof of its origin.

Level Two: THE STUDY OF DREAMS

In *Level Two* our study looks at some things that are derived from the Scripture, but a reference Bible will prove helpful in locating material.

1. Is there an explanation of the dream in the text?
2. Is the dream applied to actions in the setting?
3. Is the dream recurrent?

1. *Is there an explanation of the dream in the text?* This is determined by reading the text and looking for parallel citations or references. Very often the dream is interpreted or explained immediately, but that is not always the case. Joseph's dreams in Genesis 37 were not explained in the text, but were understood by his brothers

and Jacob, so that an explanation is available as the dream is seen by the family. Nebuchadnezzar's dreams are interpreted by Daniel, but no meaning was given to Nebuchadnezzar until Daniel gave him the word that the Lord could make the matters known to him.

The dream of the Midianite warrior in Judges 7:13 was understood by one of his colleagues, and, when Gideon overheard the conversation, he took the dream to be a guiding factor for himself.

When no meaning is assigned, it seems best not to attempt to be definitive and make the dream into a theological foundation. A partial illustration of this occurrence may be seen in Genesis 28:12*ff*. The Lord will renew the covenantal obligation in this section, but the ladder part of the dream is not, I think, explained.

Some very elaborate interpretations are available in the commentaries but when the explanation is not in the text, the interpretations cannot be final.

2. *Is the dream applied to actions in the setting?* By this we refer to the way in which the dream immediately affects what is going on. Does the dream cause a change in the direction of some aspect of the situation in the text? The dream recited in the hearing of Gideon produced an almost immediate reaction concerning his soon attack, and the fear that spread among his enemies. Gideon could quickly rally his forces and attack.

Joseph's boyhood dreams irritated his brothers and led to their eventual animosity towards him, but at the time of the telling they did nothing. Later, when they speak of him as a dreamer, they will take action in a way that seems almost irrelevant in the nature of the dream.

3. *Is the dream recurrent?* As a general rule, dreams recorded in the Bible are not recurrent—they are one-time experiences. But the continuity of dreaming, such as in the case of Nebuchadnezzar and, somewhat later, Zechariah, indicates that God may use the process in a repeated way even if the dream is not the same.

Reading from Deuteronomy 13:1*ff*, there appears to have been a class of "dreamers" in the Israelitish society. They were persons who interpreted dreams for others, no doubt, and had guiding dreams for themselves. We have no record of their actual work in the Hebrew community, but persons engaged in this sort of work depend on recurrent dreams.

The sort of recurrence evidenced in Isaiah 29:8 is a repetition of ideals and not a repeat performance of the same dream. This is also true of the two dreams of Pharaoh in Genesis 41. In both cases, the repetition of the ideal is meant to show the importance of the situation and to direct the parties to proper action. It is a point for the student's observation and where a dream, in whole or in part is reemphasized, that suggests an urgency in the meaning.

3 Level Three: THE STUDY OF DREAMS

Level Three concerns itself with some ideological matters in this order:

1. What parts of the dream are symbolic or typical?
2. What is the outcome of the dream in biblical history?
3. Is there any indication the dream has been influenced or altered by occultic forces?

1. *What parts of the dream are symbolic or typical?* This will refer to objects seen in the dream that symbolize other matters. In the dream of Pharoah, the "cows" that are healthy symbolize plenty, while those that are unhealthy symbolize want. In the dream, literal realities are seen, but the actual meaning is a symbolization of the national economy of Egypt. Likewise in the dream of Nebuchadnezzar in Daniel 2:34, the "stone" is a symbol of a power that will master the other kingdoms. (The whole dream is full of symbolism, of course).

When we come to Messianic passages such as Psalm 118:22, we find that "stone" in a symbolic sense often refers to the Messiah (*cf.* Psalm 27, "my rock"). So it is not hard to see how "stone" in Daniel 2 refers to the coming of the kingdom of the Lord and His mastery over the nations. Be careful not to create symbols, however, but to discover them as they have been used by the Bible writers.

2. *What is the outcome of the dream in biblical history?* Consideration of this point will do two things: it will show the read-

er the importance of the dream, and something of the sovereignty of
God in the affairs of people. Pharaoh's dreams, as interpreted by
Joseph, will allow for better economics in Egypt and eventually pre-
pare for the fulfillment of the promise God made to Abraham in
Genesis 15:13*ff*. This knowledge is obtained through reading the text
as well as having access to a good commentary or reference Bible.

   3. *Is there any indication the dream has been influenced or
altered by occultic forces?* As a practical rule, if the dreams depart
from the truths of the Bible or tend to lead people from the Lord, it
may be concluded that some occultic power is at work. If there is no
evidence of contradictory Bible teaching, it is not likely that a
demonic influence is present. Some dreams that occur to those who
are not the people of God may show an occultic influence after the
pattern of the prophecies of Hananiah in Jeremiah 28, although this
is not a dream situation.
   The Lord has used dreams at His will with many people to show
a particular course of action. Illustrations may be seen in the life of
Laban (Gen. 31:24), Pharaoh's household servants (Gen. 41), the
refusal to give Saul guidance by a dream (1 Sam. 28), and the grant-
ing of guidance and prophetic dreams to Nebuchadnezzar in the
book of Daniel. By them God spoke to people within the family of
God, and outside of it as well.
   Today we believe our guidance will come from the Word of God.
But there is no proof that God cannot make use of dreams if it is in
His province to do so. Where the Word of God is common and available, it should serve as a guide that all can study. Where it is not
available, the grace of God may be expressed in other ways.
   From the biblical accounts, we do not learn anything about interpreting dreams—we see what God has done and do not try to pre-
tend we have miraculous powers. But if the Lord is pleased to speak
in one of the ancient ways, who can say He should not? But when a
claim is made as to what He has said or shown, it must be measured
by the Scriptures, since there are many false spirits in the world and
some are very capable of deceiving us.
   The advice in this quarter is to be guided by the Word and the
sound principles it outlines. But remember that God has omnipotence as His tool, and if this were the place to do it, many accounts

could be related with regard to moves of God in these personal ways. This is not the place for that discussion, however, although it is the place to work on the study of dreams in the Old Testament.

THE STUDY OF VISIONS

Visions and dreams obviously have much in common. But whereas a dream occurs during a period of sleep, visions often occur when one is awake (there is some overlap and some confusion with night visions, etc. but this premise is generally valid).

A vision is a graphic display intended to give direction or guidance to the subject in some matter requiring action. The vision is "seen," to to speak, and it may or may not be startling to the viewer.

The Hebrew term for "vision" being used in the text is not necessary to identify one, as the visual occurrence is the main thing.

Ezekiel's vision (ch. 1, etc.) is one of the better known Old Testament visions, as is the vision of Isaiah (ch. 6) and there are a great many others. The term is not used in the Bible as we use it today to describe one's outlook on life or perhaps ambition or far-sightedness. It applies only to a setting in which something is seen, something remarkable or something given remarkable stature at the time. A pictorial display is what captures the attention of the subject.

Visions have a good bit in common with dreams, miracles, and wonders, but they are properly in a class of their own and have enough distinct features to make them a very interesting and even necessary study. Our approach to them will follow the standard arrangement utilized for this writing.

Level One: THE STUDY OF VISIONS

The major items at the ground level in vision study are these:

1. What is portrayed in the vision?
2. To whom is it shown?
3. What is its apparent purpose?

1. *What is portrayed in the vision?* Is it a scene depicting a person, a place, an object, an action, a combination of these things, or

something utterly different? The object of the vision needs to be
carefully identified, for in this identification may be found the purpose of its being shown.

When angels are seen in the Old Testament, that is a form of
vision. When Joshua meets the captain of the Lord's host, that is a
vision. Ezekiel has a gallery of visions, some of which are not easily described in terms of our experience. This is also true in some of
the visions of Zechariah. One can know what appears in the vision
but not understand what it means. Comparative study in other
Scriptures may help, but, in general, a knowledge of the historic setting is most helpful. Nevertheless, whether one can define the meaning of the objects or not, it is important to see what the objects are
in the vision, and identify them for present and future study.

2. *To whom is the vision shown?* As with dreams, the visions are
usually personal. Both may be reported to others, but the actual
sighting of the vision is largely done to an individual. The student
identifies the individual in the expectation that the context will give
some added light to the meaning of the vision.

3. *What is the apparent purpose in the vision?* Visions normally
function as guides for some action, an explanation of a particular situation, a challenge in some area of faithfulness, or a means of reas-
suring the recipient of God's care and direction. Other purposes may
become apparent as the student reads and rereads the text in which
the vision is reported.

Understanding the purpose may help the student in identifying
some aspects or parts of the vision. A study of the Book of Ezekiel
is especially rewarding on this line as one considers the visions[13]
first given in chapter 1, and the chore that was given to Ezekiel in
the will of God.

Level Two: THE STUDY OF VISIONS

Level Two seeks to develop the ideas of Level One, and is mostly
a matter of the study of the biblical text. Commentaries and reference Bibles are again a good source of help. The items seen in this
level are these:

1. What action is necessitated by the vision?
2. How does the subject respond?
3. What symbols or symbolic actions are seen in the vision?

1. *What action is necessitated by the vision?* Largely a matter of understanding what the vision is sent to accomplish, the student should see what the subjects are told to do or to understand. Since there are many purposes that may be involved in the vision, different actions may be in view. Basically the idea is, "What should the subject do when the information in or about the vision has been passed to them?"

2. *How does the subject respond?* Discerned in the text, the student will observe that at times the subject moves heartily to whatever action is given, or sometimes needs more advice and direction; at other times the subject appears perplexed and/or indecisive. The nature of the response in its context will offer some understanding of the Lord's intention and will also help us in understanding our own call in God's service. The vision of Isaiah in Isaiah 6 is a good illustration of a clear vision, an understandable instruction, and a clear, proper response.

3. *What symbols or symbolic actions are seen in the vision?* We seek to identify these, as they may indicate a secondary meaning that is important in future service and understanding. These are not always easily understood or identified. The visions shown to the prophet in the fourth chapter of Zechariah, for example, are not plain in their meaning to the prophet. He inquires of the angel as to their meaning and is never really told! (My opinion—not all agree). It is plain they are symbols but not so plain as to what they represent.

The symbolic actions in the visions of Isaiah 6, however, are very easily understood and become teaching symbols for all of God's people, then and now.

Level Three: THE STUDY OF VISIONS

In *Level Three* we are interested in two aspects:

1. Does the vision occur more than once?
2. Does the vision deal only with the immediate, or does it have a predictive cast?

To the greater extent, these are matters that are dealt with in the Bible itself, and our greatest need in all of these studies is a keen reading of the Scripture.

1. *Does the vision occur more than once?* The vision may be recurrent in two ways: 1) that it is given repeatedly to a party; or 2) that the same—or a similar—vision is given to different people at different times. In the case of the former, Ezekiel's vision is a good example; in the case of the latter, the appearing of the Angel of the Lord is a proper example. A better understanding is given to the vision when all occurrences are viewed and the total teaching regarding them is at hand.

2. *Does the vision deal only with the immediate or does it have a predictive cast?* Daniel was told to *seal the vision* of chapter 8 (v. 26) for it was not for many days. In chapter 12, he is told to *shut the book* of his prophecy until the proper time will come for it. In such cases we realize that the vision has an immediate teaching regarding the Lord's will, but that the fulfilling of it is for a distant time. My opinion is that most visions have chiefly an almost immediate application, but many have added predictive elements as, for example, that found in Isaiah 6. There the prophet is told to give out the Word of God, but the time of the fulfillment of the vision is a long ways off.

IN CONCLUSION

A word may be said about dreams and visions together as they have much in common. They are not equally normative for all, in that they provide direction for individuals in particular settings that may never be duplicated. From them we learn the general truth of being sensitive to God's will and leading. I have known several persons who were assured that God had offered them guidance in one of these ways, although it has never been my personal experience.

One of the more notable dream-visions in Church history was that of Patrick who, in a dream, saw the people in Ireland who had formerly enslaved him; they were entreating him to return and teach them the way of life. On the strength of that experience, he did return, and gave the rest of his life to the spiritual needs of that land.

But, as noted earlier, with both of these phenomena, the careful guidance is to be found in the Word of God. It measures the truthfulness of every other experience or enlightenment.

ENDNOTES

I. PREFACE AND HISTORICAL MATERIALS

1. Page 20: BIBLIOGRAPHY (APPENDIX II). In this Appendix the attempt is made to identify helpful books on this subject. Many of them are written by theologians and linguists who do not maintain our position on inspiration, etc. Therefore the reader must evaluate carefully ideologies that are inconsistent with verbal/plenary inspiration. In any reference book one must assume the writer is giving an honest appreciation of his point of view, but it is good to know what is true of that author's viewpoint.

Mention in the BIBLIOGRAPHY does not imply endorsement of the totality of any work. There is, however, a giant amount of work available for the studies in this subject.

2. Page 25: R. Laird Harris: *Inspiration and Canonicity of the Scriptures.* Revised Edition, 1995. Greenville, SC. An enormously helpful book written with candor and directness.

3. Page 37: Excellent reading regarding the speech devices is in A. Berkeley Mickelsen: *Interpreting the Bible.* Eerdmans Publishing Company, Grand Rapids, 1963. Sections VIII, IX, and X are particularly useful at this point.

4. Page 45: Speech Figures (APPENDIX I). Brief definitions of a selected number of speech figures and devices are the subject of this Appendix.

II. OLD TESTAMENT POETRY

1. Page 48: Of particular help is C. Hassell Bullock: *An Introduction to the Old Testament Poetic Books*; Moody Press, Chicago. 1988 (revised and expanded edition). Very well written and touching on the most important subjects.

Smaller and more concise but with less directive help is D.L. Peterson and K.H. Richards: *Interpreting Hebrew Poetry.* Augsburg Fortress, Minneapolis. 1992. A number of other books are suggested in the BIBLIOGRAPHY.

2. Page 52: F.C. Jennings: *Studies in Isaiah.* New York: Loizeaux, 1935.

3. Page 52: Parallelism. My discussion is hopelessly over-simplified. It is a complex study and, while the basic ideas are understood as they are presented here, there is a wide ranger of alternate interpretations and applications. The works cited in Endnote 1 have helpful discussions. A very interesting and developed discussion is found in J.L. Kugel: *The Idea of Hebrew Poetry: Parallelism and its History:* Yale University Press: New Haven. 1981. This is a formidable book. While the discussions are very thorough, a small knowledge of Hebrew is almost necessary to follow the full presentation.

4. Page 53: Of books on Hermeneutics, Mickelsen, *op cit.*, is highly recommended.

5. Page 60: Note the books discussing the Psalms in the BIBLIOGRAPHY.

6. Page 61: Bullock: *op cit.* p. 120

7. Page 62: J. W. Thirtle: *The Titles of the Psalms:* Froude, New York. 1904. The ground-breaking work in this area. Thirtle wrote other books on Hebrew poetry as well. The general suggestion is that many of the song titles or superscriptions really belong to the preceding psalm and not the following. One must remember that in the ancient manuscripts there were neither verse nor chapter divisions and texts often run together. I have not been convinced of Thirtle's idea, but it is one that must be considered in the study of the song titles or introductory statements. These titles are sufficiently old to be witnessed in the Psalm texts taken from Qumran.

8. Page 62: Isaiah 38:5-8. The Psalms of Degrees are variously interpreted. The term "degrees" (KJV) is derived from the Hebrew

verb meaning "to go up" and has the derivative meaning of steps or stairs. Many scholars suggest that these psalms were sung as the people of God returned from Babylon, stage by stage. More popular is the concept that they reflected the steps taken by God in Hezekiah's recovery. I prefer the first view but it is not something over which we need feel aggressive.

9. Page 66: For Ellipsis, see APPENDIX I, Group 1

10. Page 69: *The Companion Bible* was a work of Ethelbert Bullinger. Bullinger's theological posturing resulted in later editions of the Bible without his name! The current work is published by Zondervan, Grand Rapids. It is a source book of an enormous amount of material and textual data. Bullinger's chronology is no longer accepted, but the text data and linguistic helps in *The Companion Bible* make it a very valuable tool.

11. Page 76: See APPENDIX I, Group 3 for discussion of the collocation.

12. Page 78: Information on this material may be had from J.B. Pritchard: *Ancient Near Eastern Texts Relating to the Scriptures.* Princeton University Press, Princeton. 1969 (revised and updated). This is a primary source; others are listed in the BIBLIOGRAPHY.

13. Page 79: The "fool" in Psalm 14:1 is the Hebrew word *nabal* and suggest moral insensibility. The term in Proverbs 26 is *casil*, suggesting a dullard who makes poor decisions or reacts with weak judgment, or of his casual or uncaring sort of life rather than out of any academic loss.

14. Page 83: See APPENDIX III for a discussion of Job's wife and her retort as it is seen in the Septuagint, the Greek translation of the Old Testament.

15. Page 85: *The Companion Bible, op cit.* APPENDIX 33. The changes introduced by the "Sopherim" were thought to protect the name or character of God. Our knowledge of this work is not total, but it is obvious in the Job passage that no one gets the wrath of God for "blessing" Him.

16. Page 86: The BIBLIOGRAPHY contains titles and resource materials on the Wisdom books.

17. Page 91: The mergers of culture in antiquity were apparently greater than was earlier believed. Grecian coins have been found in the Persian period before the later conquests, and it seems unlikely

that the ethnic ties of any of the groups was so strong as to inhibit the interchange of cultural ideas.

18. Page 92: Pritchard, *op cit. et al.*

19. Page 94: See APPENDIX II for literature on the Song of Solomon, *et al.*

20. Page 96: H.A. Ironside: *Addresses on the Song of Solomon.* New York: Loizeaux, n.d.

21. Page 101: See 2 Chronicles 36 and Jeremiah 39.

III. OLD TESTAMENT PROPHECY

1. Page 103: Daniel's place in the Canon is a point of discussion. Scholars who do not hold a verbal/plenary inspiration view of the Scriptures are prone to indicate Daniel's place in the Canon shows that the book was written late and is not genuine. This view is refuted in Harris: *Inspiration and Canonicity, et al.* It is thought that the historical character of Daniel caused the placing of this book in the Sacred Writings. Some evangelical scholars believe Daniel, although a prophet, did not hold the "office" of a prophet and consequently his work was placed in the historical section. Better information on this view may be seen in E. J. Young: *The Prophecy of Daniel.* Eerdmans; Grand Rapids. 1949, and in his companion work, *My Servants the Prophets.* Eerdmans: Grand Rapids. 1952. In our studies the concept of a prophetic office is defined by what one does and not how one is officially recognized. Anyone who prophecies is a prophet and there seems to be no state recognition of that function.

2. Page 106: Isaiah 7. This passage exhibits a fine demonstration of the perspective of prediction and the use of early predictions to give validity to later ones. In the meeting with Ahaz and Isaiah, the first prophecy (v. 7) is to the effect that the plot of the kings of Israel and Syria against Ahaz will not succeed. This is a prophecy to be fulfilled in a very short time. Verse 8 notes that within 65 years Ephraim will not be a recognized country and eventually God will come to dwell with His people (v. 14) in a very distinctive way. The fulfillment of the first two "shorter term" prophecies constitutes the evidence that the third part will come to pass as well, but it is more futuristic.

3. Page 107: As in Note 1, it is maintained in out study that the

prophet is such when declaring the intention and will of God. Otherwise that person is just another person, although it cannot be denied that one would gain a reputation for prophesying, and in that sense might be thought of publicly as a "prophet."

4. Page 110: Isaiah 11:9, as understood by literalists, indicates a time of universal peace and blessing. The designations "holy mountain" and "earth" are thought to be synthetic so that the picture is one of peace throughout the world—not one of peace in Zion while the rest of the world fights. That it is a picture of the church is difficult unless it is only referring to the saints who have gone to heaven. The saints who remain on the earth are often at war (even with one another!).

5. Page 114: A quick chart outlining the reigns of the kings of Judah and Israel as well as the periods of prophetic activity is found in Samuel J. Schultz: *The Old Testament Speaks.* Harper: New York. 1960. p. 154.

6. Page 122: The Israelite/Assyrian relationship is summarized in Schulz: *ibid:* p. 154 and Chapter IX.

7. Page 124: Data on Hebrew self-help courses is to be found in APPENDIX III.

8. Page 125: This is a remarkable prophecy. The "goings forth" term is difficult in translation, but should not be understood in the sense of "origin," meaning that the coming king began at some point. If "origin" is understood to mean the beginning of a ministry or career, it would be thought acceptable. But the idea is something like a little boy with a screen door—he was always coming in and going out, perpetually active in the universe.

9. Page 128: Distinctions in this magnitude are necessary. The same is true of the church as a body politic. We are reminded in Timothy that the Lord knows His own; that is enough reassurance for us. But there is a world of difference between the Israel of God and the Israel of the world.

10. Page 131: It is apparent that the promises of judgment are as much a part of the covenantal relationship as the promises of blessing.

11. Page 136: All of the "kingdom" views have responsible advocates. All have problems in varied sorts and none of those mentioned in this work should be thought of as "heresy" or "false doctrine."

Diversities of understanding by persons committed to the truth of the Bible grow from our particular dispositions. Polemics is the academic science that deals with these things, and this work is not intended to be polemical, although the author is certainly welcome to state his opinion.

12. Page 159: Nineveh. The history of this Assyrian capitol is fascinating. Useful summary material may be had in Howard Vos: *Archaeology in Bible Lands.* Moody Bible Institute Press: Chicago. 1977. pp. 102-104, 118-120. Most Bible dictionaries also give excellent coverage. An enormously important city, it was virtually lost to history for more than 2,000 years.

V. STUDYING OBJECTS OR SUBJECTS

1. Page 162: Romeo and Juliet were worried about their family names.

2. Page 166: Biographical study of persons in the Bible is rewarding in seeing how they served God and how they failed God. The persons in the Bible become both models and phantoms for us, and we must remember the truth of Romans 15:4, "these things are written" that we might be better servants.

3. Page 167: See Jeremiah 35:2*ff* and 1 Kings 10:15.

4. Page 175: Zechariah 4 gives us three instances of this particular matter (vv. 5, 11, 12). The latter have caused interpreters considerable anguish ever since.

5. Page 180: *cf.* Exodus 25*ff.* Note the New Testament reference to the Tabernacle in Hebrews 9:1*ff.*

6. Page 181: Compare the ideology 2 Chronicles 24:1-14 with Exodus 36:6-7. Keep both accounts in proper context and one has a good idea of what the people can do in the work of God if they are "willing."

7. Page 199: The great theme of the Bible is redemption. From Genesis to Revelation it dominates the narratives. Different aspects within the theme are seen, and they may develop into further themes. The developed theme of Exodus, for example, is "God's deliverance" and the resultant dealings with God and His people will establish many sub-themes. But whether sub- or major, all themes may be treated in the same manner.

8. Page 205: The history of doctrines is a fascinating study. Historical theology has many insights to benefit us today. A good beginning is Louis Berkhof: *History of Doctrines.* Eerdmans: Grand Rapids.

9. Page 208: The student should be guarded against the temptation to explain miracles. That is not to say we cannot study the subject. But critical explanations as to how and why and what may be involved in the miracle usually result in the virtual denial of the miracle. Explaining that Jesus walking on the water was an example of poor perception and He was really standing on the shore at the edge of the water is a rationalization that destroys the character of the Scripture. This is only one example of how miracle explaining becomes a liability to the faith.

10. Page 216: From a practical point of view, we may treat them as virtually synonymous. The particular words may be found in a major concordance (See BIBLIOGRAPHY).

11. Page 219: The sign to Noah is found in Genesis 9:13. The sign also occurs in Ezekiel and Revelation. The sign is a spectacular display of colors and a reminder of God's promise with regard to mankind.

12. Page 220: Three major things are involved in the prophetic test: 1) it must come to pass (be true, that is); 2) is must lead to the Lord and not away from Him; and 3) it must agree with the known will of God as given.

13. Page 230: The student will note that the great vision occurs before the major trials that will take up the life of the prophet (Ezek. 10:1, *e.g.*).

VI
SUPPLEMENTARY MATERIALS

Appendix I
SPEECH FIGURES & LITERARY DEVICES

AN EXPLANATORY NOTE

Speech figures are literary tools that enable more graphic language to be employed in the description of almost anything. The speech figures represent a picture in words intended to enhance the subject. There are many, many of them. Ethelbert Bullinger (see BIBLIOGRAPHY) produced the most exhaustive work on speech figures. His work is a massive tome that could hardly be mastered by anyone outside of a very committed literary elite. But some speech figures are very common and are used daily in discourse—generally without the user knowing what had been done.

In the Introduction to his work, Bullinger urged the reader to treat language literally until something in it seemed overly demonstrative or psychologically demanding. Then one should suspect a speech figure. The Bible abounds in the use of figures, but when one studies it, the thrust should be on its teaching, not on its form. The speech figures, however, are often critical in determining the teaching. That is why they are stressed in almost all literature courses.

For this work the speech tools are divided into three groups. The first group is identified with the term "normative," meaning these speech figures are very common. A second group is called "exceptional," indicating that they are seen less but are still important. A third group gathers the "devices" that color a shade of meaning but are less explicit than the figures. What is presented is adequate to enrich our study.

In all three groups the treatment follows alphabetical order and illustrations are offered with the definitions. It is hoped the reader will be advanced in the understanding of language and, if nothing else, will add some interesting terms to one's vocabulary. The words identifying the speech figures are mostly derived from Greek compounds (a little Latin sneaks in at times). Further definition can be found for these in the *Oxford Dictionary of the English Language.*

GROUP ONE: Normative Speech Figures

1. **APOSTROPHE**: words addressed to a party aside or a representative of the cause. For example, 2 Samuel 1:21, "Ye mountains of Gilboa." *Apostrophe* may be combined with *Personification* (Item 8). The mountains are addressed as side witnesses and the assumption is that they can hear!

2. **ELLIPSIS**: a concept or an action is not fully stated; the reader must supply a term to complete the thought. In the King James Version, *Ellipsis* is usually shown by words in italics. And 2 Samuel 1:21 also supplies an illustration. The text reads, "neither *let there be* dew, neither *let there be* rain upon you." The italicized words are brought into the text to make the thought more complete and to give it a more organized place in the message.

3. **EUPHEMISM**: a word substitution in which a "softer" term is used in place of a "harder" term. "Death" is called "sleep" in 1 Corinthians 15:51. Our definition is minimal as there are several forms of euphemistic speech.

4. **HYPERBOLE**: a calculated over-statement reflecting a situation in which the literal concept cannot be known (as a rule). See 1 Samuel 13:5, "and people as the sand which is on the sea shore in multitude." *Hyperbole* is seen in the count of the people who accompanied the horsemen and the army. It is combined in this passage with *Simile* (Item 9).

5. **LITOTES** (also known as *Meiosis*): a calculated minimizing understatement in which the comparison is intended to diminish one party while elevating the other. An example may be seen in 1 Samuel 24:14, "After whom is the king of Israel come out? after whom dost thou pursue? after a dead dog? after a flea?" David diminishes his own importance—a dog, a flea—while elevating Saul, calling him the king of Israel.

6. **METAPHOR**: an implied comparison—not definitely stated but obvious. Hosea 7:8 provides an example when the Lord speaks of Ephraim as a "cake not turned."

7. **METONYMY**: basically the change of a name or a name substitution. There is an example in the Hosea passage (Item 6) where the name "Ephraim" is used for all of the kingdom of Israel (the northern kingdom). There are several varieties of *Metonomies*; it is one of the most common speech figures.

8. **PERSONIFICATION**: the attribution of life realities to non-living objects. A clear example is seen in 1 Kings 13:2 where the prophet of God addresses the altar of Jeroboam and says: "Altar, Altar, thus saith the Lord..." The message is then given as if to the altar, but the king and the attendants know for whom it is intended.

9. **SIMILE**: a stated comparison usually having the terms "like" or "as" to indicate the comparative nature. Note Psalm 1:3, 4. *Similies* and *Metaphors* differ chiefly in the explicit designation of the comparison points. The simile is exact while the metaphor is suggestive. Parables are extended *Similies* while the allegories are developed *Metaphors*.

10. **SYNECHDOCHE**: a figure that uses the part to speak for the whole. This speech figure covers a lot of ground and has varied attachments. Note James 1:27 as it speaks of pure religion and undefiled as "visiting the fatherless and the widows in their affliction" and this phrase represents all who are helpless. Thus the part mentioned is suggestive of the whole. It does not mean one could be cruel to the lame and the blind!

These ten figures are the most common as well as the most easily recognized. For that reason I have labeled them normative.

GROUP TWO: Exceptional Speech Figures

As indicated earlier, these speech figures are no less important but may be seen less frequently. The terminology is one of convenience and the following figures are also treated in alphabetical order. Some of these are identifiable chiefly in the Hebrew text and are marked with an asterisk* and the abbreviation (Heb).

1. **ANACRUSIS**: a word outside the metre at the beginning of a line or sentence. One may be seen in Lamentations 1:1 with the word "How!"* (Heb.).

2. **ANADIPLOSIS**: repetition of words at the end of one sentence and the beginning of another. Note Genesis 1:1-2, "God created the heaven and the earth…And the earth…" The continuation of the narrative is assured in this way rather than running the risk of a new thought being introduced. See also Psalm 121:1-2 (English Bible) "…from whence cometh my help? My help cometh from the Lord." While seeing this text, note the *Ellipsis*.

3. **ANABASIS**: a writing that shows a progression of thought by adding steps to a proposition or foundation. Psalm 24:3-5 offers a good example:

> Who shall ascend into the hill of the Lord? or who shall stand in His holy place?
> He that hath clean hands
> > And a pure heart
> Who hath not lifted up his soul to vanity
> > Nor sworn deceitfully
> He shall receive the blessing.

4. **ANAPHORA**: the repetition of a word or words at the beginning of successive clauses. Note Deuteronomy 28:3-6 for the word "blessed" and compare with 28:16-19 for "cursed."

5. **ANTHROPAPATHEIA** (wow!): human passions or faculties attributed to the Lord. There are many of these. Try Psalm 2:4, "he shall laugh" and verse 7, "this day have I begotten thee." A note of practical advice: most people do not even think about this sort of thing. If one is in a Bible study with a few serious-minded Bible students, it would be proper to point out this sort of speech figure. If one is teaching a class or preaching a sermon and suddenly bursts out with "this verse features an *anthropapatheia*," the speaker knows too much and is being pedantic.

6. **APOSIAPESIS**: a sudden halt or cessation in a discourse in which the speaker seems reluctant to complete the thought. Exodus 32:32 in the King James Version has Moses saying, "Yet now, if thou wilt not forgive their sin—; and if not,…" There is no special word in the Hebrew text but the nature of Moses' prayer demands such a

break: "If you will—and if you will not…"

7. **ASTERISMOS**: a speech figure for a "marking" word such as "Behold" that calls special attention to a point. See Psalm 51:5. There are many occurrences. Some are readily seen in the English Bible, some more apparent in the Hebrew.

8. **CYCLOIDES**: a phrase or sentence repeated at spaced intervals. Psalm 136 is the classic example: "His mercy endureth forever." See also 2 Samuel 1:19, 25, 27.

9. **EPIZEUXIS**: duplication or repetition of a word for emphasis as in Isaiah 6:3 "Holy, holy, holy." It is of some interest to note that in the Isaiah manuscript from Qumran, the term "holy" occurs twice, while in the Masoretic text (used in most of the English translations) the critical mark *paseq* is placed after the first "holy" and, in effect, says "don't miss this one."

10. **EPLANADIPLOSIS**: the repetition of the same word or words at the beginning and ending of a sentence. Ecclesiastes 1:2 states, "Vanity of vanities, saith the Preacher, vanity of vanities, all is vanity."

11. **EROTESIS**: the asking of questions without waiting (or perhaps expecting) an answer. There are several classes in this general grouping, including the rhetorical question. Psalm 79:5 asks, "How long, Lord? Wilt thou be angry forever?" This particular speech figure is very common in the ministry of the Lord Jesus—some say it is the most common speech figure used by Him.

12. **HYPOCATASTASIS**: an implied resemblance or representation. In Psalm 69:1 we read, "Save me, O God, for the waters are come in unto my soul." The resemblance of his spiritual difficulty is likened to one who is drowning. This is very common.

13. **PARANOMASIA**: indicates words that sound alike but are different in origin and meaning. See Deuteronomy 32:18* (Heb.).

14. **PERIPHRASIS**: is the concept of talking around something without actually naming it. In classical form, the expression "the face that launched a thousand ships" identified Helen of Troy whether she was named or not! Psalm 50:20 offers an illustration: "thou sittest and speakest against thy brother, thou slanderests thine own mother's son." No one is named, but anyone might know who was intended.

15. **PLEONASM**: the use of more words than needed, as in Psalm

89:30-31 in which the thoughts of the verses are synonymous and the judgment could rest with verse 30 by itself. Verse 31 adds nothing to the charge but reiterates the general state.

16. **POLYSYNDETON**: the repetition of conjunctions in close succession as may be seen in Psalm 80:2, with the conjunction "and" being used three times in close succession although not grammatically required. The opposite of this term is *asyndeton,* meaning a lack of conjunctions. You may want to supply some.

17. **METALEPSIS**: is a double *metonymy,* and an example may be seen in Proverbs 1:ll, "lay wait for blood, lurk privily for the innocent" is the suggestion of the wicked. They will kill someone for gain, and the two expressions say the same thing in a rather concealed way.

18. **TAPEINOSIS**: a lessening in a proposition in order to increase a point. See Genesis 27:44 where Rebecca's advice to Jacob is to go to Haran and stay there for a "few days" which in actuality will be several years. The speech figure allows one to imagine a short time rather than considering how long it will actually be.

19. **PROSOPOPOEIA**: a form of *personification* in which things not human (on the whole) are represented as human beings. There are plenty of them in the Scripture and typical of the lot is Psalm 35:10, "All my bones shall say..." There are several other things that are represented as human including animals, places, etc.

20. **HENDIADYS**: a sufficiently complicated speech figure in which 1) an idea is expressed by two nouns connected by "and" in which one noun modifies the other; and 2) two nouns or two verbs are joined by "and" but with one meaning. Genesis 1:26 is helpful and the terms "image" and "likeness" are the key words. It is pointless to distinguish between them but to see rather that they indicate the one true God who is the Creator.

We are indebted to Bullinger's study of speech figures which is vastly longer and more complicated than this short list. The student should not lose sleep over them in trying to remember them all, but should watch for places in the text where it is enhanced by colorful or descriptive language. This is true generally in the whole of the Old Testament, especially in the Poetic works.

GROUP THREE: Literary Devices

The naming of literary devices is an artificial designation, but one that tends to allow a distinction between classes of literature and the speech figures that generally depict something in short form. The devices discussed below are those which are most commonly met and so are the most valuable to the student.

1. **ACROSTIC**: a device whereby things are presented in some alphabetical order of which Psalm 119 is the great example.

2. **ALLITERATION**: a series of words beginning with the same letter. This is seen rarely in English, but is more common in Hebrew, and it is sometimes hard to tell if it is intentional or accidental. It is a favorite tool of some preachers, however.

3. **ALLEGORY**: an extended *metaphor* in which the comparisons are implied. The *metaphor* is a brief comparison while on the whole the *allegory* is drawn out somewhat. There are many *allegories* in the Old Testament. One of the better recognized one is the poem of old age in Ecclesiastes 12. A number are found in Ezekiel among other places.

4. **ASSONANCE**: the rhyming of words in which two words sound alike, although the meanings may be very different. This is less important in our English Bibles but frequently occurs in the Hebrew text. In English think of words such as "wurst" and "worst" as well as "warship" and "worship."

5. **CHIASMOS** (Chiastic Structure): The device is a variety of introversion in which the items are arranged in an order described as ABBA. The first and fourth lines harmonize while the second and third harmonize. It is illustrated in modern speech when we say things such as this:

> (A) I told you not to do it
> (B) But you did it anyway
> (B) You did it just the same,
> (A) Although I told you not to do it.

The Chiastic structure may be much longer—six lines, even chapters or books, as the writer desires, but the lines will match one another in a similar pattern: A, B, C—C, B, A. Probably the best known biblical *Chiasm* is Matthew 7:6.

> (A) Give not that which is holy unto dogs
>> (B) Neither cast ye your pearls before swine
>> (C) Lest they trample them under their feet
> (A) And turn again and rend you.

The device will be seen in the Psalms and the prophetic literature but is not always easily discerned. Bullinger notes a chiastic structure in Psalm 23 based on the occurrence of the pronouns. Verse 1-3 use the first and third pronoun (the A line), while verse 4 uses the first and second pronoun, as does verse 5 (the B lines) while 6 returns to the first and third person (the second A line). The development of intimacy based on the observation of the Lord's shepherding work is the point of the structure. The term is taken from the Greek letter CHI, an "x" figure showing the crossing of ideas.

5. **CLIMAX**: when there is a repetition of words in the manner of *anadiplosis*. The phrases as repeated build to a given end. An illustration is found in Joel 1:3-4. In verse 3, "children" is the repetitive word while in verse 4 the concept of "eaten" dominates the teaching.

6. **COLLOCATION**: numerical extensions which indicate an ongoing scenario without an increase in intensity. The collocation of Proverbs 6:16-19 is a popular example as the Lord tells the things He hates. Exodus 20:5 should also be noted.

7. **ENIGMA**: a perplexing piece of information that defies immediate understanding, although there may be clues as to its meaning in contextual places. Zechariah 4 offers illustrative material in the illustration of the lampstand, the questions posed by Zechariah to his informer, and the vague responses of the latter.

8. **FABLE**: The Bible is not a book of fables, but a fable is a fabricated story to conceal or reveal some point of truth. The account in Judges 7 with the teaching lesson of Jotham is close to a pure fable. In modern literature, scholars who do not approve the inspiration of the Bible "find" many fables. It is unfortunate that unbelief can take so much of the time of incredulous persons.

9. **INTERROGATION**: a form of question in which one seeks information, unlike *erotesis* (see Group 2, Item 11). This form expects an answer as the Lord spoke to Moses in Exodus 4:3 and said: "What is that in thine hand?" And Moses said: "A rod."

10. **IRONY**: a form of speech in which what is said is not what is meant and, in fact, is often the opposite. Amos 4:4-5 finds the prophet inviting Israel to further its sins, for that is what it likes to do. The invitation is ironic; it is exactly the opposite of what the prophet wants done! The Lord often speaks in Scripture with irony. In my mind it is a first cousin to *sarcasm*.

11. **MYSTERY**: the concept is that of presenting a situation or fact that is hard to understand or the meaning of which is not clear. The New Testament often speaks of *Mysteries* while the Old Testament mentions things that are not at the time explained but are left for the future or a distant context. Ezekiel 28:11 with the verses following presents such a *mystery*.

12. **PARABLE**: an extended *Simile*, a stated comparison of entities. The parables of the Lord are most familiar, but there are similar stories in the Old Testament in the general pattern of the *parable*. Nathan put one before David in the Bathsheba affair. The key to understanding the *Parable* is to determine what point it is making, and allow everything else to be secondary to that point.

13. **RIDDLE**: a construction intended to make one think through a point of logic and come to a conclusion. There is some confusion in the Old Testament between *Riddle* and *Enigma,* but in this work riddle is limited to things that are defined in that way (as with Samson in Judges 14).

There are, of course other literary devices and formulae, but for our study of the Bible, it is thought that these are adequate. The student is called upon, when going to the examination of Scripture, to see every word—and to see its relationship with other words. There are times when one may have a general sense of a passage, but not have the detailed information it offers. This is due to the fact that the student "sweeps" the passage and does not look at it for detail.

One should not feel defeated if one cannot remember all the figures discussed in this work, but should remain aware of the fact that language is to portray truth to us and it does so in many diversified and fascinating ways.

Appendix II
BIBLIOGRAPHIC MATERIALS

The bibliographic materials are arranged in categories, and are selected for their particular value to this work. Of the making of books there is no end, as Solomon put it in Ecclesiastes 12, and in this APPENDIX there is no attempt to be exhaustive. Each of the areas in which some mention has been made will have a much greater amount of literature than will be mentioned in this work. But the items mentioned have seemed to be especially helpful and foundational to a good supply of reference materials. The categories deal especially with Old Testament works, and are as follow:

1. Old Testament Archaeology
2. Old Testament History and Survey
3. Old Testament Introduction
4. Old Testament Parallels in Ancient Literature
5. Old Testament Poetry
6. Old Testament Prophecy
7. Bible Handbooks
8. Study Bibles, Bible Dictionaries, Concordances, etc.
9. Hermeneutics
10. Selected Special Studies
11. Commentaries

1. Old Testament Archaeology

DeVaux, R. *Ancient Israel: Its Life and Institutions.* London: Darton, Longman and Todd, 1961.

Finegan, Jack. *Light from the Ancient Past.* 2nd Edition, Princeton: Princeton U. Press, 1959.

Gordon, C. *The World of the Old Testament.* Garden City, NY 1958.

Kenyon, Frederick. *Our Bible and the Ancient Manuscripts.* 4th Edition, New York: Harper, 1958.

MacRae, A.A. *Biblical Archaeology.* Marshallton, Delaware: National Foundation for Christian Education, 1967.

Mazar, Amihai. *Archaeology of the Land of the Bible: 10,000-586 BC.* New York: Doubleday, 1990.

Millard, Alan. *Treasures from Bible Times.* Belleville: Lion Publishing Co. 1985.

Shanks, Herschel, ed. *Ancient Israel* (revised edition). Washington, DC. Biblical Archaeological Society, 1999.

Vos, Howard. *Archaeology in Bible Lands.* Chicago: Moody Press, 1977.

2. Old Testament History and Survey

Hill, A.E. and Walton, J.H. *A Survey of the Old Testament.* Grand Rapids: Eerdmans, 1991.

Jensen, Irving. *Survey of the Old Testament.* Chicago: Moody Press, 1977.

Schultz, Samuel. *The Old Testament Speaks.* New York: Harper, 1960.

3. Old Testament Introduction

Archer, G.L. *A Survey of Old Testament Introduction.* (revised edition) Chicago: Moody Press, 1985.

Ginsburgh, C.D. *Introduction to the Massoretico-Criticaln Edition of the Hebrew Bible* (reprint). New York: KTAV 1966.

Dillard, R.B. and Longman, T. *An Introduction to the Old Testament.* Grand Rapids: Zondervan, 1994.

Harrison, R.K. *Introduction to the Old Testament.* Grand Rapids: Eerdmans, 1969.

Unger, M.T. *An Introductory Guide to the Old Testament.* Grand Rapids: Zondervan,1951.

Young, E.J. *Introduction to the Old Testament.* Grand Rapids: Eerdmans, 1964.

4. Old Testament Parallels in Ancient Literature

Kitchen, K.A. *Ancient Orient and the Old Testament.* Chicago: Inter-Varsity Press, 1966.

Matthews, V. and Benjamin, Don C. *Old Testament Parallels.* New York: Paulist Press: 1991.

Pritchard, J.B. *Ancient Near Eastern Texts.* Princeton: Princeton University Press, 1955.

_____ *The Ancient Near East: Supplement Text and Pictures Relating to the Old Testament.* Princeton: Princeton U. 1969.

Thomas, D. Winton. *Documents from Old Testament Times.* New York: Harper, 1961.

5. Old Testament Poetry

Bruce, F.F. *The Poetry of the Old Testament.* In the New Bible Dictionary. Grand Rapids: Eerdmans, 1956.

Bullock, C. Hassell. *An Introduction to the Old Testament Poetic Books.* Chicago: Moody Press, 1988.

Fisch, H. *Poetry with a Purpose.* Bloomington, IN: Indiana University Press, 1990.

Kugel, J. *The Idea of Biblical Poetry.* New Haven. Yale University Press, 1981.

OConnor, M. *Hebrew Verse Studies.* Winona Lake: Eisenbrauns, 1980.

Peterson, D.L and Richards, K.H. *Interpreting Hebrew Poetry.* Minneapolis: Fortress Press, 1992.

6. Old Testament Prophecy

Bullock, C. Hassell. *An Introduction to the Old Testament Prophetic Books.* Chicago: Moody Press, 1986.

Culver, R.D. *Daniel and the Latter Days.* Chicago: Moody Press, 1954.

Heschel, A. *The Prophets.* New York: Harper Collins, 1955.

Kirkpatrick, A.F. *The Doctrine of the Prophets* (reprint). Grand Rapids: Zondervan, 1958.

MacRae, A.A. *The Gospel of Isaiah.* Chicago: Moody Press, 1977.

Newman, R.C. *The Evidence of Prophecy.* Hatfield, PA.: IBRI 1982.

Randolph, W.J. *Help for Understanding Bible Prophecy.* Dresher, PA: Shiloh Publications, 1989.

Walvoord, J.F. *Prophecy Knowledge Handbook.* Wheaton: Scripture Press (Victor Books), 1990.

Young, E.J. *My Servants, the Prophets.* Grand Rapuds: Eerdmans, 1952.

_____ *The Prophecy of Daniel.* Grand Rapids: Eerdmans, 1949.

7. Bible Handbooks

Alexander, D. *Eerdman's Handbook to the Bible.* Grand Rapids: Eerdmans, 1974.

Halley, H.H. *Bible Handbook.* Grand Raids: Zondervan, 1957.

Smith, C. *The Everyday Guide to the Bible.* Uhrichsville, Ohio: Humble Creek, 2002.

Taylor, Mark. *The Complete Book of Bible Literacy.* Wheaton: Tyndale, 1992.

8. Study Bibles, Bible Dictionaries, Concordances, etc.

Bullinger, E.W. *The Companion Bible.* (reprint) Grand Rapids: Zondervan, n.d.

Douglas, J.D., ed. *New International Dictionary of the Bible,* Revised edition. Grand Rapids: Zondervan, 1987.

Elwell, W.A. *Baker Encyclopaedia of the Bible.* Grand Rapids: Baker Book House, 1988.

Freedman, D.N., ed. *Eerdman's Dictionary of the Bible.* Grand Rapids: Eerdmans, 2000.

Grollenberg, L.H. *Atlas of the Bible.* New York: Nelson, 1956.

_____(editor) *The Anchor Bible Dictionary.* New York: Doubleday, 1992.

Harris, R.L. , G. Archer, and B. Waltke. *Theological Wordbook of the Old Testament.* Chicago: Moody, 1980.

Lindsell, H., ed. *The Harper Study Bible.* New York: Harper and Row, 1964.

Ryrie, C.C. *The Ryrie Study Bible.* Chicago: Moody Press, 1978.

Scofield, C.I. *The New Scofield Reference Bible:* Ed: E. Schuyler English. New York: Oxford Press. 1967.

Strong, J. *The Exhaustive Concordance to the Bible.* New York: Abingdon, 1890.

Tenney, M. *The Zondervan Pictorial Bible Dictionary.* Grand Rapids: Zondervan 1967.

Wood, D.W. *The New Bible Dictionary: 3rd edition.* Downers Grove, IL: InterVarsity Press. 1996.

Young, R. *Analytical Concordance to the Bible.* Grand Rapids: Eerdmans, n.d.

(*Author's Note:* The concordances listed are for the KJV Bible but there are concordances available for all of the modern translations. There are also several other Atlas productions, including Rand McNally and Westminster.)

9. Hermeneutics

Barr, J. *The Semantics of Biblical Language.* London: Oxford University Press, 1961.

Berkhof, L. *Principles of Biblical Interpretation.* Grand Rapids, Baker Book House, 1950.

Ellis, E. *Paul's Use of the Old Testament.* Grand Rapids: Eerdmans, 1957.

Farrar, F.W. *History of Interpretation.* New York: E.P.Dutton, 1886.

Mickelsen, A.B. *Interpreting the Bible.* Grand Rapids, Eerdmans, 1963.

Minear, P.S. *Eyes of Faith.* London: Lutterworth Press, 1948.

Ramm, B. *Protestant Biblical Interpretation* (Revised edition) Boston: W.A. Wilde Co., 1956.

Stuart, D. *Old Testament Exegesis.* Philadelphia: Westminster Press, 1984.

Terrey, M.S. *Biblical Hermeneutics.* Grand Rapids: Zondervan, n.d.

Young, E.J. *Thy Word is Truth.* Grand Rapids: Eerdmans, 1957.

10. Selected Specialties

Archer, G.L. *Encyclopaedia of Bible Difficulties.* Grand Rapids. Zondervan. 1982.

Baron, D. *Types, Psalms and Prophecies in the Old Testament.* London: Hodder & Stoughton, 1907. reprint: Minneapolis: Klock and Klock, 1981.

Brotzman, E.P. *Old Testament Textual Criticism.* Grand Rapids: Baker Book House, 1994.

Crockett, W.D. *A Harmony of the Books of Samuel, Kings, and Chronicles.* Grand Rapids: Baker Book House, 1954.

Fairbairn, P. *The Typology of Scripture.* Grand Rapids, Zondervan, n.d.

Freeman, J.M. *Manners and Customs of the Bible.* Plainfield, NJ: Logos, 1973.

Haley, J.W. *Alleged Discrepancies of the Bible* (reprint) Grand Rapids: Baker Book House, 1874.

Harris, R.L. *Inspiration and Canonicity of the Bible.* Grand Rapids, Zondervan, 1984.

Hengstenberg, E.H. *Christology of the Old Testament.* (reprint) Grand Rapids: Kregel, 1970.

Murphy, R.E. *The Tree of Life.* New York: Doubleday, 1990.

Payne, J.B. *The Theology of the Older Testament.* Grand Rapids, Zondervan, 1952.

Pfeiffer, C., ed. *Baker's Bible Atlas.* Grand Rapids: Baker Book House, 1961.

Sailhammer, J.H. *Introduction to Old Testament Theology.* Grand Rapids: Zondervan, 1995.

Thiele, E. *The Mysterious Numbers of the Hebrew Kings.* Grand Rapids: Eerdmans, 1965.

Torrey, R.A. *Difficulties and Alleged Errors and Contradictions in the Bible.* New York: Revell, 1907.

Wilson, R.D. *A Scientific Investigation of the Old Testament.* (revised edition) Chicago: Moody Press, 1959.

Wurthwein, Ernst. *The Text of the Old Testament.* (Translated by Peter Ackroyd) Oxford: Blackwell, 1957.

11. Commentaries

The commentary material is voluminous. This Bibliography is shortened in this category by giving some general references and a few specific commentaries for individual portions.The commentaries are in three groupings: 1) Series commentaries on the Old Testament; 2) Single volume commentaries on the Old Testament; and 3) Particular commentaries on the Old Testament books arranged in the order of the Old Testament divisions. Commentaries found in sets are not double-listed. All commentaries are subject to meaningful scrutiny—the final word is the Scripture.

Series Commentaries on the Old Testament

(Many authors may contribute in the series commentaries; this list identifies only the editor of the series.)

Albright, W.F. and D.N. Freedman. *The Anchor Bible.* Garden City, New York: Doubleday, 1964.

Barnes, A. *Bible Commentaries on the Old Testament.* reprint, Grand Rapids: Baker Book House, 1957.

Baxter, J.S. *Explore the Book.* Grand Rapids: Zondervan, 1960.

Clement, R.E. and M. Black. *New Century Bible Commentary.* Grand Rapids: Eerdmans, 1982.

Clenderen, E. Ray, ed. *The New American Commentary.* Nashville: Broadman and Holman. 1999.

Gaebelein, F.E. *The Expositor's Bible Commentary.* Grand Rapids: Zondervan, 1992.

Harrison: R.K. *New International Commentaries on the Old Testament.* Grand Rapids: Eerdmans, 1969.

Hubbard, D.A. and G.W. Barker. *The Word Bible Commentary.* Waco, TX: Word Books, 1987.

Wiseman, D.J. *Tyndale Old Testament Commentaries.* Chicago: InterVarsity, 1968.

(*Author's Note:* The older commentary series such as Lange, Keil and Delitzsch, etc., are very worthwhile but require some understanding of the original languages for maximum usefulness.)

Single Volume Commentaries on the whole Old Testament

Barker, K., ed. *Wycliffe Exegetical Commentary.* Chicago: Moody Press, 1990.

Church, L.F., ed. *Matthew Henry's Commentary in One Volume.* Grand Rapids: Zondervan, 1961.

MacDonald, W. *Believer's Bible Commentary: Old Testament.* Nashville: Nelson, 1990.

Pfeiffer, C.E. and E.F. Harrison. *Wycliffe Bible Commentary.* Chicago: Moody, 1962.

Walvoord, J.F. and R.B. Zuck. *The Bible Knowledge Commentary.* Wheaton: Scripture Press, 1985.

Particular Commentaries on Old Testament Books

THE PENTATEUCH

Allis, O.T. *The Five Books of Moses.* Philadelphia: Presbyterian and Reformed, 1943.

Bonar, H.A. *Commentary on the Book of Leviticus.* (reprint) Evansville, IN: Jay Green, 1959.

Bush, G. *Notes on Exodus.* reprint Minneapolis: Klock and Klock,1976. 2 volumes.

Cumming, J. *The Book of Deuteronomy* (reprint) Minneapolis: Klock and Klock, 1982.

Davis, J.D. *Moses and the Gods of Egypt.* Grand Rapids: Baker second edition 1986.

McIntosh, C.H. *Notes on the Pentateuch.* New York: Loizeaux, n.d.

North, G. *Leviticus: An Economic Commentary.* Tyler, TX: Institute for Christian Economics, 1994.

Ross, A.P. *Creation and Blessing.* Grand Rapids: Baker, 1988.

Sacks, R.D. *A Commentary on the Book of Genesis.* Lewiston: Mellen Press, 1990.

THE FORMER PROPHETS

Barber, C. *Judges: A Narrative of God's Power.* Neptune, NJ: Loizeaux, 1990.

Blaikie, W.G. *The First Book of Samuel* (reprint) Minneapolis: Klock and Klock, 1978.

_____ *The Second Book of Samuel* (reprint) Minneapolis: Klock and Klock, 1983.

Inrig, G. *Hearts of Iron, Feet of Clay (Judges).* Chicago: Moody Press, 1979.

Hess, D.S. *Joshua: an Introduction and Commentary.* Downers Grove: InterVarsity, 1996.

Nelson, R.D. *Joshua: A Commentary.* Louisville: Westminster John Knox Press, 1997.

THE LATTER PROPHETS: Major

Jennings, F.C. *Studies in Isaiah.* New York: Loizeaux, 1935.

Laetsch, T. *Jeremiah.* St. Louis: Concordia, 1952.

Ellison, H.E. *Ezekiel, the Man and His Message.* Grand Rapids: Eerdmans, 1956.

Thompson, J.A. *The Book of Jeremiah.* Grand Rapids: Eerdmans, 1980.

White, R.E.O. *The Indomitable Prophet: Jeremiah.* Grand Rapids: Eerdmans 1992.

THE LATTER PROPHETS: Minor

Baldwin, J.G. *Haggai, Zechariah, Malachi.* Downers Grove, IL: InterVarsity Press. 1972.

Baron, D. *Visions and Prophecies of Zechariah.* reprint. Grand Rapids: Kregel, 1975.

Conant, N.C. *Cheating God. Malachi.* Ft. Washington, PA: CLC, 1985.

Gaebelein, F.E. *Four Minor Prophets.* Chicago: Moody, 1970.

Howard, J.K. *Amos Among the Prophets.* Grand Rapids: Baker, 1967.

Laetsch, T. *Minor Prophets.* St. Louis: Concordia, 1956.

Pusey, E.B. *The Minor Prophets.* reprint. Grand Rapids: Baker, 1956.

Unger, M.F. *Zechariah.* Grand Rapids: Zondervan, 1963.

THE SACRED WRITINGS: Poetry: Psalms/Proverbs/Job

Alexander, J.A. *The Psalms.* New York: Baker and Scribner, 1851.

Andersen, F.I. *Job: An Introduction and Commentary.* London: InterVarsity, 1976.

Bonar, A. *Christ and His Church in the Book of Psalms.* reprint. Grand Rapids: Kregel, 1978.

Bridges, C. *Psalm 119.* reprint. Carlisle, PA. Banner of Truth Trust.

_____ *An Exposition of Proverbs.* reprint. Grand Rapids: Zondervan, 1959.

Crenshaw, J.L. *Old Testament Wisdom: An Introduction.* Atlanta: John Knox, 1981.

Dahood, M. *Psalms: The Anchor Bible.* Garden City: New York, 1970.

Ellison, H.L. *From Tragedy to Triumph.* London: Paternoster, 1958.

Jensen, I. *The Psalms, A Self-Study Guide.* Chicago, Moody, 1968.

Kidner, D. *The Proverbs.* Downers Grove, IL. InterVarsity, 1964.

Kirkpatrick, A.F. *The Book of Psalms* (Cambridge Bible for Schools and Colleges) Cambridge: Cambridge Univ. Press 1910.

Leupold, H.C. *Exposition of the Psalms.* Columbus, OH: Wartburg, 1959.

Lewis, C.S. *Reflections on the Psalms.* New York: Harcourt, Brace and World, 1958.

_____ *The Problem of Pain.* New York, Macmillan, 1965.

Perowne, J.J.S. *The Book of Psalms.* Grand Rapids, Zondervan, 1966.

Scroggie, W.G. *The Psalms.* London: Pickering and Inglis, 1950.

Spurgeon, C.H. *The Treasury of David.* New York: Funk and Wagnalls, 1881.

Thirtle, J.W. *The Titles of the Psalms: Their Nature and Meaning Explained.* London: Frowde, 1904.

THE SACRED WRITINGS: The "Rolls"—Ruth, Esther, Song of Solomon, Ecclesiastes, Lamentations

Adeney, W.T. *Ezra and Nehemiah.* reprint. Minneapolis: Klock and Klock, 1980.

Barber, C.J. *Nehemiah and the Dynamics of Effective Leadership.* Neptune, NJ: Loizeaux 1976.

Grabbe, L.L. *Ezra-Nehemiah.* London, Routledge, 1998.

Bridges, C. *An Exposition of Ecclesiastes,* reprint. London: Banner of Truth Trust, n.d., (original publication, 1859).

Ginsburg, C.D. *The Song of Songs and Koheleth.* reprint. New York: KTAV, 1970.

Hocking, C.E. *Rise Up, My Love.* Neath, West Glamorgan, UK: Precious Seed, 1988.

Ironside, H.A. *Addresses on the Song of Solomon.* New York: Loizeaux, n.d.

Kidner, D. *A Time to Mourn and a Time to Dance.* Downers Grove, IL: InterVarsity Press. 1976.

Morris, L. *Judges and Ruth.* Chicago, InterVarsity, 1968.

Provan, Iain. *Lamentations* (The New Century Bible Commentary). Grand Rapids: Eerdmans, 1991.

Van Selns, A. *Job: A Practical Commentary.* Grand Rapids: Eerdmans, 1992.

Zuck, R.B., ed. *Sitting with Job.* Grand Rapids: Baker, 1992.

THE SACRED WRITINGS: Histories

Johnstone, W. *1-2 Chronicles* (2 vols). Sheffield: Sheffield Press, 1997.

Luck, G.C. *Ezra and Nehemiah.* (In the Everyman's Commentary Series) Chicago: Moody Press 1961.

MacRae, A.A. *The Prophecies of Daniel.* Singapore: Christian Life Publishers, 1991.

Newell, P.R. *Daniel.* Chicago: Moody Press, 1962.

Wood, L.A. *A Commentary on Daniel.* Grand Rapids, Zondervan, 1972.

Appendix III
SOME SPECIAL HELPS

1. A NOTE ON THE OLD TESTAMENT TEXT

As we know, the Old Testament was written mostly in Hebrew; there are just a few Aramaic portions. Aramaic is a member of the Semitic family and very close to Hebrew. The Hebrew text used almost exclusively today is known as the **Masoretic** text and is the product of a body of traditional Jewish scholars who, in the Christian era, feared their sacred Scriptures might be lost or corrupted. The Masoretic period covers several hundred years and represents an enormous amount of very meticulous work in copying and checking the Old Testament Hebrew texts.

Part of the zeal in this work came from the fact that much of the Christian community made use of a Greek translation of the Hebrew Scriptures that was prepared well before the coming of the Christian era. This work is known as the **Septuagint**—a name associated with the means whereby the translation was done.

Translations from one language to another are always marked with difficulty, and the Hebrew community at large did not think the Greek translation was totally trustworthy. Therefore the continued monitoring of Hebrew texts and the extremes taken to make sure no erroneous material was inserted was very intense. It is a study of considerable interest, and much longer that can be analyzed now.

The Septuagint is considerably longer than the Masoretic text, embodying many additional notes, and eventually including the Apocryphal books to which the Hebrew community never ascribed inspiration or canonical acceptance.

With regard to our discussion of useful matters, it is important to know that this text variance occurs, but it is not something which is of major importance at this time. Here are two examples, however, of Septuagint additions. From them one may glean an appreciation for the problems that come in preserving a text. The italicized words indicate the Greek additions to the text.

> **Genesis 4:8** And Cain talked with Abel his brother and he said: *Let us go into the field.* And it came to pass, when they were in the field...

> **Job 2:9** Then his wife said to him: How long wilt thou hold out saying, *Behold yet I wait a little while, expecting the hope of my deliverance? For behold thy memorial is abolished from the earth, even thy sons and daughters, the pang and pains of my womb which I bore in vain with sorrows...and thou thyself sittest down to spend the nights in the open air among the corruption of worms, and I am a wanderer and a servant from place to place and house to house, waiting for the setting of the sun, that I may rest from my labors and my pangs which now beset me:* but say some word against the Lord and die...

The translation is from Brenton: *The Septuagint with Apocrypha Greek and English.* (Grand Rapids, Zondervan reprint 1980). In the Septuagint as edited by Alfred Rahlfs (New York: American Bible Society) the passage is versified as 9-a-e, indicating the text is about four verses longer than the standard Hebrew text.

This writer is a follower of the Masoretic text, but this Greek passage in Job gives the reader some idea of the anguish in the life of Job's wife's. The student does not have to solve these text matters, but should know that the text we have for the Old Testament (and for the New Testament as well!) is an excellent text, carefully guarded through the years by the care of men and the divine influence of the Holy Spirit.

2. HOW HEBREW HELPS THE STUDENT

In the nature of our earlier discussions in the study of the Old Testament, I have often mentioned that a working knowledge of Hebrew is a great aid to the student. It is not a *sine qua non* factor, however. While it is preferable to have such knowledge, the author has known some very gifted and capable Bible teachers who did not have it; on the other hand, he has known some who did have it but were neither capable nor comprehensive in their teaching. It must be noted, then, that there is a great deal more to Bible study and teaching than academics.

At this point some concepts are presented in which the help of Hebrew is a great aid. It is hoped that in simply seeing some of the concepts, more of our Bible students would take the opportunity to study Hebrew and, of course, Greek—but that is for the New Testament portion of useful materials in study.

The items that follow have been observed in my own study and are illustrated with the help of the Hebrew Grammar of Dr. Fred Putnam of the faculty of Biblical Seminary (*An Introduction to the Grammar and Syntax of Biblical Hebrew.* Frederick C. Putnam. Hatfield, PA., Biblical Seminary, 2003.) Used by permission.

The great service of the biblical languages is that we are allowed to scrutinize the text more closely and to understand and apply it more fully. The study of these languages is not like a sudden illumination that overcomes intellectual darkness, but is more a matter of insight and quiet understanding that will then allow for a better or fuller application of the material studied.

Hebrew is especially helpful to this end since, in the Old Testament, we are dealing with a different culture and a linguistic style that is moved some distance from the Greek and Latin world. In other words, we are changing a style of thinking. This becomes apparent to the Hebrew student when one learns that reading is from right to the left and, in classical Hebrew, either has no vowels designated or finds them with curious marks under the letters. This simply means that the thinking is oriental rather than occidental.

Our Bibles were translated by persons who mastered the original languages but they could only give us the benefit of their own understanding. I am not suggesting that we are in any way superior to them, but in working with the enciphering languages we very often catch a gleam of a feature that will not show in translation. It is in this area that Hebrew is a special help to the student. The areas that are mentioned are only indicative of the quantity and quality of ideals that are seen in the text but not printed in the letters and words. I will mention a few of the things that have been of special interest to me in my studies. There are many more, but these will serve for an introductory thrust at the potential field. Grammarians will differ in their understanding of some, but all will agree that there are enriching concepts and the basic tool for discovery is the original language as the expressions are studied in adequate context.

1. Hebrew helps us to understand conditions expressed in sentences by words such as *if*, and, *since*, etc., by the use of particles and the tense sense understood in verbal constructions. The student reading 1 Kings 11:28 will smile when he sees that Micaiah said to the wicked king Ahab, *"If you return in peace..."* for the student knows that the condition is highly unlikely to be fulfilled. The king is not coming back in peace or, even better, perhaps not at all.

2. The character of negation is clarified to a certain extent by Hebrew, again by the particles used and the syntactical constructions. This involves recognizing an absolute denial in contrast with a permissive denial. There is a wide difference between the *"thou shalt not"* of Deuteronomy 5:11 and *"be not afraid"* in Joshua 1:9. The Lord speaks in both cases but with a special emphasis distinguished in each case. The first is an **absolute ordinance** while the second is a **petitioned request.** We can understand it in English with some effort, but in Hebrew the forms are much clearer.

3. We are better able to understand volition by virtue of the occurrence of untranslatable particles and verb forms. This may affect what we want to do, intend to do, or are told to do. One will see some of this expression in passages like Genesis 41:35 where Joseph tells Pharaoh what the people should do in the face of the oncoming famine period. The translator shows this with the term, *"let the people,"* where the concept is to not only *give the people permission* but also *use urgency* in what must be done.

There is a similar usage for the first person ("I") with regard to indicating the strong intention of doing something as opposed to the incidental doing. Some translators will show this by using the term surely or some form of self-intention.

4. The simple conjunctions *and, but, now,* etc., become syntactical tools in understanding sentence and phrase construction. A student will realize that, in a given text, a conjunction might be intended to reverse an action rather than continue it. This point may be disputed in a passage, of course, due to the feeling of a student or translator, but the potential is there, and may well be considered. Careful notice of the conjunctions may alert us to sequences of events, etc., that are observable in English but maximized when seen in Hebrew.

5. Reading the Hebrew text, one may become aware of sound similarity that calls attention to a special feature. Dr. Putnam (*Grammar,* p. 76) notes how the verbs in Psalm 100 call our attention to their significance and cumulative effect simply by repetition of a common ending. The verbs are there, of course, regardless of endings, but it is easy to read and miss the total effect.

6. Interrogation is sometimes rendered more forceful in the Hebrew text by virtue of syntactical forms and affixes. In Judges 4:6, Deborah poses a question of Barak that allows us to know that Barak had received instruction from God about the deliverance he should bring to Israel, but, by implication, he had dragged his feet on the matter.

7. Very often the understanding of Hebrew enables one to grip the emphasis on words and ideas stressed through syntax. Infinitives and participles are most commonly used in this way, and since these are often abused or ignored in our own English language, it is not surprising that they are not maximized in translation. The force of a verbal expression and the intended outcomes are often indicated by these constructions.

Much more could be said. There are many Bible translations to help our understanding, but without the knowledge of Hebrew we may be left to the tired mercies of pedantic patrons!

3. SOME ADDITIONAL STUDY HELPS

Hebrew Self Study

There are several of these programs on the market today, and, while no one should be deceived about the time and work involved, valuable help can be had by all that I have seen. One of the better programs, in my judgment, is that Dr. Randall Buth: **www.biblical ulpan.org**. Information may also be had from 101 Language, 408 S. Pasadena Ave., Department BAR, Pasadena, CA 91105. All of the programs have an expense factor, of course.

Biblical Charts

Two excellent charts for Old Testament study have been designed by Dr. John Whitcomb and are available from Moody Press in Chicago. They are: *Old Testament Patriarchs and Prophets* and *Old Testament Kings and Prophets*. Some fine charts are available from Rose Publishing, 4455 Torrance Blvd., Torrance, CA 90503

Electronic Material

Many modern helps are available in this area. I am not able to offer decisive judgment but a good place to start is with *Bibleworks*. The e-mail address is **www.bibleworks.com**.

A number of Bible Commentaries have been made available. The *Entire Word Bible Commentary* series is published by Nelson: **www.nelsonreference.com** and in this computer age the cost is really diminished. But what will be practical for one scholar may not suit another.

4. NOTES ON TYPOLOGY

The science of interpretation is called *hermeneutics*, a word derived from the Greek word that means to explain something by words or to interpret. Interpretation is particularly necessary when translating from one language to another, or when explaining the meaning of words in context. *Typology* is generally considered to be a branch of hermeneutics in which the object is to show the relationship between events or persons in that the first object teaches or depicts the second object. The first object is a *type* and the second is the *antitype*.

As a hermeneutical tool, typology is a method of biblical interpretation showing how various objects from the Old Testament correspond or prefigure objects in the New Testament This is thought to show a continuity of salvation history, in particular, from the Old Testament to the New Testament so that God's plan of redemption is foreseen in the Old Testament in persons, events, etc., that will find their fulfillment in the New Testament. It is thought that this approach gives credence to the unity of the Bible, and is one of the arguments that is used early in the history of the New Testament Church to show its fulfillment of the spiritual aspects of the Old Testament.

Justin Martyr, while making very much of fulfilled prophecy as a basis for continuity, also resorted to typology studies, as may be seen in his work known as the *Dialogue with Trypho*. The pseudopigraphic work known as the Epistle of Barnabas may be the earliest non-biblical literature displaying this hermeneutic, but I am not certain of the comparative dates.

Within the Bible itself, one may see examples of this in Romans 5 (Adam and Christ) and Hebrews 9 (the sacrifices of the tabernacle and the work of Christ). The term itself comes from the Greek word *tupos,* and this word has a variety of meanings in the New Testament, although all have in common the idea of transference of one image to another.

The basic idea seems to have been that of a pattern and the print made from it as in the striking of an image. Beyond this, however, the term is used in 1 Corinthians 10:6 and 11 (translated *"examples"* in the KJV) to warn believers about falling into the pattern of past sins. It is seen in Hebrews 8:5 (*"example"*) as depicting the worship in heaven through an earthly medium, while in 1 Peter 5:3 it is used to encourage a pattern of life on the part of the elders that will guide the flock in holy living. Similar usage is seen in Philippians 3:17, 1 Timothy 4:12, and 2 Thessalonians 3:9. The pre-figuring aspect is clearly seen in Romans 5:14 (KJV translates the term as *"figure"*). From all aspects, the concept of typology is developed to describe the way in which one item depicts another.

There are various schools of typologists: some thinking that a

type must be identified as such in the New Testament before it can
be accepted; some thinking that any correspondence or resemblance
of two entities indicates a type; others who think that the term can
only apply to prophetic matters or must be predictive in character.
This does not define all the views of typology but it seems that the
fact of typological significance cannot be denied and the interpretation will depend much on the orientation of the student.

In dealing with types, whether plainly stated or suggested, the
approach recommended in this work is as follows:

Level One: OLD TESTAMENT TYPES

In *Level One*, these three points seem basic:

1. Identify the item one conceives as a type
2. Note all that the Bible tells about it in its context
3. Identify the antitype

1. *Identify the item one conceives to be a type:* For most Bible students, the suggestion of a type will arise from reading a commentary
or a study Bible. There is nothing wrong in this because we do not
all see things as quickly, and we who read today are benefited by the
learning of previous generations—not only in biblical studies but in
all the academic fields with which I am familiar! One may, however, simply be impressed when reading the Bible that an object is suggested as a type.

An illustration of this is seen in John 3:14 where the Lord Jesus
explicitly states: *"As Moses lifted up the serpent in the wilderness,
even so must the Son of Man be lifted up."* The Old Testament reference is Numbers 21:9 in a full context. The type, then, is identified
as the action of lifting up the serpent for the healing of those who
would look to it at the direction of God; the antitype is the lifting up
of the Lord Jesus who would save all who looked to Him. The type
is not the serpent *per se*, but the action that depicts the dealing of
God in salvation. The student simply needs to identify the type.

2. *Note all that the Bible tells about it in its context:* This calls for
the intense study of the object identified. It includes physical fea-

tures, characteristic actions, symbolic ideas, etc. The type and anti-type do not need to be absolutely identical. There may be points where significant difference is seen, but the part that is depicted must correspond. In our illustration from John 3, the serpent is made of brass; Jesus is flesh and blood. But brass is often an object symbolizing judgment, and the cross shows judgment in a passionate sense. The pole of Numbers is not shaped as was the cross, but that is insignificant in the light of the action and the result.

It goes without saying that there is a danger in pressing matters too far. This is something that only the student can judge—although those he teaches may pass judgment that is more severe! Some years ago, I heard a preacher discussing the "Good Samaritan" as a New Testament type of the dealing with sinners about the gospel. The donkey was made to be a type of the Holy Spirit and no further comment can be made at this time, although I am sure it was a popular idea with the speaker.

3. *Identify the antitype:* Obviously the type does not exist alone. The student must identify the antitype as to whether it is the fulfillment of a type in an entity, an action, or a combination of these. Is the ark of Noah a type of God's means of providing salvation for His people in a difficult or unbelieving age? See 2 Peter 2:5 for help in deciding this matter.

Level Two: OLD TESTAMENT TYPES

Level Two calls for a more concentrated Bible study, and promotes these lines:

1. Does the Bible itself identify this type as such?
2. Is there a predictive inference in the item?

This level calls for a good bit of Bible knowledge, although study Bibles and commentaries will prove helpful. It is one of the reasons that the Bible student should keep an up-to-date notebook of things he/she sees and finds of special interest in the daily reading.

1. *Does the Bible itself identify this type as such?* The identifica-

tion might be direct or might be implied. One can hardly read
Leviticus 1–5 without seeing the implications of these sacrifices of
the Old Testament for the New Testament believer.

If one discerns the biblical identification, then the student must
determine the degree to which the comparisons extend. The ark typ-
ifies (in my judgment) the protection God offers His people in a time
of great trial that seems in 2 Peter not to refer to our common trials
but to an eschatological standing. But does the fact that eight people
were saved give us any symbolic ideal, or does it simply depict the
fact that all, regardless of number, who enter God's protective care
through faith in the Lord Jesus, will be delivered. Typologists often
identify the life of Joseph as a type of the life of the Lord, and, while
this is never stated flatly in Scripture, many points of resemblance
encourage that view. As with many other matters discussed in our
work, the student must have a charitable heart towards other teachers as well as a devoted concern for the Word of God.

2. *Is there a predictive element in the type?* Once again, this does
not need to be stated in a blunt fashion, but one must look to discern
the possibility. When Moses elevates the serpent, does it predict that
God will one day lift up a salvation standard to the whole world? It
is doubtful that Moses would have understood this, but is it possible
that we can understand it? In terms of the teaching of John 3, it
would seem to be necessary to understand it in this fashion.

If there is no predictive element, it may be that the resemblance is
just one of consequence rather than planned information, but there
is just enough left unsaid on this subject to keep us humble students.

At this point, we may advance to **Level Three,** where we find
some other intricate matters of discussion:

1. What is the relation between typology and allegory?
2. What is the contribution of typology to salvation history?
3. How many types are there in the Bible?

1. *What is the relation between typology and allegory?* Allegory
as a type of language, and speech figure has been discussed in the
chapters about prophecy. Essentially it is the idea of giving a sec-

ondary meaning to an entity, an action, etc. First Corinthians 10:4 gives a clear allegorical thrust when Paul speaks of the wanderers in the wilderness, and declares that the rock that followed them was Christ! The rock was a solid piece of sediment, but it typified Christ, and that conclusion cannot be avoided. The student will come to the conclusion that typology often involves allegory, but not all allegories are types.

2. *What is the contribution of typology to salvation history?* Salvation History is the great theological theme of the Bible—the grace of God reaching out to mankind in mercy, justice,and grace. Typology allows this message to be communicated graphically. The sacrificial lambs of the Old Testament vigorously portray the *"lamb of God who takes away the sin of the world."* With the use of types and symbols, the work of God is given pictorially and is gripping on the mind of people. Somewhat in the non-biblical quotation, "A single picture is worth a thousand words."

3. *How many types are there in the Bible?* The obvious answer is that no one knows for sure. Different scholars have arrived a different answers. A certain number (such as that in John 3) will be recognized by all. But there is a wide diversity of agreement on many others. If the student thinks he has found one, he should check the criteria mentioned and go ahead with the study. He is warned about being dogmatic with it, and encouraged to be sure he is teaching the Word of God and not some highly imaginative idea.

For literature regarding typology, the following items are mentioned, while the reference books noted are listed in the BIBLIOGRAPHY:

Alsup, John A. *Typology in the Anchor Bible Dictionary.* Doubleday: New York, 1992.

Eerdmans' Dictionary of the Bible. Eerdmans: Grand Rapids, 2000.

Goppelt, L. *Typos: The Typological Interpretation of the Old Testament.* Grand Rapids, 1992.

McNeill, Brian. *Typology in the Dictionary of Biblical Interpretation,*
    SCM Press: London, 1990.

When consulting other Bible dictionaries, etc., the student may need to look under Hermeneutics, as some regard typology a subheading.

Printed in the United States
54078LVS00004B/1-102